China Accounting Standards

Lorenzo Riccardi

China Accounting Standards

Introduction and Effects of New Chinese Accounting Standards for Business Enterprises

Springer

Lorenzo Riccardi
Shanghai
China

ISBN 978-981-10-0004-1 ISBN 978-981-10-0006-5 (eBook)
DOI 10.1007/978-981-10-0006-5

Library of Congress Control Number: 2015952994

Springer Singapore Heidelberg New York Dordrecht London

Printed on acid-free paper

Springer Science+Business Media Singapore Pte Ltd. is part of Springer Science+Business Media (www.springer.com)

Contents

Chapter 1
Introduction to New Accounting Standards for Business Enterprises

The process of increasing economic openness and liberalization has been particularly prevalent in the past decade. Recently, this process has been making China increasingly integrated into the world economy. Perspectives are changing and a growing extent of investors are demanding financial statements; this demonstrates a higher level of transparency, objectivity, and accuracy, particularly in mainland China. Keeping up to date with international accounting standards is crucial in order to meet increasingly demanding global requirements. In fact, the process of harmonization and integration of reporting standards can bring a twofold advantage. First, it provides transparency and promotes confidence among foreign investors, the major aim of latest Chinese economic policies. Second, an internationally integrated system makes it easier for companies to raise capital and it reduces the risk of financial crisis.

The very beginning of the Chinese Accounting System refers to 1949, when the People's Republic of China was established. In that period, the framework was mainly related to the Soviet Union's Accounting Standards. The development of a centrally controlled system was aimed at implementing the economic policy for a socialist economy. In 1978, while prompting the economic reform and encouraging foreign investments, the policymakers realized that the previous reporting system was quite useless in the managerial decision-making process. To put it otherwise, the archaic Soviet Union-inspired standards were more suitable for providing information to planning and control activities run by central, instead of paving the way for the implementation of Deng's "Open-Door" Policy. Since then, a large extent of reforms has occurred.

The first introduction of Western practices in firms operating in China took place in 1985 as the Regulations on Accounting System for Sino-Foreign Joint Ventures was issued by the Ministry of Finance (MoF). For the first time, the new regulation introduced international principles to the greatest possible extent under China's socialist economy. In the same year, the introduction of the Accounting Law defined the functions of accounting, the organization of accounting work, and the power and legal responsibilities of accounting personnel. The featuring purpose of this initiative was to establish operational methods, procedures, and financial reporting requirements for different enterprises. At the same time, the system for

L. Riccardi, *China Accounting Standards*,
DOI 10.1007/978-981-10-0006-5_1

domestic companies still centered around the socialist framework, leading to a two-sided accounting environment.

A third key change occurred in the 1990s, following the establishment of Shanghai and Shenzhen Stock Exchanges. After 1991, listed companies previously issuing only A-shares to domestic investors were now allowed also to issue B-shares to overseas investors. Furthermore, state-owned enterprises (SOEs) were now allowed to be shareholding entities with limited liabilities through corporatization and shares issue listed to the public. The discrepancy between the Chinese economic environment and the backward-oriented accounting standards now became blatant, and a reform in the reporting system was necessary.

In 1992, the MoF released new accounting standards to replace completely the Soviet Union's model and to merge the dual system into one common system. On July 1, 1993, the Accounting Standards for Business Enterprises (ASBE) were applicable to all Chinese enterprises regardless of their ownership structure. Despite the great extent of efforts deployed, there were still significant differences between the Chinese standards and those adopted abroad. The lack of a common way led to a seamless flow of reforms aimed to add, cancel, and amend the Accounting Law from 1999 onward.

This reforming activity culminated in February 2006, when the MoF formally announced the issuance of revised ASBE. The revision referred to the promulgation of 22 new standards and the amendment of 16 principles. New ASBE cover almost all the most relevant topics under the International Financial Reporting Standards (IFRSs) and make the most recent regulation compulsory for all listed companies. However, all types of companies are strongly encouraged to adopt new principles (Table 1.1).

Table 1.1 Revision of accounting standards of business enterprises

No.	Title and ASBE basic standard	Remarks
1	Inventories	2006
2	Long-term equity investments	Revised
3	Investment property	2006
4	Fixed assets	2006
5	Biological assets	2006
6	Intangible assets	2006
7	Exchange of non-monetary assets	2006
8	Impairment of assets	2006
9	Employee compensation	2006
10	Enterprise annuity fund	2006
11	Share-based payments	2006
12	Debt restructuring	2006
13	Contingencies	2006
14	Revenue	2006

(continued)

Table 1.1 (continued)

No.	Title and ASBE basic standard	Remarks
15	Construction contracts	2006
16	Government grants	2006
17	Borrowing costs	2006
18	Income taxes	2006
19	Foreign currency translation	2006
20	Business combinations	2006
21	Leases	2006
22	Recognition and measurement of financial instruments	2006
23	Transfer of financial assets	2006
24	Hedging	2006
25	Direct insurance contracts	2006
26	Reinsurance contracts	2006
27	Extraction of petroleum and natural gas	2006
28	Changes in accounting policies and estimates, and correction of errors	2006
29	Events after the balance sheet date	2006
30	Presentation of financial statement	2006
31	Cash flow statement	2006
32	Interim financial reporting	2006
33	Consolidated financial statement	Revised
34	Earnings per share	2006
35	Segment reporting	Revised
36	Related party disclosures	2006
37	Presentation of financial instruments	Revised
38	First-time adoption of accounting standards for business enterprises	2006
39	Fair value measurement	New
40	Joint venture arrangements	New
41	Disclosure of interest	New

The new ASBE represent a higher level of convergence with IFRS. Most of the newly issued and revised standards are equivalent to the IFRS and adopt similar principles and treatments. As a result, the financial reports prepared with the new ASBE are more comparable with those prepared in accordance with IFRS than they would have been in previous years.

Being adopted since January 2007, the new Chinese ASBE fueled the convergence between Chinese Accounting Standards and IFRSs. In this process of integration with world economy, China is benefiting from different advantages. The increased confidence in the Chinese capital market and the financial reporting system will spur the attractiveness for both domestic and overseas investments. Moreover, the Chinese companies operating in international environment will improve their acceptance in foreign markets and reduce the cost of complying with the accounting regimes in the different countries they operate.

Chapter 2
ASBE's Main Features and General Differences of New China GAAP Versus US GAAP and IFRS

At first glance, the major changes introduced by new principles embrace a set of basic standards which are now more in line with IFRSs. First, in accordance with international standards, new ASBEs reintroduce the generally agreed definition of assets and liabilities. In all cases, accounting elements shall be recognized only when their definition is made and the established recognition conditions are satisfied. Some other main features have been introduced: first the definition of "gains" and "losses" and second the method of historical cost as general requirement when measuring accounting elements. Deviations from the latter provision are replacement cost, net realizable value, and fair value, which can be adopted in the case of reliable determination.

A great extent of intervention refers to guidelines to draw financial statement. The principle of "substance over form" still finds application. At the same time, a minor difference with IFRSs involves the exercise of prudence in the presentation of financial reports. Prudence means that assets and income items might not be overstated and liabilities and expenses not understated. Specifically, while new ASBEs prescribe to follow a prudential approach in the recognition, measurement, and reporting of transaction, IASB's Framework for the Preparation and Presentation of Financial Statements considers prudence as a simple qualitative characteristic in terms of a not biased evaluation.

The cornerstones of the last version of the ASBEs can be summarized with the following key features:

- First and most importantly, new ASBEs introduce for Chinese companies the generally agreed concept of fair value measurement for all categories of Assets. ASBEs No. 3 (Inventory Property), 11 (Share-Based Payments), 20 (Business Combination), and 22 (Recognition and Measurement of Financial Assets) apply this subject.
- A consistent intervention has involved business combinations and form of consolidated financial statements. ASBEs No. 20 (Business Combination) and 30 (Presentation of Financial Statements) carry on accounting standards and detailed guidelines addressing these purposes.

L. Riccardi, *China Accounting Standards*,
DOI 10.1007/978-981-10-0006-5_2

- ASBE No. 22 (Recognition and Measurement of Financial Assets) makes some previously off-balance-sheet items, compulsory to be recorded in the balance sheet.
- Specialized industries, mainly in financial and insurance sectors, face new dedicated regulation. ASBEs No. 5 (Biological Assets), 10 (Enterprise Annuity Fund), 25 (Direct insurance contracts), 26 (Reinsurance contracts), 36 (Related party disclosures), and 37 (Presentation of financial instruments) introduce new standards for those companies falling within these industries.
- According to the ASBE No. 8 (Impairment of assets), impairment loss cannot be reversed in future financial periods.
- The compliance with IFRS finds highest and strictest level of application in ASBEs No. 28 (Changes in accounting policies and estimates, and correction of errors), 30 (Presentation of financial statements), 34 (Earnings per share), 35 (Segment reporting), 36 (Related party disclosure), and 37 (Presentation of financial instruments).
- Finally, ASBE No. 38 (First time adoption of Accounting Standards for Business Enterprises) allows transitional provisions for first time adoption of new standards.

The new ASBE do not simply extend the disclosure requirements. As they operate meaningful and profound changes to the previous Mainland China General Agreed Accounting Procedures (GAAPs), they could result in significant differences of end-year results or Asset valuation in financial statements. The major changes occurred are listed in Table 2.1.

This stage shows evidence of the increasing parallelism of Chinese systems with international standards. The process started in 1993 with the very first adoption of the ASBEs; this represents an important step in an increasing integration of China with the world economy. However, despite the fundamental convergence of the new ASBEs with IFRS, there are a few exceptions that are still recognized in certain subjects, notably due to Chinese particular economic circumstances.

First of all, Chinese Accounting Standards prescribe the generally established requirement of fair value in many cases. However, when accounting for Assets, some exceptions are allowed. In particular, ASBEs No. 4 (Fixed Assets) and 6 (Intangible Assets) permit only the cost model for the measurement of reported categories of assets. This provision is clearly in contrast to IFRSs where revaluation model is allowed.

Biological assets (ASBE No. 5) remark just a lighter difference with IFRS. In this case, the fair value is the exception to the cost method. On the contrary, IAS 41 envisages the general approach of fair value unless for the single case, it is clearly unreliable. Another major difference refers to the record of land use. Under the ASBEs, this right is classified as intangible asset instead of operating lease. In case land-use rights meet a set of criteria in order to be recognized as an investment property, the cost model should be the most appropriate principle.

ASBE No. 2 (Long-Term Equity Investments) disposes the equity method as the only accepted way to manage jointly controlled entities, whereas IFRSs allow both

Table 2.1 Introductions under the new ASBEs in details

Item	Provision under new ASBE
Share-based transactions	Their settlement must be measured at the fair value as expenses in the income statement.
Business combination	For entities that are not under common control it is disposed the acquisition method. Assets and liabilities of acquired enterprise should be carried at the fair value.
Goodwill	Its treatment is not different from indefinite life intangible assets. Likewise, it is not amortized, but the value is annually scrutinized for the impairment test.
Discount on business acquisition	It is treated similarly to the "credit balance of equity investment difference." The discount value should be immediately recorded as a profit.
Minority interests	They should be presented within equity.
Non-monetary assets	A grant related to this kind of assets should be presented as deferred income and split evenly over the useful life of the asset.
Reversal of impairment loss	This category is prohibited to a large extent both for tangible and intangible assets.
Development costs	Following trends in international standards, now this category of costs should be capitalized.
Borrowing costs	The expenses incurred for general borrowing should be presented as deferred income and recognized as income along the useful life of the underlying asset.
Derivative instruments	They must be recognized on the balance sheet with changes in fair value taken to income statement. This provision is applied unless these financial instruments are proved to be effective hedging instruments.
Investment property	The fair value is the criteria to be followed in the evaluation of this item.
Non-monetary transactions	Should be carried according to fair value if the commercial substance can be substantiated.
Debt restructuring	Gains from debt restructuring operations should be recognized in profit or loss.
Financial lease assets	Financial lease assets should be recognized by the lessee at the lower of fair value and the present value of minimum lease payments.
Taxes	The tax payable method is prohibited. Instead, the tax effect accounting method should be adopted to record the tax effect of temporary differences.
Hybrid instruments	A financial instrument featuring both debt and equity components needs to be split and the two components accounted separately.

Source RSA Asia

proportionate consolidation and equity method. At the same time, state-controlled entities are exempted from the regulation of related parties due to their state-owned stake. As a matter of facts, this special provision is not met under the IFRS.

In accordance with ASBE No. 8 (Impairment of Assets), the reversal of impairment losses is generally prohibited (excluding inventories and trade receivables), whereas IAS 36 forbids this practice only for the reversal of impairment of goodwill. Capitalization method should be applied to those borrowing costs, which meet certain criteria. On the contrary, IFRSs leave the option to measure borrowing costs as expenses. ASBE No. 20 (Business Combination) includes and addresses in the same scope all business combinations involving entities under common control. The same *Article* does not embrace reverse acquisition.

Specific accounting treatments refer to "Reinsurance contracts" and "Extraction of Petroleum and natural Gas" (respectively ASBEs No. and), whereas no counterpart is disposed under IFRSs. To the same extend, IFRSs specifically refer to "Non-current assets held for sale and discontinued operation." No equal treatment is adopted in new ASBEs.

Finally, ASBEs as a general principle restrict the options available for the measurement of several expenses. Some cost items should be analyzed by function for income statement presentation purposes. In this case, the direct method is required for cash flow statements and only the gross presentation is allowed for government grants related to assets.

Chapter 3
Impact and Results on Financial Statements

Although new principles have affected firms to a different extent, analysts argue Chinese companies under new ASBEs to be benefited mostly in terms of comparability. This point could lead in turn to an increased level of volatility of financial results due to the greater use of fair value principle. Both differences in adoptions of standards and increased volatility in end-year results should be explained in financial statement and disclosure to stakeholders.

At the same time, loan covenants based on ratios from financial statements may be broken, or become much tighter, leading to uncertainty about the availability of finance. Accordingly, a timely review of agreements intended to identify potential issues is a possible measure to cope with this drawback.

Another relevant area concerns with the implementation of ASBEs. Internal reporting systems now have to recognize what data are no longer required under new principles. Generally speaking, modifications and other requirements must be identified early to enable identification of records. Also, staff and other members involved in operational decisions, in particular those charged with governance, are expected to have an in-depth knowledge and understanding of ASBEs.

Finally, the introduction of ABSEs has substantially inferred over dividend policies and tax treatment of enterprises. To the one hand, entities had to communicate to shareholders the degree of change in dividends and the impact on the global payout policy. To the other hand, financial disclosure needed to show in details an accurate assessment of the full tax implications. Despite these provisions, precise appraisals of how these dividends and taxations changed were available only the immediate financial year-end, as their impact come realized.

Over years, many empirical researches have been conducted to investigate how ASBEs influence results in Chinese enterprises. On this purpose, Heng and Noronha (2011) take into analysis a sample of some 1500 companies (either A-share or B-share) listed in Shanghai Stock Exchange and Shenzhen Stock Exchange.

Starting with financial performances, results show how more than half of firms selected reported higher operating revenue under new ASBEs than under old standards. Up to 30 % maintained the same operating revenue under both sets of standards, whereas only a residual part significantly decreased operating revenue under new ASBEs.

L. Riccardi, *China Accounting Standards*,
DOI 10.1007/978-981-10-0006-5_3

With regard to profit, the majority of firms achieved higher results. This outcome could be referred to as the treatment of debt restructuring. In fact, new ASBE No. 12 recognizes positive differences resulting from a fair value in Debt Restructuring, as gains to be recorded in the profit and loss. The same principle holds for ASBE No. 22 “Recognition of Financial Instruments” with all changes in fair value to be recognized in the income statement of the period. Furthermore, new treatments provisioned both for Borrowing Costs (ASBE No. 17) and for Intangible Assets (ASBE No. 6), allow enterprises to capitalize expenditures, while these were totally recorded as period expenses under prior standards.

Lastly, in 60 % of cases, basic earnings per share increased under new ASBEs, and 13 % of firms showed the same figures. A possible answer to this pattern could be provided by changes in net profit attributable to shareholders of ordinary shares and adjustments in weighted-average number of outstanding shares. An interesting example is referred to the distribution of stock dividends during the reporting period. Wider differences can be assessed when comparing Profit before tax and Net Profit before Extraordinary items, where up to 70 % of enterprises achieved higher results.

Findings are quite different when comparing differences that occurred in Cash Flow under new ASBEs. In considering Net Cash Flow from Operating Activities and Net Cash Flow from Operating Activities per Share, more than 40 % of entities did not show any appreciable change in their results. The remaining portion of companies (around 55 %) looks equally shared between increased and decreased results.

Finally, in regard to the Total Assets (current and non-current) and Equity Items, 70 % of companies recorded an increase in total assets and total assets per share under new ASBEs. The remaining percentage is mostly referred to those entities facing a decreased value in total assets and total assets per share, while few companies have left unchanged their value. Accounting for the possible causes, the focus centers on ASBE No. 1 (Inventories), ASBE No. 3 (Investment Property), ASBE No. 4 (Fixed Assets), ASBE No. 5 (Biological Assets), ASBE No. 6 (Intangible Assets). First of all, Inventories result in a higher valuation, due to the new provision of ASBE No. 1 which no longer permits LIFO (Last-In-First-Out) for evaluating stock. With raising prices, only those items which came later are considered. With regard to both tangibles and intangibles (ASBEs No. 3, 4, 5, and 6), the major modifications occurred in terms of fair value valuation and cost capitalization lead in many cases to a substantial increase of recorded value of Assets. A similar distribution is followed in the pattern of Shareholders’ Funds Attributable to Equity Shareholders. Here relevant principles deal with ASBE No. 11 (Share-based Payments) and ASBE No. 22 (Recognition and Measurement of Financial Instruments). Still, the new prevision states that payments settled through Shares have to be recorded at the fair value of share. At the same time, the Recognition at the fair value of financial instruments disposes any gain from the difference between fair value and book value to adjust the beginning shareholders’ funds.

Chapter 4
Effects of the New PRC GAAP

At a glance, new ASBEs have introduced substantial innovation in accounting principles and measurement requirements, such as the adoption of fair value. This change enhances the relevance of accounting information as it closely connects the external financial markets with the performance of companies. Despite that the actual implications of fair value could turn into difficulties in a clear determination of a reliable fair value for enterprises, leading to volatility.

The big effort put in place by the Ministry of Finance has really made financial reports from Chinese entities closely comparable to those under IFRS. Still, some key differences stand between ASBEs and IFRS largely deemed to the unique characteristics featuring the Chinese economy. These disparities should be regarded as a further point for triggering harmonization of systems.

Irrespective of the formal aim of new ASBEs, it is equally important to underline how new standards have played an important role to boost relevance of information in financial statements. Another improvement reflected the required disclosure of financial risk management policies, especially the obligation for companies to disclaim if hedge policies have taken in accordance with hedge accounting requirements of new standards. All previous aspects have led to the modification and improvement of internal control systems (for instance, the establishment of internal control to monitor transactions of derivative instruments).

The following work is aimed at providing guidelines and explanations to describe the new Chinese ASBEs. The next sections cover each *Article*, providing the regulatory dispositions introduced in 2007 (in accordance with the original text) and **COMMENTS** on the most important changes with past version and differences against IAS/IFRS. Finally, some basic examples are introduced to help readers understand the different issues and rationale underlying the new provisions.

L. Riccardi, *China Accounting Standards*,
DOI 10.1007/978-981-10-0006-5_4

Chapter 5
Accounting Standards for Business Enterprises No. 1—Inventories

5.1 Chapter I: General Provisions

Article 1 These Standards are formulated in accordance with the Accounting Standards for Enterprises—Basic Standards for the purpose of regulating the recognition of the inventories, measurement, and disclosure of related information.

Article 2 Other relevant accounting standards shall apply to such items as follows: (1) The Accounting Standard for Business Enterprises No. 5—Biological Assets shall apply to the consumptive biological assets. (2) The Accounting Standard for Business Enterprises No. 15—Construction Contracts shall apply to the costs of the inventories together through construction contracts.

5.2 Chapter II: Recognition

Article 3 The term “inventories” refers to finished products or merchandise possessed by an enterprise for sale in the daily course of business, or work in progress in the process of production, or materials and supplies to be consumed in the process of production or offering labor service.

Article 4 The inventories shall not be recognized unless they satisfy such conditions simultaneously as follows: (1) The economic benefits pertinent to the inventories are likely to flow into the enterprise and (2) the cost of the inventories can be measured reliably.

L. Riccardi, *China Accounting Standards*,
DOI 10.1007/978-981-10-0006-5_5

5.3 Chapter III: Measurement

Article 5 The inventories shall be initially measured in light of their cost. The cost of inventory consists of purchase costs, processing costs, and other costs.

Article 6 The purchase costs of inventories consist of the purchase price, relevant taxes, transport fees, loading and unloading fees, insurance premiums, and other expenses that may be relegated to the purchase costs of inventories.

Article 7 The processing costs of inventories consist of the direct labor and production overheads allocated according to a particular method. The "production overheads" refers to all indirect expenses incurred in the process of manufacturing products and providing labor services by an enterprise. According to the nature of the production overheads, an enterprise shall choose the reasonable method for the allocation of production overheads. If two or more kinds of products are manufactured in the same production process, and the processing cost for each product is unable to be separated from that of others directly, the processing costs shall be allocated among the products in a reasonable way.

Article 8 "Other costs of inventories" refers to those costs, other than purchase costs and processing costs, incurred in bringing the inventories to their present location and condition.

Article 9 The following expenses shall be recognized as current profits and losses as they happen, which shall not be included in the cost of inventories: (1) the direct materials, direct labor, and production overheads that are abnormally consumed; (2) the storage expenses (excluding the expenses which are necessary in the production process to reach the next production stage); and (3) other expenses that cannot be included in the cost of bringing the inventories to their present location and condition.

Article 10 The borrowing costs, which shall be included in the cost of inventories, shall be disposed in accordance with the Accounting Standard for Enterprises No. 17—Borrowing costs.

Article 11 The cost of inventories invested by an investor shall be ascertained in accordance with the value as stipulated in the investment contract or agreement, unless it is not stipulated fair in the contract or agreement.

Article 12 The cost of agricultural products in the harvest and the cost of inventories obtained by the exchange of non-monetary assets, recombination of liabilities, and merger of enterprises shall be ascertained in accordance with the Accounting Standard for Business Enterprises No. 5—Biological Assets, Accounting Standard for Business Enterprises No. 7—Exchange of Non-monetary Assets, Accounting Standard for Business Enterprises No. 12—Debt Restructurings, and Accounting Standard for Business Enterprises No. 20—Business Combinations, respectively.

Article 13 Where an enterprise provides labor service, the direct labor expenses, other direct expenses as well as the indirect expenses included thereto shall be included in the cost of inventories.

Article 14 An enterprise shall confirm the actual cost of sending out inventories by employing the first-in first-out method, the weighted average method, or the specific identification method. The cost of sending out inventories of items with similar nature and purpose shall be confirmed by employing the same cost calculation method. Generally, the cost of non-substitutable inventories, goods purchased and produced, labor services offered for specific projects, and the cost of sending out shall be confirmed by employing the specific identification method. As to the inventories, which have been already sold, their costs shall be carried forward as the current profits and losses and the relevant provision for the loss on decline in value of inventories shall also be carried forward.

Article 15 On the date of the balance sheet, the inventories shall be measured as either the cost or the net realizable, whichever is lower. If the cost of inventories is higher than the net realizable value, the provision for the loss on decline in value of inventories shall be made and be included in the current profits and losses. In the daily business activity, the net realizable value refers to the amount after deducting the estimated cost of completion, estimated sales expense, and relevant taxes from the estimated sales price of inventories.

Article 16 An enterprise shall confirm the net realizable value of inventories on the ground of reliable evidence obtained, taking into consideration the purpose for holding inventories and the effects of events occurring after the date of the balance sheet. The materials held for production shall be measured at cost if the net realizable value of the finished products is higher than the cost. If a decline of the value of materials shows that the net realizable value of the finished products is lower than the cost, the materials shall be measured at the net realizable value.

Article 17 The net realizable value of inventories held for the execution of sales contracts or labor contracts shall be calculated on the ground of the contract price. If an enterprise holds more inventories than the quantities subscribed in the sales contract, the net realizable value of the excessive part of the inventories shall be calculated on the ground of the general sales price.

Article 18 Ordinarily, an enterprise shall make provision for the loss on decline in value of inventories on the ground of each item of inventories. For inventories with large quantity and relatively low unit prices, the provision for the loss on decline in value of inventories shall be made on the ground of the categories of inventories. For the inventories related to the series of products manufactured and sold in the same area, with an identical or similar final use or purpose, and difficulty to be measured by separating them from other items, the provision for the loss on decline in value of inventories shall be made on a combination basis.

Article 19 An enterprise shall confirm the net realizable value of inventories on the balance sheet date. If the factors causing any write-down of the inventories have disappeared, the amount of write-down shall be resumed and be reversed from the provision for the loss on decline in value of inventories that has been made. The reversed amount shall be included in the current profits and losses.

Article 20 An enterprise shall amortize the easily consumed products of low value and packing by employing the one-off write-off method or equal-split amortization method and bring it in the cost of the relevant assets or in the current profits and losses.

Article 21 For any damage to the inventories of an enterprise, the enterprise shall include the amount after deducting the book value and relevant taxes from the disposal income in the current profits and losses. The book value of inventories shall refer to the amount after deducting the accumulative provision for the loss on decline in value of inventories from the cost of inventories. The loss of inventories shall be included in the current profits and losses.

5.4 Chapter IV: Disclosure

Article 22 An enterprise shall, in the notes, disclose the information concerning to inventories as follows: (1) the book value of all inventories at the beginning and end of the period; (2) the methods to confirm the cost of sending out inventories; (3) the basis for confirming the net realizable value of inventories, the methods to make provision for the loss on decline in value of inventories, the amount of the provision for the loss on decline in value of inventories to be reversed in the current period as well as the relevant information about the making and reversion of the provision for the loss on decline in value of inventories; and (4) the book value of inventories used for a guarantee.

5.5 Comments

According to the regulatory disposition, inventories are those assets held for sale in the ordinary course of business, in the process of production aimed for sale, or in the form of materials or supplies to be consumed in the production process or while providing services.

When accounting for their value, inventories shall be initially measured at their cost. The cost of inventories consists of the "purchase price, relevant taxes, transport fees, loading and unloading fees, insurance premiums, and other expenses that may be relegated to the purchase costs of inventories." Additionally, the initial cost shall account for other indirect costs, labor cost in case of internally produced goods, and borrowing costs in accordance with ASBE No. 17.

Inventories shall be carried at the lower cost value and net realizable value. The net realizable value is estimated to be the selling value of good on a daily business activity after deducting "the estimated cost of completion, estimated sales expense, and relevant taxes from the estimated sales price of inventories."

If the net realizable value of inventories is less than their cost (supposing that they have been initially carried at their cost), the company shall proceed to write off the difference between cost and net realizable value. In case of successive revaluation of inventories, the company may recover their value up to their initial amount. If inventories are damaged, this shall be recorded in profits and losses.

As a general provision, new ASBEs allow different options to evaluate the cost of inventories except LIFO, in line with IAS 2.

The inventories contributed by an investor (unless it is not possible to clearly determine their fair value) should be evaluated according to the value determined in the investment contract or agreement. Finally, the methods used to evaluate inventories produce a standardized result as the exemption for commodity distribution companies has been removed.

ASBE No.1 briefly explains some important information about inventory evaluation, providing dispositions very close to IAS 2.

5.6 Examples

For the sake of ease, let us assume that Company X purchases the following amounts of goods during the year and has no initial inventories:

- 30/01/Year: 1000 pieces, unit price 10 RMB;
- 30/05/Year: 500 pieces, unit price 15 RMB;
- 30/09/Year: 2500 pieces, unit price 8 RMB;

End-of-year inventories: 1500 pieces.

Now try to calculate end-year value for inventories under FIFO (first in first out), LIFO (last in first out), and WAC (weighted average cost) in case the specific identification of good is not feasible.

FIFO: The final inventories totally refer to the last batch (2000 pieces, unit price 8 RMB), so their value is $1500 \times 8 = 12{,}000$ RMB.

LIFO—The final inventories are shared between the first batch (1000 pieces, unit price 10 RMB) and the second batch (500 pieces, unit price 15 RMB). The final value is $(1000 \times 10) + (500 \times 15) = 10{,}000 + 7500 = 17{,}500$ RMB.

WAC—The final inventories are evaluated on an average cost weighted according to the different purchases. The final value is $1500 \times (1000/4000 \times 10 + 500/4000 \times 15 + 2500/4000 \times 8) = 1500 \times 9.375 = 14{,}062.5$.

To sum up, Company X shall adopt either FIFO (12,000 RMB) or WAC (14,062.5 RMB) as final evaluation for inventories. On the contrary, after 2007, LIFO evaluation (17,500 RMB) is no longer allowed.

Chapter 6
Accounting Standards for Business Enterprises No. 2—Long-Term Equity Investments

6.1 Chapter I: General Provisions

Article 1 In order to regulate the recognition and measurement of long-term equity investments, and disclosure of relevant information, these Standards are formulated in light of the Accounting Standards for Enterprises—Basic Standards.

Article 2 Other relevant accounting standards shall apply to such items as follows: (1) The Accounting Standards for Enterprises No. 19—Foreign Currency Translation shall apply to the translation of long-term equity investments in foreign currencies and (2) the Accounting Standards for Enterprises No. 22—Recognition and Measurement of Financial Instruments shall apply to the long-term investments which have not been dealt with by the present standards.

6.2 Chapter II: Initial Measurement

Article 3 The initial cost of the long-term equity investment formed in the merger of an enterprise shall be ascertained in accordance with the following provisions: (1) For the merger of enterprises under the same control, if the consideration of the merging enterprise is that it makes payment in cash, transfers non-cash assets, or bears its debts, it shall, on the date of merger, regard the share of the book value of the owner's equity of the merged enterprise as the initial cost of the long-term equity investment. The difference between the initial cost of the long-term equity investment and the payment in cash, non-cash assets transferred as well as the book value of the debts borne by the merging party shall offset against the capital reserve. If the capital reserve is insufficient to dilute, the retained earnings shall be adjusted. If the consideration of the merging enterprise is that it issues equity securities, it shall, on the date of merger, regard the share of the book value of the owner's equity of the merged enterprise as the initial cost of the long-term equity investment. The total

L. Riccardi, *China Accounting Standards*,
DOI 10.1007/978-981-10-0006-5_6

face value of the stocks issued shall be regarded as the capital stock, while the difference between the initial cost of the long-term equity investment and total face value of the shares issued shall offset against the capital reserve. If the capital reserve is insufficient to dilute, the retained earnings shall be adjusted. (2) For the merger under different control, the merging party shall, on the date of merger, regard the merger costs ascertained in accordance with the Accounting Standards for Enterprises No. 20—Merger of Enterprises as the initial cost of the long-term equity investment.

Article 4 Besides the long-term equity investments formed by the merger of enterprises, the initial cost of a long-term equity investment obtained by other means shall be ascertained in accordance with the provisions as follows: (1) The initial cost of a long-term equity investment obtained by making payment in cash shall be the purchase cost which is actually paid. The initial cost consists of the expenses directly relevant to the obtainment of the long-term equity investment, taxes, and other necessary expenses. (2) The initial cost of a long-term equity investment obtained on the basis of issuing equity securities shall be the fair value of the equity securities issued. (3) The initial cost of a long-term equity investment of an investor shall be the value stipulated in the investment contract or agreement except the unfair value stipulated in the contract or agreement. (4) The initial cost of a long-term investment obtained by the exchange of non-monetary assets shall be ascertained in accordance with the Accounting Standards for Enterprises No. 7—Exchange of Non-monetary Assets. (5) The initial cost of a long-term equity investment obtained by recombination of liabilities shall be ascertained in accordance with the Accounting Standards for Enterprises No. 12—Debt Restructuring.

6.3 Chapter III: Subsequent Measurement

Article 5 The following long-term equity investments shall, in accordance with *Article 7* of these Standards, be measured by employing the cost method: (1) A long-term equity investment of an investing enterprise that is able to control the invested enterprise. The term "control" refers to the power to determine the financial and operating polices of an enterprise and obtain benefits from its operating activities. If the investing enterprise can control an invested entity, the invested entity as its subsidiary company shall be included in the consolidation range of the consolidated financial statements. For a long-term equity investment on the subsidiary company of an investing enterprise, the investing enterprise shall be accounted for by employing the cost method as prescribed by these Standards and shall make an adjustment by employing the equity method when it works out consolidated financial statements. (2) A long-term equity investment of the investing enterprise that does not do joint control or does not have significant influences on the invested entity has no offer in the active market, and its fair value cannot be reliably measured. The term "joint control" refers to the control over an economic activity, in accordance with the contracts and agreements, which does not exist unless the investing parties of the economic activity with one an assent on sharing the control power over the relevant important financial and operating decisions. Where an investing enterprise and other parties do joint control over an invested entity, the invested entity shall be their joint enterprise. The term "significant influences" refers to the power to participate in making decisions on the financial and operating policies of an enterprise, but not to control or do joint control together with other parties over the formulation of these policies. Where an investing enterprise is able to have significant influences on an invested entity, the invested entity shall be its associated entity.

Article 6 When ascertaining whether or not it is able to control or have significant influences on an invested entity, an enterprise shall take into consideration the invested enterprises' current convertible corporate bonds and current executable warrants held by the investing enterprise and other parties, as well as other potential factors concerning the voting rights.

Article 7 The price of a long-term equity investment measured by employing the cost method shall be included at its initial investment cost. If there are additional investments or disinvestments, the cost of the long-term equity investment shall be adjusted. The dividends or profits declared to distribute by the invested entity shall be recognized as the current investment income. The investment income recognized by the investing enterprise shall be limited to the amount received from the accumulative net profits that arise after the invested entity has accepted the investment. Where the amount of profits or cash dividends obtained by the investing entity exceeds the aforesaid amount, it shall be regarded as recovery of initial investment cost.

Article 8 A long-term equity investment of the investing enterprise that does joint control or significant influences over the invested entity shall, in accordance with *Articles 9* through *13* of these Standards, be measured by employing the equity method.

Article 9 If the initial cost of a long-term equity investment is more than the investing enterprise's attributable share of the fair value of the invested entity's identifiable net assets for the investment, the initial cost of the long-term equity investment may not be adjusted. If the initial cost of a long-term equity investment is less than the investing enterprise's attributable share of the fair value of the invested entity's identifiable net assets for the investment, the difference shall be included in the current profits and losses and the cost of the long-term equity investment shall be adjusted simultaneously. The fair value of the identifiable net assets of the invested entity shall be ascertained by referring to the relevant provisions of the Accounting Standards for Enterprises No. 20—Merger of Enterprises.

Article 10 After an investing enterprise obtains a long-term equity investment, it shall, in accordance with the attributable share of the net profits or losses of the invested entity, recognize the investment profits or losses and adjust the book value of the long-term equity investment. The investing enterprise shall, in light of the profits or cash dividends declared to distribute by the invested entity, calculate the proportion it shall obtain, and shall reduce the book value of the long-term equity investment correspondingly.

Article 11 An investing enterprise shall recognize the net losses of the invested enterprise until the book value of the long-term equity investment and other long-term rights and interests which substantially form the net investment made to the invested entity are reduced to zero, unless the investing enterprise has the obligation to undertake extra losses. If the invested entity realizes any net profits later, the investing enterprise shall, after the amount of its attributable share of profits offsets against its attributable share of the unrecognized losses, resume to recognize its attributable share of profits.

Article 12 The investing enterprise shall, on the ground of the fair value of all identifiable assets of the invested entity when it obtains the investment, recognize the attributable share of the net profits and losses of the invested entity after it adjusts the net profits of the invested entity. If the accounting policies and accounting periods adopted by the invested entity are different from those adopted by the investing enterprise, an adjustment shall be made to the financial statements of the invested entity in accordance with the accounting policies and accounting periods of the investing enterprise and recognize the investment profits or losses.

Article 13 Where any change is made to the owner's equity other than the net profits and losses of the invested entity, the book value of the long-term equity investment shall be adjusted and be included in the owner's equity.

Article 14 For a long-term equity investment for which there is no offer in the active market and of which the fair value cannot be reliably measured, if the investing enterprise has not joint control or significant influence over the invested entity any more as a result of the decrease of investment or other reasons, the cost method shall be employed in the measurement, and the book value of the long-term equity investment employing the equity method shall be regarded as the initial investment cost to be measured by employing the cost method. If an enterprise is able to do joint control or significant influence, which does not constitute control, over the invested entity as a result of additional investment or other reasons, the equity method shall be employed in the measurement, and the book value of the long-term equity investment measured by employing the cost method or the book value of investment ascertained in accordance with the Accounting Standards for Enterprises No. 22—Recognition and Measurement of Financial Instruments shall be regarded as initial investment cost measured by employing the cost method.

Article 15 The impairment of a long-term equity investment which is measured by employing the cost method as prescribed in these Standards, for which there is no offer in the active market and of which the fair value cannot be reliably measured, its impairment shall be disposed in accordance with the Accounting Standards for Enterprises No. 22—Recognition and Measurement of Financial Instruments. The impairment of any other long-term equity investment measured in accordance with these Standards shall be disposed in accordance with the Accounting Standards for Enterprises No. 8—Asset Impairment.

Article 16 When disposing of a long-term equity investment, the difference between its book value and the actual purchase price shall be included in the current profits and losses. If any change other than the net profits and losses of the invested entity occurs and it is included in the owner's equity, the portion previously included in the owner's equity shall, when disposing of a long-term equity investment measured by employing the equity method, be transferred to the current profits and losses according to a certain proportion.

6.4 Chapter IV: Disclosure

Article 17 An investing enterprise shall, in the notes, disclose the information concerning long-term equity investments as follows: (1) the name list of its subsidiary companies, joint ventures, and associated enterprises, consisting of the names, registration places, and business nature, proportions of shares, and proportions of voting rights of the investing enterprises; (2) the main financial information of the joint ventures and associated enterprises, consisting of the aggregate amounts of assets, liabilities, incomes, expenses, etc.; (3) the information about the restriction of the invested entity' s capacity of transferring funds to the investing entity; (4) the current period and accumulative amounts of unrecognized investment losses; and (5) the contingent liabilities or the investments in the subsidiary companies, joint ventures, and associated enterprises.

6.5 Comments

The aim of ASBE No. 2 is to ameliorate and integrate the accounting procedures referring to long-term investments. In particular, it focuses on accounting requirements for parents, and controlled or associated enterprises.

Under new ASBEs, a subsidiary shall be recorded in the separate financial statement of the parent company when using the cost method instead of the equity method. In order to assess an enterprises' ability to control or significantly influence another enterprise, the main driver to be considered is the "potential voting right."

An important change regarding the initial measurement requirements for long-term equity investment involving entities under the same control. In fact, in the case of "common control" (namely both entities are controlled by the same parties both before and later and in a non-transitory time extent), the amount of acquired entity should be adjusted to consider the share of net assets and any difference referred to capital surplus or retained earnings according to the circumstances.

New ASBEs also introduce the equity method as an accounting method for the invested company. Accordingly, the investor entity, after having proceeded to adjust the value of identifiable assets at the moment of acquisition, shall recognize its share of profits.

ASBE No. 2 also presents several differences from equivalent dispositions under IAS/IFRS. As stated before, new Chinese standards largely account for the equity method and dispose a separate financial statement only if the case of cost method is used. IAS 27 addresses this point requiring subsidiaries, associates, and jointly controlled entities to be stated in separate financial statements regardless if under cost or equity method. Furthermore, ASBE No. 2 does not allow the proportionate consolidation to recognize interests and does not provide indication about the control of joint operations/assets.

6.6 Example

Referring to two entities under the same control, let us assume that Company X purchases a 40 % stake in Company Y for 1,000,000 RMB. In such a situation, we assume that Company X exercises a significant influence over Company Y requiring the equity method.

Scenario 1 The original carrying amount of net assets of Company Y is assessed to be worth 2,000,000 RMB (hence, the share of net assets is 800,000 RMB). In this scenario, the exceeding amount of 200,000 RMB shall be accounted as capital surplus.

Scenario 2 The original carrying amount of net assets of Company Y is assessed to be worth 750,000 RMB (hence, the share of net assets is 1,100,000 RMB). In this second scenario, we record an exceeding amount of 100,000 RMB to be recorded as retained earnings.

Still figuring out this example, suppose a final net profit of 100,000 RMB for Company Y. Now assume two different scenarios for the end-year value of identifiable assets at the time of acquisition.

Scenario 1 The end-year value of original assets for Company Y shows a loss of 150,000 RMB. The share of profits Company X shall recognize is (200,000–150,000) × 40 % = 20,000 RMB.

Scenario 2 The end-year value of original assets for Company Y shows a gain of 100,000 RMB. The share of profits Company X shall recognize is (200,000 + 100,000) × 40 % = 120,000 RMB.

Chapter 7
Accounting Standards for Business Enterprises No. 3—Investment Real Estates

7.1 Chapter I: General Provisions

Article 1 In order to regulate the recognition and measurement of the investment real estates and disclosure of the relevant information, these Standards are formulated in light of the Accounting Standards for Enterprises—Basic Standards.

Article 2 The term "investment real estates" refers to the real estates held for generating rent and/or capital appreciation. The investment real estate shall be measured and sold, respectively.

Article 3 These standards shall apply to the following investment real estates: (1) The right to use any land which has already been rented; (2) The right to use any land which is held and prepared for transfer after appreciation; and (3) The right to use any building which has already been rented.

Article 4 The following items are not included within the scope of investment real estates: (1) The real estates for self-use, that is to say, the real estates held for manufacturing commodities, rendering labor services, or business management; and (2) The real estates regarded as inventories.

Article 5 Other relevant accounting standards shall apply to the items as follows: (1) The Accounting Standards for Enterprises—Construction Contracts shall apply to the real estates built by enterprises for others; and (2) The Accounting Standards for Enterprises No. 21—Leasing shall apply to the income from rents of investment real estates and the leaseback of investment real estates.

L. Riccardi, *China Accounting Standards*,
DOI 10.1007/978-981-10-0006-5_7

7.2 Chapter II: Recognition and Initial Measurement

Article 6 No investment real estate shall be recognized unless it meets the following requirements simultaneously: (1) The economic benefits pertinent to this investment real estate are likely to flow into the enterprise; and (2) The cost of the investment real estate can be reliably measured.

Article 7 The initial measurement of the investment real estate shall be made at its cost. (1) The cost of an investment in real estate by acquisition consists of the acquisition price, relevant taxes, and other expenses directly relegated to the asset. (2) The cost of a self-built investment real estate composes of the necessary expenses for building the asset to the hoped condition for use. (3) The cost of an investment real estate obtained by other means shall be recognized in accordance with the relevant accounting standards.

Article 8 For the follow-up expenses pertinent to an investment real estate, if they meet the recognition conditions as mentioned in *Article 6* of these Standards, they shall be included in the cost of the investment real estate; otherwise, if they fail to meet the recognition conditions as mentioned in *Article 6* of these Standards, they shall be included in the current profits and losses when they are incurred.

7.3 Chapter III: Follow-Up Measurement

Article 9 An enterprise shall make a follow-up measurement to the investment real estate through the cost pattern on the date of the balance sheet except that the investment real estate complies with the provisions of *Article 10* of these measures. The Accounting Standards for Enterprises No. 4—Fixed Assets shall apply to the follow-up measurement of a building measured through the cost pattern. The Accounting Standards for Enterprises No. 4—Intangible Assets shall apply to the follow-up measurement of the right to the use of the land measured through the cost pattern.

Article 10 Where any well-established evidence shows that the fair value of an investment real estate can be obtained in a continuous and reliable way, a follow-up measurement may be made to the investment real estate through the fair value pattern. To make a measurement through the fair value pattern, the following conditions shall be met simultaneously: (1) There is an active trading market of real estate in the location of the investment real estate; and (2) The enterprise is able to obtain the market prices of the identical or similar real estates and other relevant information from the trading market of real estate, so as to be able to estimate the fair value of the investment real estate.

Article 11 For the investment real estate measured through the fair value pattern, where there is no accrual depreciation or amortization made for it, its book value shall be adjusted on the basis of its fair value on the date of the balance sheet, and the difference between the fair value and its original book value shall be included in the current profits and losses.

Article 12 Once an enterprise's pattern for the measurement of the investment real estate is decided, it shall not be changed randomly. If the enterprise replaces the cost pattern by the fair value pattern, it shall be considered that it has changed its accounting policy, which shall be disposed in accordance with the Accounting Standards No. 28—Changes in Accounting Policies and Estimates and Correction of Errors. For an investment real estate that has been measured through the fair value pattern, the pattern of its measurement shall not be changed from the fair value pattern to the cost method.

7.4 Chapter IV: Conversion

Article 13 Where an enterprise which has well-established evidence to indicate that the purpose of the real estate has changed, it shall convert the investment real estate to other assets or vice versa, when it meets any of the following conditions: (1) The investment real estate begins to be used for its own; (2) The investment real estate for inventory is changed for rent; (3) The lands with the right to self-use are changed for generating rents or capital appreciation; or (4) The buildings with the right to self-use are changed for rent.

Article 14 Under the cost pattern, the book value of the real estate prior to the conversion shall be the entry value after conversion.

Article 15 Where an investment real estate measured through the fair value pattern is converted into self-use real estate, the fair value on the date of conversion shall be the book value of the self-use real estate. The difference between the fair value and the original book value shall be included in the current profits and losses.

Article 16 When any self-use real estate or real estate for inventory is converted to investment real estate to be measured through the fair value pattern, the investment real estate shall valuate under the fair value on the date of the conversion. If the fair value on the date of the conversion is less than the original book value, the difference shall be included in the current profits and losses. If the fair value on the date of the conversion is more than the original book value, the difference shall be included in the owner's rights and interests.

7.5 Chapter V: Disposal

Article 17 If an investment real estate is disposed of, or if it withdraws permanently from use and if no economic benefit will be obtained from the disposal, the recognition of it, as an investment real estate, shall be terminated.

Article 18 When an enterprise sells, transfers, or discards any investment real estate, or when any investment real estate of an enterprise is damaged or destroyed, the enterprise shall deduct the book value of the investment real estate as well as the relevant taxes from the disposal income and include the amount in the current profits and losses.

7.6 Chapter VI: Disclosure

Article 19 An enterprise shall, in the notes, disclose the information concerning the investment real estates as follows: (1) The type, amount, and measurement pattern of the investment real estates; (2) The information on the depreciation or amortization as well as the provision for the impairment of the investment real estates measured through the cost pattern; (3) As to the investment real estate measured through the fair value pattern, its basis and pattern for the recognition of the fair value, and the relevant effects of changes of the fair value on the profits and losses; (4) The information about the conversion of the real estates and the relevant reasons, as well as the effects on the profits and losses or the owner's rights and interests; and (5) The investment real estates disposed currently and the relevant effects on the profits and losses.

7.7 Comments

As stated in *Article 2*, investment property is a category of properties (regardless the nature of the real estate) held to earn rental income, to gain capital appreciation, or both. An investment property shall be measured initially at its cost (including transactions costs). In order to evaluate the investment property, both fair value and cost models are permitted.

An investment property shall be eliminated from the balance sheet both in case of disposal or when the property is withdrawn permanently from use and there are no future economic benefits expected from its disposal. Gains or losses arising from the retirement or disposal of investment property are determined between the net disposal proceeds and the net carrying value of the property. The value of profits/losses shall be recognized in the period of retirement/disposal of the property.

The principal innovation upon the existing ASBEs refers to an additional line item to indicate separately the "investment properties" category. They are accounted for using the cost method in the same manner as fixed assets. Under the precedent version, investment properties were recorded as either fixed assets or other long-term assets.

In accordance with the new provision, if there is clear evidence that the fair value of an investment could be reliably recognized on a continuing basis, the fair value model shall be used. Under the fair value method, no depreciation or amortization is provided: For such properties, the difference between the fair value and the carrying amount should be computed directly in profit or loss.

From the IAS/IFRS perspective, some differences deserve attention. First, IAS 40 extends the scope of ASBE 3 including also land held for undetermined use and under certain criteria property interests deriving from operating leases. Secondly, IAS 40 disposes that a company shall maintain the same accounting criteria for all categories of its properties. On this point, ASBE 3 does not provide similar requirements.

Finally, IAS 40 classifies use rights held for rental purpose as an investment property under the fair value model adopted. ASBE 3 allows land-use rights held for the same purpose to be classified either using the cost model or fair value method (in the last case if this model can be reliably determined on a continuing basis).

7.8 Examples

Company X has an investment property with a carrying amount of 1,000,000 RMB (According to AASB 140, carrying amount is defined as the amount which an asset is recognized in the statement of financial positions). Assuming that the conditions that reliably recognize the fair value of the property are met, let us figure out the following scenarios at 31/12/Y.

Case 1 According to the fair value method, the property is assessed to be worth 1,200,000 RMB. At the end of the fiscal year, Company X shall recognize a positive income item of 200,000 RMB.

Case 2 Still according to the fair value method, the property is assessed 850,000 RMB. At the end of the fiscal year, Company X shall recognize a negative income item of 150,000 RMB.

Chapter 8
Accounting Standards for Business Enterprises No. 4—Fixed Assets

8.1 Chapter I: General Provisions

Article 1 In order to regulate the recognition and measurement of the fixed assets, and disclosure of the relevant information, these Standards are formulated in light of the Accounting Standards for Enterprises—Basic Standards.

Article 2 Other relevant accounting standards shall apply to the items as follows: (1) The Accounting Standards No. 3—Investment Real Estates shall apply to the buildings as investment real estates; and (2) The Accounting Standards No. 5—Biological Assets shall apply to the productive biological assets.

8.2 Chapter II: Recognition

Article 3 The term "fixed assets" refers to the tangible assets that simultaneously possess the features as follows: (1) They are held for the sake of producing commodities, rendering labor service, renting, or business management; and (2) their useful life is in excess of one fiscal year. The term "useful life" refers to the period of time over which a fixed asset is expected to be used, the quantity of products expected to be produced, or services expected to be rendered through the fixed asset.

Article 4 No fixed asset may be recognized unless it simultaneously meets the conditions as follows: (1) The economic benefits pertinent to the fixed asset are likely to flow into the enterprise; and (2) the cost of the fixed asset can be measured reliably.

Article 5 The components of a fixed asset have different useful lives or cause economic benefits for the enterprise in different ways and to which different depreciation rates or depreciation methods apply, and they shall be recognized as fixed assets on an individual component basis.

L. Riccardi, *China Accounting Standards*,
DOI 10.1007/978-981-10-0006-5_8

Article 6 If the subsequent expenses related to a fixed asset meet the recognition conditions as described in *Article 4* of these Standards, they shall be included in the cost of fixed asset; otherwise, they shall be included in the current profits and losses.

8.3 Chapter III: Initial Measurement

Article 7 The initial measurement of a fixed asset shall be made at its cost.

Article 8 The cost of a purchased fixed asset consists of the purchase price, the relevant taxes, freights, loading and unloading fees, professional service fees, and other expenses that bring the fixed asset to the expected conditions for use and that may be relegated to the fixed asset. If a certain payment is made for purchasing several fixed assets not priced separately, the cost of each fixed asset shall be ascertained by allocating the payment according to the proportion of fair value of each fixed asset to the total cost of all assets acquired. If the payment for a fixed asset is delayed beyond the normal credit conditions and it is of financing nature in effect, the cost of the fixed asset shall be ascertained based on the current value of the purchase price. The difference between the actual payment and the current value of the purchase price shall be included in the current profits and losses within the credit period, unless it shall be capitalized in accordance with the Accounting Standards No. 17—Borrowing Costs.

Article 9 The cost of a self-constructed fixed asset shall be formed by the necessary expenses incurred for bringing the asset to the expected conditions for use.

Article 10 The borrowing costs, which shall be included in the cost of a fixed asset, shall be disposed in light of the Accounting Standards No. 17—Borrowing Costs.

Article 11 The cost invested to a fixed asset by the investor shall be ascertained in accordance with the value as stipulated in the investment contract or agreement, other than those of unfair value as stipulated in the contract or agreement.

Article 12 The costs of fixed assets acquired through the exchange of non-monetary assets, recombination of liabilities, merger of enterprises, and financial leasing shall be, respectively, ascertained in accordance with the Accounting Standards No. 7—Exchange of Non-monetary Assets, Accounting Standards for Enterprises No. 12—Debt Restructuring, Accounting Standards for Enterprises No. 20—Merger of Enterprises, and Accounting Standards for Enterprises No. 21—Leases.

Article 13 The expected discard expenses should be taken into consideration in the ascertainment of the cost of a fixed asset.

8.4 Chapter IV: Subsequent Measurement

Article 14 An enterprise shall make depreciation for all its fixed assets. However, the fixed assets that have been fully depreciated but are still in use and the land that is separately measured and included shall be excluded. The term "depreciation" refers to the systematic amortization of the depreciable amount through a definite method during the useful life of the fixed asset. The term "depreciable amount" refers to the amount of deducting its expected net salvage value from the original price of the fixed asset to be depreciated. For a fixed asset of which the provision for depreciation has been made, one shall deduct the accumulative amount of the provision for impairment of the depreciated fixed asset that has been already made. The "expected net salvage value" refers to the expected amount that an enterprise may obtain from the current disposal of a fixed asset after deducting the expected disposal expenses at the expiration of its expected useful life.

Article 15 An enterprise shall, in accordance with the nature and use of a fixed asset, reasonably ascertain its useful life and expected net salvage value. Once an enterprise decides the useful life or expected net salvage value of the fixed asset, it shall not change it randomly except that the provisions of *Article 19* of these Standards are met.

Article 16 When the useful life of a fixed asset is ascertained, the enterprise shall take into consideration the factors as follows: (1) the expected production capacity or output of physical objects; (2) the expected tangible and intangible loss of the asset; and (3) limits of statutory or similar provisions on the use of asset.

Article 17 An enterprise shall reasonably select a depreciation method for a fixed asset in accordance with the expected form for the realization of the economic benefits concerning the fixed asset. The available depreciation methods consist of the straight-line method, unit of production method, double declining balance method, sum of the years digits method, etc. Once an enterprise ascertains the method of depreciation of the fixed asset, it shall not change it randomly, except that the provisions of *Article 19* of these Standards are met.

Article 18 Depreciation shall be made for the fixed assets on a monthly basis and shall, in accordance with the purposes of the fixed assets, be included in the cost of the relevant assets or in the current profits and losses.

Article 19 An enterprise shall, at least at the end of each year, have a check on the useful life, expected net salvage value, and the depreciation method of the fixed assets. If there is any difference between the expected useful life and the previously estimated useful life of a fixed asset, the expected useful life of the fixed asset shall be adjusted. If there is any difference between the amount of expected net salvage value and the previously estimated amount of the net salvage value, the expected net salvage value shall be adjusted. If any significant change is made on the form of the realization of the expected economic benefits concerning a fixed asset, the method for the depreciation of the fixed asset shall be changed. If any change is made to the useful life, expected net salvage value, or the depreciation method of a fixed asset, it shall be regarded as a change of the accounting estimates.

Article 20 The impairment of a fixed asset shall be disposed in light of the Accounting Standards for Enterprises No. 8—Asset Impairment.

8.5 Chapter V: Disposal

Article 21 Where a fixed asset meets either of the conditions as follows, the recognition of it as a fixed asset shall be terminated: (1) The fixed asset is in a state of disposal; or (2) the fixed asset is unable to generate any economic benefits through use or disposal as expected.

Article 22 An enterprise shall adjust its expected net salvage value of the fixed assets it holds for sale.

Article 23 When an enterprise sells, transfers, or discards any fixed asset, or when any fixed asset of an enterprise is damaged or destroyed, the enterprise shall deduct the book value and relevant taxes from the disposal income and include the amount in the current profits and losses. The book value of the fixed assets is the amount after deducting the accumulative depreciation and accumulative impairment provision from the cost of the fixed assets. The losses of inventories of the fixed assets shall be included in the current profits and losses.

Article 24 Where an enterprise includes the subsequent disbursements for a fixed asset in the cost of the fixed asset in accordance with *Article 6* of these Standards, the book value of the substituted part shall be terminated the recognition as the cost of the fixed asset.

8.6 Chapter VI: Disclosure

Article 25 An enterprise shall, in the notes, disclose the information concerning fixed assets as follows: (1) the conditions of recognition, classifications, measurement basis, and depreciation methods for the fixed assets; (2) the useful lives, expected net salvage values, and depreciation rates of the various fixed assets; (3) the original prices at the beginning and the end, the amount of accumulative depreciation, and accumulative amount of the impairment provisions for fixed assets; (4) the current recognition of the depreciation disbursements; (5) the limits on the ownership of the fixed assets, the amount of the fixed assets, and the book value of fixed assets used for guarantees; and (6) the name, book value, fair value, expected disposal expenses, expected disposal costs and the expected time for disposal, etc.

8.7 Comments

ASBE No. 4 applies to property, plant, and equipment excluding investment properties which fall under ASBE No. 3. Different categories of assets such as Biological and Intangible Assets fall under devoted ASBE No. 5 and ASBE No. 6.

Fixed assets are defined as tangible items that are held for use in the production or supply of goods or services for administrative purposes. They are expected to be used in company operations for more than one accounting period. The cost model is the permitted method to record the carrying amount of the assets. It is measured at cost less depreciation and eventual impairment (which is recognized as an expense).

Fixed assets, also in accordance with IAS 16, shall be recognized if they simultaneously meet the following conditions: "(1) The economic benefits pertinent to the fixed asset are likely to flow into the enterprise; and (2) the cost of the fixed asset can be measured reliably."

Fixed assets are initially recorded at their cost of purchase. The cost consists of "the relevant taxes, freights, loading and unloading fees, professional service fees, and other expenses that bring the fixed asset to the expected conditions for use and that may be relegated to the fixed asset. In case of bundled purchase of several assets upon only one payment, the cost of each single asset shall be computed. With regard to borrowing costs burden to purchase fixed assets, further explanation will be provided in ASBE No. 17. The cost of a self-constructed fixed asset shall be computed by the necessary expenses incurred to make the asset suitable for the conditions of use.

An important issue is related to depreciation. Its amount is referred as yearly loss in carrying value of the asset, due to operating activity. It shall be calculated on a systematic basis and be recorded as an expense in the income statement. Depreciation also depends on the expected useful life (usage) of the asset. The depreciation should reflect the pattern according to which the asset's useful life is forecasted.

As already seen for inventories, items of property, plant, and equipment, they shall be derecognized on disposal or when no future economic benefit is expected from its use. Any difference between proceeds from disposal and carrying amount of asset should be recognized as an item on the income statement for the period.

Under the new regulatory statement of ASBE No. 4, two separate recognition principles for initial costs and subsequent expenditure are provisioned. Firstly, for the initial costs, they should be capitalized when it is probable that future economic benefits will flow to the enterprise and the initial cost can be measured reliably. Secondly, the subsequent expenses occurred after the fixed assets have taken part to enterprise's operations should be capitalized only if their expenditure will improve the asset's condition beyond its originally assessed standard of performance. In both cases, ASBE No. 4 provides the first recognition principle to measure both initial costs and subsequent expenditures. According to this perspective, under new ASBEs, dismantling and removal expenses shall be included in the cost of the fixed asset.

With regard to the payment, if it is deferred beyond normal credit terms, then the difference between the original price equivalent and the total payment due (namely, the interest expense) is recognized either as an interest over the period of credit or capitalized according to ASBE No. 17 (Borrowing Costs).

New ASBE No. 4 also restates the concept of residual value as "an amount an enterprise would currently receive for the asset if the asset were already of the age and in the condition expected at the end of its useful life." In addition, it prescribes to periodically revise at least each financial period of the estimation of residual value and the depreciation method as well. Precedent correspondent GAAP required only a periodic review of above subject.

Also, the carrying amount of each component of a fixed asset which has been replaced shall be derecognized, and the cost of replacement included in the carrying amount of the asset. Finally, unless the terms of contract are not fair, the cost of fixed assets contributed by investors shall be determined according to the value stipulated in the investment contract or agreement.

The most important difference to IAS/IFRS equivalent dispositions refers to the revaluation. In fact, IAS 16 allows for fixed assets both the cost model and the revaluation model. In the second case, if any item belonging to property, plant, and equipment is revaluated, the entire category shall be revaluated. New ASBE 4 only allows the cost model.

8.8 Examples

Company X purchases equipment worth 2,000,000 RMB. After the installation process requiring an additional disbursement of 100,000 RMB, the equipment is ready to use for the last six months of the year. Finally, according to its usage, it is expected to depreciate on a straight-line basis on next 10 years. The initial book value of the assets is its cost plus additional setup expenses 2,100,000 RMB.

The depreciation for the first year is (2,100,000/10)/2 = 105,000 RMB (the share of depreciation referred to six months), and the carrying value is 1,995,000 RMB.

Assuming no impairment occurred over years, at the beginning of year 3 Company X bears additional 500,000 RMB of costs to improve the expected performance of the equipment. Since the net carrying vaule of depreciation for the equipment is 1,785,000 RMB (estimated as 2,100,000–105,000–210,000), the expenses of 500,000 RMB increase the carrying value for the equipment up to 2,285,000 RMB.

Chapter 9
Accounting Standards for Business Enterprises No. 5—Biological Assets

9.1 Chapter I: General Provisions

Article 1 In order to regulate the recognition and measurement of biological assets related to the agricultural production, and the disclosure of relevant information, these Standards are formulated in accordance with the Accounting Standards for Enterprises—Basic Standards.

Article 2 Biological assets refer to living animals and plants.

Article 3 Biological assets have a classification of consumptive biological assets, productive biological assets, and public welfare biological assets.

The consumptive biological assets refer to the biological assets held for sale or biological assets to be harvested as agricultural products in the future, consisting of growing field crops, vegetables, commercial forests, livestock on hand, etc.

The productive biological assets refer to the biological assets held on the purpose of producing agricultural products, rendering labor services, renting, etc., consisting of the economic forests, fuel forests, productive livestock, draught animals, etc. The public welfare biological assets refer to the biological assets for the main purpose of protection or environmental protection, consisting of windbreak and sand fixation forests, water and soil conservation forests, water conservation forests, etc.

Article 4 Other relevant accounting standards shall apply to the items as follows: (1) The Accounting Standards for Enterprises No. 1—Inventories shall apply to the agricultural production of the harvest; and (2) The Accounting Standards for Enterprises No. 16—Governmental Subsidies shall apply to the governmental subsidies concerning the biological assets.

L. Riccardi, *China Accounting Standards*,
DOI 10.1007/978-981-10-0006-5_9

9.2 Chapter II: Recognition and Initial Measurement

Article 5 No biological asset shall be recognized unless it meets the following conditions simultaneously: (1) An enterprise possesses or controls the biological asset as a result of past transaction or event; (2) the economic benefits or service potential concerning this biological asset is likely to flow into the enterprise; and (3) the cost of this biological asset can be measured reliably.

Article 6 The initial measurement shall be made to the biological asset at its cost.

Article 7 The cost of a purchased biological asset consists of the purchase price, the relevant taxes, freight, insurance premium, and other expenses that may be directly attributable to the purchase of this asset.

Article 8 The cost of any consumptive biological asset by way of self-planting, self-cultivating, and self-breeding shall be ascertained in accordance with the provisions as follows: (1) The cost of self-planting crops and vegetables consists of the necessary expenses for the materials such as the seeds, fertilizers, and pesticides, labor, indirect apportionment, etc., prior to the harvest; (2) the cost of consumptive biological asset such as self-cultivating forest consists of the necessary expenses for forestation, forest tending, forest operating facilities, testing of good species, investigation and design, indirect apportionment, etc; (3) the cost of self-breeding livestock raised exclusively for meat production consists of the necessary expenses for feed, labor, indirect apportionment, etc., prior to the sale; and (4) the cost of breeding aquatic animals and plants consists of the necessary expenses for materials such as seedlings, feedstuffs, and fertilizers, labor, indirect apportionment, etc., prior to the sale or the storage.

Article 9 The cost of self-breeding productive biological asset shall be ascertained in accordance with the provisions as follows: (1) The cost of self-planting productive biological assets as forests consists of the necessary expenses for forestation, forest tending, forest operating facilities, testing of good species, investigation and design, indirect apportionment, etc., before accomplishing the expected objective of production and operation; and (2) the cost of self-breeding productive livestock and draught animals consists of the necessary expenses for feedstuffs and labor, indirect apportionment, etc., before accomplishing the expected objective of production and operation (being grown up). The phrase "accomplishing the expected objective of production and operation" refers that the productive biological assets may produce agricultural products, render labor services, and be rented out stably for several consecutive years after they enter into the normal production period.

Article 10 The cost of self-cultivating public welfare biological assets shall be ascertained in accordance with the necessary expenses for forestation, forest tending, forest protection, forest operating facilities, testing of good species, investigation and design, indirect apportionment, etc., prior to the close canopy.

Article 11 The borrowing costs, which shall be included in the cost of biological assets, shall be disposed in accordance with the Accounting Standards for Enterprises No. 17—Borrowing Costs. The borrowing costs of consumptive biological assets such as forests shall be stopped from being capitalized at the close canopy.

Article 12 An investor shall ascertained the cost of a biological asset in accordance with the value as stipulated in the investment contract or agreement, unless the unfair value is stipulated in the contract or agreement.

Article 13 The cost of a biological asset sourced from the nature shall be ascertained in accordance with its nominal amount.

Article 14 The cost of biological assets obtained from the exchange of non-monetary assets, recombination liabilities, and merger of enterprises shall be ascertained in accordance with the Accounting Standards for Enterprises No. 7—Exchange of Non-monetary Assets, Accounting Standards for Enterprises No. 12—Debt Restructuring, and Accounting Standards for Enterprises No. 20—Merger of Enterprises, respectively.

Article 15 The subsequent expenses for the biological assets as additional forest planting as a result of selective felling, intermediate felling, or tending and improvement felling shall be included in the cost of the biological asset as forests. The subsequent expenses for the management and protection or for the breeding of a biological asset after canopy closure or after the accomplishment of the expected objective of production and operation shall be included in the current profits and losses.

9.3 Chapter III: Subsequent Measurement

Article 16 An enterprise shall make subsequent measurements for the biological assets in accordance with the provisions from *Article 17* to *Article 21* of these Standards except for the items as prescribed in *Article 22* of these Standards.

Article 17 An enterprise shall, in accordance with the schedule, make the depreciation charges of any productive biological asset whose expected objective of production and purpose has been accomplished, and shall, based on the use of the biological asset, include it in the cost or current profits and losses of the relevant asset.

Article 18 An enterprise shall, in accordance with the nature of a productive biological asset, the information about the utilization, and the form of realization of the relevant expected economic benefits, reasonably ascertain the useful life, expected net salvage value, and depreciation methods of this productive biological asset. The depreciation methods available consist of the straight-line method, unit-of-production method, unit-of-output method, etc. Once an enterprise ascertains the useful life, expected net salvage value, or depreciation method of a productive biological asset, it shall not change it randomly, unless it meets the provisions prescribed as in *Article 20* of these Standards.

Article 19 When an enterprise ascertains the useful life of a productive biological asset, it shall take into consideration the factors as follows: (1) The expected output capacity or output of physical objects; (2) the expected tangible loss of the asset such as decrepitude of productive livestock and draught animals and the aging of economic forests; and (3) the expected intangible loss of the asset, such as the relative decrease or degrade in the production capacity of the productive biological asset, or the quality of the agricultural products produced thereby as a result of appearance of new products, the relative outmode of the agricultural products of the productive biological asset as a result of the change of market demands.

Article 20 An enterprise shall, at least at the end of each year, have a check on the useful life, expected net salvage value, and depreciation method of the productive biological assets. If there is any difference between the expected useful life or the amount of expected net salvage value and that of the previously estimated in a fixed asset, or if any significant change is made on the form of realization of the relevant economic benefits, it shall be regarded as a change of the accounting estimates, and thus, the useful life or the expected net salvage value or depreciation method of the productive biological asset shall be adjusted or changed in accordance with the Accounting Standards for Enterprises No. 28—Changes in Accounting Policies and Estimates, and Correction of Errors.

Article 21 An enterprise shall, at least at the end of each year, examine the consumptive biological assets and productive biological assets. If any well-established evidence indicates that the realizable net value of any consumptive biological asset or the recoverable amount of any productive biological asset is lower than its book value as a result of natural disaster, plant diseases and insect pests, animal disease, or change of market demand, the enterprise shall, based on the difference between the realizable net value or the recoverable amount and the relevant book value, make provision for the loss on decline in value of or for the impairment of the biological asset and shall include it in the current profits and losses. The aforesaid realizable net value and recoverable amount shall be ascertained in accordance with the Accounting Standards for Enterprises No. 1—Inventories and Accounting Standards for Enterprises No. 8—Asset Impairment, respectively. If the factors causing any impairment of a consumptive biological asset have disappeared, the amount of write-down shall be resumed and shall be reversed from the provision for the loss on decline in value of the consumptive biological asset that has been made. The reversed amount shall be included in the current profits and losses. Once the provision for impairment of a productive biological asset is made, it shall not be reversed. No provision shall be made for public welfare biological assets.

Article 22 Where any well-established evidence indicates that the fair value of a biological asset can be obtained in a reliable and continuous way, the biological asset shall be measured at the fair value. If a biological asset is to be measured at fair value, it shall meet the following conditions simultaneously: (1) There is an active biological asset trading market; and (2) the identical or similar market prices of biological assets and other relevant information can be obtained from the trading market, so as to make a reasonable estimate on the fair value of the biological asset.

9.4 Chapter IV: Harvest and Disposal

Article 23 The cost of a consumptive biological asset shall, at the time of harvest or sale, be carried over in accordance with its book value. The methods available for the carryover of cost consist of the weighted average method, specific cost identification method, stock volume proportion method, fixed number of years within rotational felling period method, etc.

Article 24 The cost of agricultural products harvested by a productive biological asset shall be ascertained in accordance with the necessary expenses for the materials, labor, indirect apportionment, etc., during the course of output or gathering. The book value of the productive biological asset shall be carried over as the cost of agricultural products by employing such methods as the weighted average method, specific cost identification method, stock volume proportion method, fixed number of years within rotational felling period method, etc.

The agricultural products harvested shall be disposed in light of the Accounting Standards No. 1—Inventories.

Article 25 The cost of the biological asset of which the purpose has been changed shall be ascertained at the previous book value when its purpose has not been changed.

Article 26 For a biological asset, when conditions such as sale, inventory loss, death, damage, or destroy appear, its balance after deducting the book value and the relevant taxes from the disposal income shall be included in the current profits and incomes.

9.5 Chapter V: Disclosure

Article 27 An enterprise shall, in the notes, disclose the information concerning the biological assets as follows: (1) The categories of biological assets, quantities of physical output, and book value of various biological assets; (2) the accumulative amount of provision for loss on decline in value of various consumptive biological assets, and the useful life, expected net salvage value, depreciation method, amount of accumulative depreciation, and accumulative amount of provision for impairment; (3) the categories, obtainment methods, and quantities of physical goods of the biological assets sourced from the nature; (4) the book value of the biological assets used as guaranties; and (5) the information about the risks related to the biological assets and the relevant management measures.

Article 28 An enterprise shall, in the notes, disclose the information concerning the increase and decrease of biological assets as follows: (1) The increase of the biological assets as a result of a purchase; (2) the increase of the biological assets as a result of self-planting, self-cultivating, or self-breeding; (3) the decrease of the biological assets as a result of sale; (4) the decrease of the biological assets as a result of inventory loss, death, damage, or destroy; (5) the depreciation or provision for loss on decline in value or impairment which has been made; and (6) other alterations.

9.6 Comments

ASBE No. 5 introduces the concept of Biological Assets. *Article 3* provides three macro-categories: consumptive, productive, and welfare biological assets according to their specific destination of use.

Generally speaking, biological assets follow the provisions already met for recognizing other categories of assets. Moreover, they meet the same requirements when referring to measurement. In fact, they shall be initially measured at their cost. The cost of a purchased biological asset consists of "the purchase price, the relevant taxes, freight, insurance premiums, and other expenses that may be directly attributable to the purchase of this asset."

A major difference with fixed assets is the inherit feature of biological assets. In case of self-breeding, self-cultivated, and self-plated biological assets, their cost evaluation ascertains directly to agricultural operations. In case of reduction in value of biological assets, an impairment loss shall be disposed (with the only exception of welfare biological assets).

Apart from the weighted average method and the specific cost identification method, specific cost methods are introduced for evaluating inventories. Among them, *Article 23* mentions the stock volume proportion method and fixed number of years within rotational felling period method.

Under new ASBEs, "Biological Assets" represent an additional line item to be separately presented in the balance sheet. The cost model should be used for this category of assets unless there is a clear evidence that the fair value of them can be determined on a continuing basis. To this extent, ASBE No. 5 formalizes the practices adopted under the past system and provides more guidance on how to account for different types of biological assets using the cost model.

The main changes introduced by the new ASBE No. 5 embrace the consideration of impairment losses. Three different cases are provisioned. Impairment losses in respect to consumable biological assets (i.e., biological assets held for sale, or biological assets to be harvested for future agricultural production) shall be reversed if certain conditions are met. On the contrary, impairment losses occurred to bearer biological assets (i.e., biological assets held for the production of agricultural produce) shall not be reversed. Finally, no impairment loss shall be recognized for welfare biological assets (i.e., assets basically held for environmental protection purposes).

Shifting the focus on International Standards, ASBE No. 5 differs from IAS 41 on two main points. Firstly, as stated above, new ASBE No. 5 disposes only the cost model for measuring biological assets, unless there is a clear evidence that the fair value can be reliably estimated on a continuing basis. IAS 41 allows the adoption of the fair value model for all biological assets, unless its estimation is clearly unreliable.

Second, new ASBE No. 5 encourages the provision of quantified description of biological assets with detailed distinctions between consumable and bearer biological assets, and between mature and immature biological assets. On this issue, IAS 41 does not provide any classification for "welfare biological asset."

9.7 Examples

Company X operates as an agricultural conglomerate. It holds consumable biological assets with a carrying value of 500,000 RMB, bearer (productive) biological assets with a carrying value of 1,000,000 RMB, and welfare biological assets with a carrying value of 250,000 RMB.

Following facts occur during financial year: In first months of the FY considered, Company X, due to an unexpected drought, realizes impairment losses of 100,000 RMB, 300,000 RMB, and 50,000 RMB, respectively, for its consumable, bearer, and welfare biological assets. Of these losses, Company X recovers before the end of FY 80,000 RMB, 200,000 RMB, and 20,000 RMB still, respectively, for all categories of biological assets. Let us assess the accounting records for Company X:

- With regard to consumable biological assets, Company X shall impair the carrying value for 100,000 RMB and then recover up to 80,000 RMB. The net difference on income statement is a 20,000 RMB loss.
- With regard to productive biological assets, Company X shall impair a carrying value for 200,000 RMB, accounting also in profit and losses, but recovery is permitted.
- With regard to welfare biological assets, no record is needed.

Chapter 10
Accounting Standards for Business Enterprises No. 6—Intangible Assets

10.1 Chapter I: General Provisions

Article 1 To standardize the confirmation and measurement of intangible assets and disclosure of related information, these Standards are formulated in accordance with the Accounting Standard for Business Enterprises—Basic Standards.

Article 2 The following items shall be subject to other relevant accounting standards: (1) The right to use the land as investment real estates shall be subject to the Accounting Standard for Business Enterprises No. 3—Investment Properties; (2) the business reputation formed during the merger of enterprises shall be subject to the Accounting Standard for Business Enterprises No. 8—Impairment of Assets and Accounting Standard for Business Enterprises No. 20—Business Combinations; and (3) the rights and interests related to oil and natural gas mining areas shall be subject to the Accounting Standard for Business Enterprises 27—Extraction of Petroleum and Natural Gas.

10.2 Chapter II: Confirmation

Article 3 The term "intangible asset" refers to the identifiable non-monetary assets possessed or controlled by enterprises which have no physical substance. An asset, which satisfies any of the following conditions, shall meet the identifiable standards as mentioned in the definition of intangible assets: (1) being able to separate or divide from the enterprise and being able to be sold, transferred, licensed, rented, or exchanged independently or along with the relevant contracts, assets, or liabilities; or (2) being derived from any contractual right or other statutory rights, no matter whether or not these rights can be transferred or separated from the enterprise or other rights and obligations.

L. Riccardi, *China Accounting Standards*,
DOI 10.1007/978-981-10-0006-5_10

Article 4 Intangible assets may be confirmed when it meets the conditions simultaneously as follows: (1) The economic benefits related to intangible assets are likely to flow into the enterprise and (2) The cost of intangible assets can be measured reliably.

Article 5 When making a judgment on whether or not the economic benefits generated by intangible assets is likely to flow into it, an enterprise shall make a reasonable estimation to all potential economic factors within the expected service life of intangible assets and present clear evidences.

Article 6 The expenditures for an intangible item of an enterprise shall all be recorded into the profit or loss for the current period, unless it is under any of the following circumstances: (1) the part meeting the confirmed conditions as prescribed in these Standards and consisting of the cost of intangible assets, and (2) The part obtaining from the merger of enterprises not under the same control or cannot being independently confirmed as intangible assets, or composing the business reputation confirmed on the day of purchase.

Article 7 The expenditure for its internal research and development projects of an enterprise shall be classified into research expenditure and development expenditure. The term "research" refers to the creative and planned investigation to acquire and understand new scientific or technological knowledge. The term "development" refers to the application of research achievements and other knowledge to a certain plan or design, prior to the commercial production or use, so as to produce any new material, device, or product, or substantially improved material, device, and product.

Article 8 The research and development expenditure for internal research and development projects of an enterprise shall be recorded in the profit and loss for the current period.

Article 9 The development expenditure for internal research and development projects of an enterprise may be confirmed as intangible assets when they satisfy the following conditions simultaneously: (1) It is feasible technically to finish intangible assets for use or sale; (2) it is intended to finish, use, or sell the intangible assets; (3) the usefulness of methods for intangible assets to generate economic benefits shall be proved, including being able to prove that there is a potential market for the products manufactured by applying the intangible assets or there is a potential market for the intangible assets itself or the intangible assets will be used internally; (4) it is able to finish the development of the intangible assets and able to use or sell the intangible assets, with the support of sufficient technologies, financial resources, and other resources; and (5) the development expenditures of the intangible assets can be reliably measured.

Article 10 For an ongoing research and development project which is obtained by an enterprise and has been confirmed as intangible assets, the post-obtainment expenditures shall be treated in accordance with *Articles 7–9* of these Standards.

Article 11 The self-created business reputation of an enterprise, or its internally made brand, newspaper, or magazine name, shall not be confirmed as intangible assets.

10.3 Chapter III: Initial Measurement

Article 12 The intangible assets shall be initially measured according to the cost. The cost of outsourcing intangible assets shall include the purchase price, relevant taxes, and other necessary expenditures directly attributable to intangible assets for the expected purpose. Where the payment of purchase price for intangible assets is delayed beyond the normal credit conditions, which is of financing intention, the cost of intangible assets shall be determined on the basis of the current value of the purchase price. The difference between the actual payment and the current value of the purchase price shall be recorded into profit or loss for the credit period, unless it shall be capitalized under the Accounting Standards for Enterprises No. 17—Borrowing Cost.

Article 13 The cost of self-developed intangible assets shall include the total expenditure incurred during the period from the time it meets the provisions of *Articles 4–9* of these Standards to the time when the expected purposes of use are realized, except that the expenditures which have already been treated prior to the said period shall not be adjusted.

Article 14 The cost invested into intangible assets by investors shall be determined according to the conventional value in the investment contract or agreement, except for those of unfair value in the contract or agreement.

Article 15 The costs of intangible assets acquired from non-monetary asset transactions debt recombination, government subsides, and merger of enterprises shall be determined, respectively, according to the Accounting Standard for Business Enterprises No. 7—Exchange of Non-monetary Assets, Accounting Standard for Business Enterprises No. 12—Debt Restructurings, Accounting Standard for Business Enterprises No. 16—Government Grants, and Accounting Standard for Business Enterprises No. 20—Business Combinations.

10.4 Chapter IV: Subsequent Measurement

Article 16 An enterprise shall analyze and judge the service life of intangible assets, when it obtains intangible assets. As for the intangible assets with limited service life, the enterprise shall estimate the years of its service life, or the amount of the output or any other similar measurement unit, which constitutes its service life. If it is unable to forecast the period when the intangible asset can bring economic benefits to the enterprise, it shall be regarded as an intangible asset with an uncertain service life.

Article 17 With regard to intangible assets with limited service life, the amortization amount shall be amortized within its service life systematically and reasonably. An enterprise shall amortize intangible assets from the time they are available for use to the time they are not confirmed as intangibles anymore. The method chosen by an enterprise for the amortization of intangible assets shall reflect the expected realization pattern of the economic benefits which are relevant to the intangible assets. If it is unable to determine the expected realization pattern reliably, intangible assets shall be amortized by the straight-line method. Generally, the amortized amount of intangible assets shall be recorded into profit or loss for the current period, unless there are other accounting standards.

Article 18 The reasonable amortization amount of intangible assets shall be the cost minus the expected residual value. For intangible assets with an impairment provision, the accumulative amount of impairment provision shall be deducted from the cost as well. For intangible assets with a limited service life, its residual value shall be regarded as zero, unless it is under the circumstances as follows: (1) A third party promises to purchase the intangible assets at the end of its service life and (2) the information about the expected residual value is able to obtain from the active market, and the market is most likely to remain when the service life of the intangible asset ends.

Article 19 Intangible assets with an uncertain service life may not be amortized.

Article 20 The impairment of intangible assets shall be treated in accordance with the Accounting Standards for Enterprises No. 8—Impairment of Assets.

Article 21 An enterprise shall, at least at the end of each year, check the service life and the amortization method of intangible assets with limited service life. When the service life and the amortization method of intangible assets are different from those before, the years and method of the amortization shall be changed. An enterprise shall check the service life of intangible assets with uncertain service life each accounting period. Where there are evidences to prove the intangible assets have limited service life, it shall be estimated of its service life and be treated according to these Standards.

10.5 Chapter V: Disposal and Discarding

Article 22 The difference between the price acquired and the carrying amount of intangible assets shall be recorded in the profit and loss, where an enterprise sells intangible assets.

Article 23 In the case where no economic benefit is expected to be realized from an intangible asset to the enterprise, the carrying value of intangibles assets shall be written off.

10.6 Chapter VI: Disclosure

Article 24 An enterprise shall disclose the following information related to its intangible assets according to their categories in the annotation: (1) The beginning and ending book balances, accumulative amount of amortization, and accumulative amount of provision for impairment of intangible assets; (2) the estimation about the service lives of intangible assets with limited service lives and the basis for the judgment about the uncertain service life of intangible assets with uncertain service lives; (3) the methods for the amortization of intangible assets; (4) the carrying value of intangible assets used for guarantees, the amortization amount for the current period, and other information; and (5) the amount recorded in the profit and loss for the current period and those confirmed as the research and development expenditures for intangible assets.

10.7 Comments

Article 3 affirms that "the term 'intangible asset' refers to the identifiable non-monetary assets possessed or controlled by enterprises which have no physical substance." Additionally, the same *Article* provides for "intangible assets" the feature to be separated or divided from the enterprise for being disposed and derived from any contractual right or statutory right. Still for "intangible assets," ASBE No. 6 reaffirms the two foundations of future economic benefits and reliable measurement to be recognized.

A major introduction refers to development costs. *Article 9* disposes that development costs (the application of research achievements and other knowledge to a certain plan or design, prior to the commercial production or use) shall be capitalized when they satisfy the following conditions simultaneously: (1) It is feasible technically to finish intangible assets for use or sale; (2) it is intended to finish and use or sell the intangible assets; (3) the usefulness of methods for intangible assets to generate economic benefits shall be proved; (4) it is able to finish the development of the intangible assets and able to use or sell the intangible assets; and (5) the development expenditures of the intangible assets can be reliably measured. This new feature of intangible assets makes ASBE No. 6 more in line with the correspondent IAS 38.

Among other provisions, intangible assets self-developed "shall include the total expenditures incurred during the period from the time when it meets the provisions of *Articles 4–9* of these Standards to the time when the expected purposes of use are realized."

New ASBE No. 6 introduces the depreciable amount as the cost of the intangible asset less the residual value. The past version of PRC GAAP does not consider the residual value. The amortization method shall reflect the pattern in which the asset's future economic benefits are expected to be consumed. Only if the pattern cannot be reliably established, the straight-line method should be used.

This represents another innovation since the straight-line method was the only depreciation pattern under precedent standards. Furthermore, an intangible asset with an indefinite useful life cannot be amortized. However, it should be annually tested for impairment at least annually in accordance with ASBE No. 8. This new disposition partially changes the previous one, which required both amortization and impairment test at least annually for all intangible assets.

At the same time for intangible assets with a finite life, ASBE No. 6 requires a review of the useful life and amortization method of the asset at least at the end of each financial year. For these latter type of assets, PRC GAAP until 2007 did not address how frequent the useful life or the amortization method should have been reviewed.

When purchasing an intangible asset, if payment is deferred beyond credit terms, the difference between the cash price equivalent and the total payment is recognized either as interest over the period of credit or capitalized according to the requirements of ASBE No. 17 (following the same procedure seen for fixed assets).

The major divergence to IAS 38 lays on revaluation method. Under IAS 38 allows both the cost model and the revaluation model (only in case the fair value can be determined by reference to a price quoted in an active market). As stated above, ASBE No. 6 only permits the cost model.

10.8 Examples

Company X bears during an accounting year development costs to the value of 1,600,000 RMB in order to set out a new patent. The expenses are shared across the four quarters evenly. According to deeper enquiries, it has been found that from April 1st, the expenditure meets all five requirements of developments costs to be recognized as intangible assets.

For this reason, Company X at the accounting year end (the time when the expected purposes of use are realized) shall recognize as Intangible asset the pro-quota amount of development costs 1,600,000 × 9/12 = 1,200,000 RMB.

Chapter 11
Accounting Standards for Business Enterprises No. 7—Exchange of Non-Monetary Assets

11.1 Chapter I: General Provisions

Article 1 To standardize the confirmation and measurement of non-monetary asset transactions, and disclosure of relevant information, these standards are formulated according to the Accounting Standards for Business Enterprises—Basic Standards.

Article 2 The non-monetary assets transaction is an exchange of non-monetary assets between transacting parties, mainly including the transactions of inventories, fixed assets, intangible assets, and long-term equity investments. This kind of exchange involves little or no monetary assets (namely, monetary assets are referred to as a "boot"). The term "monetary assets" refers to the monetary capital held by enterprises, the assets to be received in fixed or determined amounts of currency, including cash, bank deposits, accounts and notes receivable, and bond investments to be held to maturity. The term "non-monetary assets" refers to the assets other than monetary assets.

Article 3 Where a non-monetary assets transaction satisfies the following conditions at the same time, the fair value of the assets and relevant payable taxes shall be regarded as the transaction cost, and the difference between the fair value and the carrying value of the asset surrendered shall be recorded into the profit or loss of the current period: (1) The transaction is commercial in nature; and (2) The fair value of the assets received or surrendered can be measured reliably. If both the fair values of the assets received and surrendered can be reliably measured, the fair value of the assets surrendered shall be the basis for the determination of the cost of the assets received, unless there is any exact evidence showing that the fair value of the assets received is more reliable.

L. Riccardi, *China Accounting Standards*,
DOI 10.1007/978-981-10-0006-5_11

11.2 Chapter II: Confirmation and Measurement

Article 4 A non-monetary assets transaction, meeting any of the following conditions, is commercial in nature: (1) The future cash flow of the assets received is different from that of the surrendered assets in the aspects of risk, time and amount notably; and (2) The current values of the expected future cash flow of the assets received and surrendered is different, and the difference between them is more significant than the fair values of the assets received and surrendered.

Article 5 When determining whether or not non-monetary asset transactions are commercial in nature, an enterprise shall pay attention to whether or not the transacting parties are connected ones. The existence of the relationship between connected parties is likely to cause the loss of commercial nature of non-monetary assets transaction.

Article 6 Where any non-monetary assets transaction does not meet the conditions as prescribed in *Article 3* of these standards at the same time, the carrying value and relevant payable taxes of the assets surrendered shall be the cost of the assets received and no profit or loss is recognized.

Article 7 Where a boot is caused when an enterprise treats the fair value and relevant payable taxes as the cost of the assets received, the boot shall be accounted for according to the following circumstances, respectively: (1) The enterprise, which pays the boot, shall record the difference between the cost of the assets received and the sum of the carrying value of the assets surrendered plus the paid boot and relevant payable taxes into the profit or loss of the current period; (2) The enterprise, which receives the boot, shall record the difference between the costs of the assets received plus the received boot and the carrying value of the assets surrendered plus relevant payable taxes into the profit or loss of the current period.

Article 8 Where a boot is caused when an enterprise treats the carrying value of the surrendered assets and the relevant payable taxes as the cost of the received assets, the boot shall be accounted for according to the following circumstances, respectively: (1) The enterprise, which pays the boot, shall treat the result of the carrying value of the assets surrendered plus the paid boot and relevant payable taxes as the cost of the assets received, and no profit or loss may be recognized; or (2) The business enterprise, which receives the boot, shall treat the result of the carrying value of the assets surrendered minus the received boot and plus relevant payable taxes as the cost of the assets received, and no profit or loss may be recognized.

Article 9 Where several assets are received in a non-monetary assets transaction simultaneously, the cost of each received assets shall be determined according to the following circumstances, respectively: (1) If the non-monetary assets transaction is commercial in nature and the fair value of the assets received can be reliably measured, the cost of each received asset shall be determined by applying the proportion of the fair value of each asset received to the total fair value of the assets received to allocate the total cost of the assets received; or (2) If the non-monetary assets transaction is not commercial in nature, or it is commercial in nature, but the fair value of the assets received cannot be reliably measured, the cost of each received assets shall be determined by applying the proportion of the original carrying value of each asset received to the total original carrying value of the assets received to allocate the total cost of the assets received.

11.3 Chapter III: Disclosure

Article 10 An enterprise shall disclose the following information relating to non-monetary transactions in the annotation: (1) types of the assets received and surrendered; (2) determination method for the assets received; (3) fair values of the assets received and surrendered, as well as the carrying value of the surrendered assets; and (4) profit or loss of a non-monetary assets transaction.

11.4 Comments

In accordance with *Article 2*, the exchange of non-monetary assets are defined as a transaction involving "an exchange of non-monetary assets between transacting parties, mainly including the transactions of inventories, fixed assets, intangible assets, and long-term equity investments." On the contrary, monetary assets are referred "to the monetary capital held by enterprises, the assets to be received in fixed or determined amounts of currency, including cash, bank deposits, accounts and notes receivable, and bond investments to be held to maturity."

Article 3 prescribes that if the exchange simultaneously meets the requirements of commercial transaction and reliable measurement of fair value, the fair value method shall be applied to recognize the cost of the transaction. This is the principal innovation upon the past PRC GAAP. In case the exchange transaction involving non-monetary assets lack commercial substance, its treatment is still consistent with the previous provision of PRC GAAP. In accordance with this, the acquired asset shall be measured at the carrying amount of the asset given up. Still *Article 3* states that the difference between the fair value and additional taxes, and the carrying value of the non-monetary assets shall be reported in profit and loss.

Articles 4 and *Article 5* focus on the definition of commercial transaction. First, a commercial transaction is occurring when either or both following conditions are met: (1) The future cash flow of the assets received is different from that of the surrendered assets in the aspects of risk, time, and amount notably; and (2) The current values of the expected future cash flow of the assets received and surrendered is different, and the difference between them is more significant than the fair values of the assets received and surrendered. Second, when considering the commercial nature of a transaction, an enterprise should pay attention to the connections existing between two parties. In case of established relationship, there is a great possibility to reject the commercial nature of the considered transaction.

Major differences refer instead to the treatment of the exchange of non-monetary assets under international standards. IFRSs provide no specific standard dealing with this type of transaction. IAS 16, IAS 18, and IAS 38 contain just the requirement for different types of assets. In line with IAS 16 and IAS 38, ASBE No. 7 considers the "commercial substance" to deal with all types of non-monetary transactions (including inventories, fixed assets, intangible assets, and long-term equity investments). To a different extent, IAS 18 adopts the fair value for measuring an exchange of goods, only when the goods exchanged or the services are dissimilar.

11.5 Examples

Company X sells out to Company Y a batch of 100,000 pieces of inventories. Let us suppose their carrying amount is estimated to be 800,000 RMB, whereas their fair value (reliably measured) is 1,000,000 RMB. There are no additional taxes on the transaction.

Case 1 The conditions for a commercial transaction are met and the exchange is measured at the fair value of the inventories. As a consequence, the difference between the fair value of inventories and their carrying amount (1,000,000 − 800,000 = 200,000) shall be measured in profit and loss.

Case 2 Due to the previously established mutual relationship between two entities, the conditions for commercial transaction do not occur. In this case, the cost of the transaction is 800,000 RMB and no record is required in profit and loss.

Chapter 12
Accounting Standards for Business Enterprises No. 8—Impairment of Assets

12.1 Chapter I: General Provisions

Article 1 To standardize the confirmation and measurement of the impairment of assets, and the disclosure of relevant information, these Standards are formulated according to the Accounting Standard for Business Enterprises—Basic Standards.

Article 2 The term "impairment of assets" refers to the recoverable amount of assets being lower than the carrying value. The assets as mentioned in these standards shall include single-item assets and group assets. The term "group assets" refers to a minimum combination of assets that may be recognized by an enterprise, by which the flow-in cash generated shall be generally independent of those by other assets or group assets.

Article 3 The following items shall be subject to other relevant accounting standards: (1) The impairment of inventories shall be subject to the Accounting Standard for Business Enterprises No. 1—Inventories; (2) The impairment of investment properties measured through the fair value method shall be subject to the Accounting Standard for Business Enterprises No. 3—Investment Properties; (3) The impairment of consumptive biological assets shall be subject to the Accounting Standard for Business Enterprises No. 5—Biological Assets; (4) The impairment of assets formed by construction contracts shall be subject to the Accounting Standard for Business Enterprises No. 15—Construction Contracts; (5) The impairment of deferred income tax assets shall be subject to the Accounting Standard for Business Enterprises No. 18—Income Taxes; (6) The impairment of the unsecured residual value of the lessor in a financial lease shall be subject to the Accounting Standard for Business Enterprises No. 21—Leases; (7) The impairment of financial assets regulated by the Accounting Standard for Business Enterprises No. 22—Recognition and Measurement of Financial Instruments shall be subject to the Accounting Standard for Business Enterprises No. 22—Recognition and Measurement of Financial Instruments; and (8) The impairment of the rights and

L. Riccardi, *China Accounting Standards*,
DOI 10.1007/978-981-10-0006-5_12

interests of unverified petroleum and natural gas mining areas shall be subject to the Accounting Standard for Business Enterprises No. 27—Extraction of Petroleum and Natural Gas.

12.2 Chapter II: Recognition of Assets with Potential Impairment

Article 4 An enterprise shall, on the day of balance sheet, make a judgment on whether there is any sign of possible assets impairment. No matter whether there is any sign of possible assets impairment, the business reputation formed by the merger of enterprises and intangible assets with uncertain service lives shall be subject to impairment test every year.

Article 5 There may be an impairment of assets when one of the following occurs: (1) The current market price of assets falls, and its decrease is obviously higher than the expected drop over time or due to the normal use; (2) The economic, technological, or legal environment in which the enterprise operates, or the market where the assets is situated, will have any significant change in the current period or in the near future, which will cause an adverse impact on the enterprise; (3) The market interest rate or any other market investment return rate has risen in the current period, and thus, the discount rate of the enterprise for calculating the expected future cash flow of the assets will be affected, which will result in great decline of the recoverable amount of the assets; (4) Any evidence shows that the assets have become obsolete or have been damaged substantially; (5) The assets have been or will be left unused, or terminated for use, or disposed ahead of schedule; (6) Any evidence in the internal report of the enterprise shows that the economic performance of the assets has been or will be lower than the expected performance, for example, the net cash flow created by assets or the operating profit (or loss) realized is lower (higher) than the excepted amount, etc.; and (7) Other evidence indicates that the impairment of assets has probably occurred.

12.3 Chapter III: Measurement of Recoverable Amount of Assets

Article 6 Where any evidence shows that there is a possible assets impairment, the recoverable amount of the assets shall be estimated. The recoverable amount shall be determined in light of the higher one of the net amount of the fair value of the assets minus the disposal expenses and the current value of the expected future cash flow of the assets. The disposal expenses shall include the relevant legal expenses, relevant taxes, trucking, as well as the direct expenses for bringing the assets into a marketable state.

Article 7 When either the net amount of the fair value of an asset minus the disposal expenses or the current value of the expected future cash flow of the asset exceeds the carrying value of the asset, it shows that no asset impairment has occurred, and it does not need to estimate another amount of the asset.

Article 8 The net amount of the fair value of an asset minus the disposal expenses shall be determined in light of the amount of the basis of the price as stipulated in the sales agreement in the fair transaction minus the disposal expenses directly attributable to the asset. Where there is no sales agreement but there is an active market of assets, the net amount of the fair value of an asset minus the disposal expenses shall be determined in light of the amount of the market price of the asset minus the disposal expenses. Generally, the market price of the asset shall be determined according to the price bidden by the buyer of the asset. Where there is no sales agreement and no active market of assets, the net amount of estimated fair value of an asset minus the disposal expenses shall be estimated in light of the best information available. The said net amount may be estimated by reference to the latest transaction prices or results of similar assets among the counterparts. Where the net amount of the fair value of an asset minus the disposal expenses cannot be estimated reliably according to the provisions as described above, the enterprise shall regard the current value of the expected future cash flow of the asset as the recoverable amount of the asset.

Article 9 The current value of the expected future cash flow of an asset shall be determined by the discounted cash with an appropriate discount rate, on the basis of the expected future cash flow generated during the continuous use or final disposal of an asset. To predict the current value of the future cash flow, the enterprise shall take into comprehensive consideration the expected future cash flow, service life, discount rate, and other factors.

Article 10 The expected future cash flow of an asset shall include the following items: (1) The cash inflow generated during the continuous use of the asset. (2) The necessary expected cash outflow for realizing cash inflow generated during the continuous use of the asset (including the cash outflow to bring the asset to the expected conditions for use). The outflow of cash shall be the outflow cash that is directly attributable to, or that may be distributed to the asset on reasonable and consistent basis. (3) At the end of the service life of an asset, the net cash flow received or paid for the disposal of the asset. The cash flow shall be, during the process of fair transaction between parties that are familiar with the situation on their own free will, the amount expected to obtain from or pay for the disposal of the asset minus the expected disposal expenses.

Article 11 When making an estimate of the future cash flow of an asset, the managers of the enterprise shall make a best estimate of the entire economic status of the asset in its remaining service life in a reasonable and well-grounded manner. The expected future cash flow of an asset shall be based on the latest financial budget or forecast data as well as the stable or regressive growth rates after the year of the aforesaid budget or forecast. When the managers can prove that the progressive growth rates are reasonable, the expected future cash flow of the asset may be based on the progressive growth rates. The expected cash flow set forth on the basis of the budget or forecast can cover 5 years at most. Where the managers can prove that a longer period is reasonable, it may cover a longer time. When making an estimate of the cash flow after the year of the budget or forecast, the growth rates adopted shall not exceed, unless the enterprise can prove that it is reasonable to adopt higher growth rates, the long-term average growth rate of the products, or the market, or the industrial field which the enterprise belongs to, or the country or region where the enterprise is located, or the long-term average growth rate of the market where the asset is situated.

Article 12 The expected future cash flow of an asset shall be based on the current status of the asset. It shall not include any possible and uncommitted recombination items or any expected future cash flow related to the asset improvement. The expected future cash flow of an asset shall not include the cash inflow or outflow generated by financing activities, or the cash flow related to the receipt or payment of income taxes. Where an enterprise has made a commitment of recombination, when determining the current value of the future cash flow of assets, the amounts of the expected future cash inflow and outflow shall reflect the expenses that can be saved in the recombination, other benefits to be brought about by the recombination, and the estimated amount of the future cash outflow that may result from the recombination. Generally, the expenses that can be saved in the recombination and other benefits that could be brought about by the recombination shall be estimated on the basis of the latest financial budget or forecast data as approved by the management of the enterprise. The amount of future cash outflow that may result from the recombination shall be estimated according to the expected amount of liabilities incurred due to the recombination as described in the Accounting Standard for Business Enterprises—Contingencies.

Article 13 The discount rate is the pre-tax interest rate, which can reflect the time value of money in the present market and the specific risks of the asset. The discount rate is the necessary return rate as required by an enterprise when it purchases or invests in the asset. Where an adjustment has been made to the specific risks of the asset when an estimate of the future cash flow of an asset is made, it does not need to take into consideration these specific risks when making an estimate of the discount rate. Where the estimate of the discount rate is based on the post-tax factors, it shall be adjusted to the pre-tax discount rate.

Article 14 Where the expected future cash flow of an asset involves any foreign currency, the current value of the asset shall, on the basis of the settlement currency of the future cash flow to be generated by the asset, be calculated with a discount rate applicable to this currency. Then, the current value of the foreign currency shall be converted at the spot exchange rate of the current day when the future cash flow of the asset is calculated.

12.4 Chapter IV: Determination of Losses of Asset Impairment

Article 15 Where the measured result of the recoverable amount indicates that an asset's recoverable amount is lower than its carrying value, the carrying value of the asset shall be recorded down to the recoverable amount, and the reduced amount shall be recognized as the loss of asset impairment and be recorded as the profit or loss for the current period. Simultaneously, a provision for the asset impairment shall be made accordingly.

Article 16 After the loss of asset impairment has been recognized, the depreciation or amortization expenses of the impaired asset shall be adjusted accordingly in the future periods so as to amortize the post-adjustment carrying value of the asset systematically (deducting the expected net salvage value) within the residual service life of the asset.

Article 17 Once any loss of asset impairment is recognized, it shall not be switched back in the future accounting periods.

12.5 Chapter V: Recognition of Group Assets and Treatments of Impairment

Article 18 Where there is any evidence indicating a possible impairment of assets, the enterprise shall, on the basis of single-item assets, estimate the recoverable amount. Where it is difficult to do so, it shall determine the recoverable amount of the group assets on the basis of the asset group to which the asset belongs. The recognition of an asset group shall be based on whether the main cash inflow generated by the asset group is independent of those generated by other assets or other group assets. Simultaneously, when recognizing an asset group, the enterprise shall take into consideration how its managers manage the production and business activities (e.g., according to the production lines, business varieties; or according to the regions or areas), and the ways of decision making for the continuous use or disposal of the assets, etc. Where there is an active market for the products manufactured by (or other outputs of) a combination of several assets, even if some or all of these products (or other outputs) are provided for the internal use, the enterprise shall also recognize this combination of assets as an asset group on the condition that the provisions of the preceding paragraph are accorded with. Where the cash inflow of the asset group is affected by the internal transfer price, the future cash flow of the asset group shall be determined on the basis of the best available estimate made by the managers of the enterprise for the future price in the fair transaction. Once an asset group is recognized, it shall be kept consistent during different accounting periods and not be changed at will. Where it is necessary to make any change, the managers of the enterprise shall prove that this change is reasonable and shall make an explanation pursuant to *Article 27* of these Standards in its annotation.

Article 19 The basis for the determination of the carrying value of an asset group shall be the same as that for the determination of the recoverable amount. The carrying value of an asset group shall include the carrying value that may be directly attributed to or may be reasonably and consistently distributed to the asset group. Generally, it shall not include the carrying amount of a liability that has already been recognized, unless it is unable to determine the recoverable amount of the asset group if not considering the amount of liability. The recoverable amount of an asset group shall be determined on the basis of the higher one of the net amount of the fair value of the asset minus the disposal expenses and the current value of the expected future cash flow of the asset. Where the purchaser is required to bear a liability (such as environment resumption liability) when an asset group is disposed of, the amount of liability has been recognized and has been recorded in the carrying value of the relevant assets, and the enterprise can only obtain the net amount of the unitary fair value of the assets and liability aforesaid minus the disposal expenses, the amount of liability that has been recognized shall be deducted from the liability when determining the carrying value and the current value of expected future cash flow of the asset group, so as to compare the carrying value with the recoverable amount of the asset group.

Article 20 The assets of the headquarters of an enterprise shall include the office buildings, electronic data processing equipment of the enterprise group, or its business departments. A conspicuous character of the assets of the headquarters is that it is difficult to generate independent cash inflow when it is separated from other assets or asset group and difficult to attribute its carrying value completely to a certain group. Where any evidence shows any possible impairment of a particular asset of the headquarters, the enterprise shall calculate and determine the recoverable amount of the asset group to which the asset group or the combination of group assets belongs to, then compare it with the corresponding carrying value of the asset so as to decide whether it is necessary to confirm the impairment loss. The term "combination of group assets" refers to the minimum combination of group assets formed by several asset groups, including the asset groups or combination of group assets, and the proportion of the assets of the headquarters allocated by a reasonable method.

Article 21 When an enterprise conducts an impairment test on a certain asset group, it shall first determine all the assets of the headquarters which are related to the asset group, then treat it according to the following circumstances, respectively, by taking into consideration whether the assets of the headquarters can be apportioned to this asset group on a reasonable and consistent basis: (1) For the part of the relevant assets of the headquarters that can be apportioned to this asset group on a reasonable and consistent basis, the enterprise shall apportion the carrying value of this proportion to this asset group, then compare the carrying value of the asset (including the carrying value of the headquarters' assets which have been apportioned to) with its recoverable amount, and treat it in pursuance of *Article 22* of these Standards. (2) Where it is difficult to apportion some assets of the related assets of the headquarters to this asset group on a reasonable and consistent basis, the enterprise shall take the following steps to treat these assets: First, without taking into consideration the relevant assets of the headquarters, estimating and comparing the carrying value with its recoverable amount of the asset group, and treating it in accordance with *Article 22* of these Standards. Second, deciding the minimum combination of asset groups formed by several asset groups. This combination of asset groups shall include the asset groups that have been tested, and the proportion of the carrying value of the headquarters' assets that can be apportioned to this combination on a reasonable and consistent basis. Finally, comparing the carrying value of the combination of asset groups it has determined (including the proportion of the "headquarters" assets that have been apportioned to) with the recoverable amount of the combination, and treats it according to *Article 22* of these Standards.

Article 22 Where the recoverable amount of an asset group or a combination of asset groups is lower than its carrying value (where the headquarters' assets and business reputation are apportioned to a certain asset group or a combination of asset groups, the carrying value of the asset group or the combination of asset groups shall include the amount of the relevant assets of the headquarters and business reputation that have been apportioned to), it shall be recognized as the corresponding impairment loss. The amount of the impairment loss shall first be charged against the carrying value of the headquarters' assets and business reputation which are apportioned to the asset group or combination of asset groups, then charge it against the carrying value of other assets in proportion to the weight of other assets in the asset group or combination of asset groups with the business reputation excluded. The charges against the carrying value of the assets above shall be treated as the impairment loss of the assets (including the business reputation) and recorded as profit or loss for the current period. The carrying value of each asset after charging against shall not be lower than the highest one of the following three: the net amount of the fair value of the asset minus the disposal expenses (if determinable), the current value of the expected future cash flow of the asset (if determinable), and zero. The amount of impairment loss that cannot be apportioned incurred thereby shall be apportioned on the basis of the weight of the carrying value of other assets in the relevant asset group or combination of the asset groups.

12.6 Chapter VI: Treatment of Impairment of Business Reputation

Article 23 The business reputation formed by a merger of enterprises shall be subject to an impairment test at least at the end of each year. The business reputation shall, together with the related asset group or combination of asset group, be subject to the impairment test. The related asset group or combination of asset groups shall be the asset group or combination of asset groups that can benefit from the synergy effect of enterprise merger, and shall be smaller than the reporting segments as determined according to Accounting Standard for Business Enterprises No. 35—Segment Reporting.

Article 24 When an enterprise makes an impairment test of assets, it shall, as of the purchasing day, apportion the carrying value of the business reputation formed by merger of enterprises to the relevant asset groups by a reasonable method. Where it is difficult to do so, it shall be apportioned to the relevant combinations of asset groups. When apportioning the carrying value of the business reputation to the relevant asset groups or combinations of asset groups, it shall be apportioned on the basis of the proportion of the fair value of each asset group or combination of asset groups to the total fair value of the relevant asset groups or combinations of asset groups. Where it is difficult to measure the fair value reliably, it shall be apportioned on the basis of the proportion of the carrying value of each asset group or combination of asset groups to the total carrying value of the relevant asset groups or combinations of asset groups. Where the report structure changes due to enterprise recombination or for any other reason, which thus has affected the structure of one or several asset group(s) or combination(s) of asset groups to which the business reputation has already been apportioned, the business reputation shall be reapportioned to the affected asset group(s) or combinations of the asset group(s), with the apportion method similar to that as provided for in the preceding paragraph of this *Article*.

Article 25 When conducting an impairment test on the relevant asset groups or combination of asset groups containing business reputation, if any of the evidence shows that the impairment of asset groups or combinations of asset groups is possible, the enterprise shall first make an impairment test on the asset groups or combinations of asset groups not containing business reputation, calculate the recoverable amount, compare it with the relevant carrying value, and recognize the corresponding impairment loss. Then, the enterprise shall make an impairment test of the asset groups or combinations of asset groups containing business reputation and compare the carrying value of these asset groups or combinations of asset groups (including the carrying value of the business reputation apportioned thereto) with the recoverable amount. Where the recoverable amount of the relevant assets or combinations of the asset groups is lower than the carrying value thereof, it shall recognize the impairment loss of the business reputation and treat them according to *Article 22* of these Standards.

12.7 Chapter VII: Disclosure

Article 26 An enterprise shall disclose the following information relevant to the impairment of assets in its annotation: (1) The amount of impairment loss of each asset recognized during the current period; (2) The accumulative amount of provision recognized for the impairment of each asset; and (3) The amount of impairment loss recognized in each reporting segment of the current period, if segment reporting information is provided.

Article 27 Where any serious asset impairment loss is incurred, the enterprise shall, in its annotation, disclose the reasons why each of the serious asset impairment losses have incurred and the amount of serious asset impairment losses recognized in the current period. (1) Where a serious impairment loss has been incurred for a single-item asset, the enterprise shall disclose the nature of the single-item asset. Where any segment of the reporting information is provided, the enterprise shall also disclose the segment of the main reporting to which this asset belongs to. (2) Where a serious impairment loss has been incurred to an asset group (or combination of asset groups, the same below), it shall disclose: (a) the basic information of the asset group; (b) the amount of impairment loss of each asset of the asset group as recognized in the current period; and (c) where the formation of the asset group is different from those in the previous period, the enterprise shall disclose the reasons for the change, as well as the constitution of the asset group in the previous period and the current period.

Article 28 With regard to any serious impairment of assets, the enterprise shall disclose the method for the determination of the recoverable amount of the assets (or asset group, the same below) in its annotation: (1) Where the recoverable amount is determined on the basis of the net amount of the fair value of the asset minus the disposal expenses, the enterprise shall disclose the basis for the estimate of the net amount of the fair value minus the disposal expenses. (2) Where the recoverable amount is determined on the basis of the expected future cash flow of the assets, the enterprise shall disclose the discount rate it adopts for estimating the current value of the assets, as well as the discount rate it adopted in the previous period when the recoverable amount of the asset in the previous period was also determined on the basis of the expected future cash flow of the asset.

Article 29 The information as described in Paragraphs 1, 2 of *Article 26* and Item 2 of Paragraph 2 of *Article 27* shall be disclosed according to different sorts of the assets. The sorts of assets shall be determined by considering whether the nature or function of the assets in production and business operation is identical or similar.

Article 30 Where the carrying value of the business reputation apportioned to a particular asset group (or intangible asset with uncertain service life, the same below) accounts for a large portion of the total carrying value of the business reputation, the enterprise shall disclose the following information in its annotation: (1) the carrying value of the business reputation apportioned to the asset group; (2) the method for the determination of the recoverable amount of the asset group. (a) Where the recoverable amount is determined on the basis of the net amount of the fair value of the asset group minus the disposal expenses, the enterprise shall disclose the method for the determination of the net amount of the fair value minus the disposal expenses. Where the net amount of the fair value of the asset group minus the disposal expenses is not determined on the basis of the market price, the enterprise shall disclose: (i) the crucial assumptions adopted by the managers of the enterprise for the determination of the net amount of the fair value minus the disposal expenses, and the basis for these assumptions; (ii) whether or not the values of the crucial assumptions as determined by the managers of the enterprise are consistent with the experiences of the enterprise or its external information; if not, the reasons shall be accounted for. (b) Where the recoverable amount is determined according to the current value of future cash flows as predicted by the asset group, the enterprise shall also disclose: (i) the assumptions for predicting the cash flows in the future and the grounds thereof made by the managers of the enterprise; (ii) when the managers of the enterprise determine the values relating to the relevant assumptions, whether they are in consistence with the experiences of the enterprise or the external information; if not, the reasons shall be accounted for; (iii) the discount rate adopted for the estimate of the current value.

Article 31 Where the total or partial carrying value of the business reputation is apportioned to several asset groups, and the proportion apportioned to each asset group to the total carrying value of the business reputation is not large, the enterprise shall describe it and offer the aggregate amount of the business reputation apportioned to the above-mentioned asset groups in its annotation. Where the carrying value of the business reputation is apportioned to the above-mentioned asset groups according to the same crucial assumptions, and the amount of business reputation apportioned to each assets group accounts for a large proportion of the total carrying value of the business reputation, the enterprise shall describe it and disclose the following information in its annotation: (1) The aggregate carrying value of the business reputation apportioned to the above-mentioned asset groups; (2) The crucial assumptions adopted, and the grounds thereof; and (3) Whether or not the values of the crucial assumptions as determined by the managers of the enterprise are consistent with the experiences of the enterprise or the source of its external information; if not, the reasons shall be accounted for.

12.8 Comments

The impairment of an asset occurs when the recoverable amount of assets is lower than its carrying value. The impairment loss shall follow an impairment test on a single asset and a group of assets as well. The term "group assets" refers to a minimum combination of assets that may be recognized by an enterprise, by which the flow-in cash generated shall be generally independent of those from other assets or group assets.

Article 3 prescribes that for inventories, investment properties, biological assets, construction contracts, deferred income taxes, lease contracts, financial instruments, and extraction of petroleum and natural gas, the relevant ASBEs provide procedure for the respective impairment treatment.

The impairment shall take place on the day of balance sheet regardless of actual signs of impairment. *Article 5* provides all possibilities in which an impairment loss can occur: "(1) The current market price of assets falls below the expected drop over time or due to the normal use; (2) Significant changes in the economic, technological, or legal environment in which the enterprise operates, or the market where the assets is situated, causing adverse outcome on the asset; (3) The market interest rate or any other market investment return rate has risen in the current period, and thus, the discount rate of the enterprise for calculating the expected future cash flow of the assets will be affected, which will result in a great decline of the recoverable amount of the assets; (4) Any evidence shows that the assets have become obsolete or have been damaged substantially; (5) The assets have been or will be left unused, or terminated for use, or disposed ahead of schedule; (6) Any evidence in the internal report of the enterprise shows that the economic performance of the assets have been or will be lower than the expected performance, for example, the net cash flow created by assets or the operating profit (or loss) realized is lower (higher) than the excepted amount, etc.; and (7) Other evidence indicates that the impairment of assets has probably occurred."

Once the conditions for an impairment loss have been determined, the next step consists of evaluating a possible recoverable value. To this extent, *Article 6* in line with disposition of IAS 36 recognizes the recoverable value as the higher amount between the fair value of the asset less costs of disposal and the current value of cash flows. In the first case, the fair value can be determined on comparable transactions for similar assets. If this comparison is not possible, the fair value can be assessed if there is an active market for the same category of assets. A third hypothesis consists of relying on the best possible information. If any of the previous methods are useful in order to obtain a reliable valuation of the asset's fair value, the recoverable value shall be based only on the current amount of future cash flows.

With regard to the cash flow approach, *Article 9–14*s indicate criteria for valuation. In particular, *Article 10* states that for a cash flow to be considered it needs: (1) the inflows should be generated during the continuous use of the asset. (2) The outflow of cash shall be the outflow cash that is directly attributable to the cash inflows or that may be distributed to the asset on reasonable and consistent basis. (3) At the end of the service life of an asset, the net cash flow received or paid for the disposal of the asset. *Article 13* requires a pre-taxes interest rate, which shall reflect the specific risk for the asset.

If the higher between the fair value net of costs of disposal and current value of cash flows is lower than the carrying value, the asset shall be impaired (on the opposite if the recoverable value is higher than carrying value, no impairment is needed).

Accordingly, the difference between the carrying value and the recoverable value should be recorded as a loss in the period income statement. The new depreciation shall be calculated on the impaired value of the asset. Most notably, new ASBE No. 8 prohibits the reversal of all previously recognized impairment losses (for the impairment losses within the scope of ASBE No. 8). This last point features the key difference with the IAS 36, which forbids only the reversal of impairment losses for goodwill.

ASBE No. 8 introduces that the recoverable amount shall be estimated for individual assets. In case it is not possible to determine the recoverable amount of an individual asset, an enterprise shall estimate the recoverable amount of the asset group to which the asset belongs. After having determined an asset group it shall not be changed arbitrarily. The previous regulation just required an impairment test to be conducted for individual assets, and the issue of "asset group" was not addressed. The new regulation provides more guidance leading to stricter requirements for impairment testing. Finally, also business reputation shall be subject to impairment test and account for Segment Report (ASBE No. 35).

12.9 Examples

Company X has machinery with a carrying value of 600,000 RMB and an estimated residual life of 5 years (10 years original life) following a straight-line pattern. The machinery is still expected to provide a net cash flow of 85,000 RMB per annum until it will be dismantled.

At the beginning of the new financial year, a sudden change in the market and technological environment leads to an accelerated obsolescence of the machinery. After the impairment test, it is found that similar transactions involving secondhand assets take place for some 420,000 RMB. The overall expenses related for dismantling and marketing the machinery are estimated to be 45,000 RMB. Furthermore, the revision of future cash flows yields values down to 65,000 RMB per annum. The estimated pre-tax rate reflecting the specific risk of the asset is 10 %.

Let us proceed with the assessment of the recoverable value for the machinery:

- Fair value net of disposal expenses: 420,000–45,000 = 375,000 RMB
- Current Value of future cash flow: $65{,}000/1.1 + 65{,}000/1.1^2 + 65{,}000/1.1^3 + 65{,}000/1.1^4 + 65{,}000/1.1^5 = 246{,}401.14$ RMB

The recoverable value is 375,000 RMB (the higher between the fair value net of cost of disposal and current amount of future cash flows). Since the recoverable value is lower than the carrying value, we record an impairment loss in profit and loss for 225,000 RMB.

Furthermore, the new annual depreciation will be 75,000 RMB.

Chapter 13
Accounting Standards for Business Enterprises No. 9—Employee Compensation

13.1 Chapter I: General Provisions

Article 1 To standardize the confirmation and measurement of the employee compensation, and the disclosure of relevant information, these Standards are formulated according to the Accounting Standards for Business Enterprises—Basic Standards.

Article 2 The term "employee compensation" refers to all kinds of payments and other relevant expenditures given by enterprises in exchange for the services offered by the employees. The employee compensation shall include the following: (1) wages, bonuses, allowances, and subsidies for the employees; (2) welfare expenses for the employees; (3) medical insurance, endowment insurance, unemployment insurance, work injury insurance, maternity insurance, and other social insurances; (4) housing accumulation fund; (5) labor union expenditure and employee education expenses;(6) non-monetary welfare; (7) compensation for the cancelation of the labor relationship with the employees; and (8) other relevant expenditures of services offered by the employees.

Article 3 The following items shall be subject to other relevant accounting standards: (1) The enterprise annuity funds shall be subject to the Accounting Standards for Business Enterprises No. 10—Enterprise Annuity Fund and (2) the compensation based on shares shall be subject to the Accounting Standard for Business Enterprises No. 11—Share-based Payment.

13.2 Chapter II: Confirmation and Measurement

Article 4 During the accounting period of an employee's providing services to an enterprise, the enterprise shall recognize the compensation payable as liabilities. Except for the compensations for the cancelation of the labor relationship with the

L. Riccardi, *China Accounting Standards*,
DOI 10.1007/978-981-10-0006-5_13

employee, the enterprise shall, in accordance with beneficiaries of the services offered by the employee, treat the following circumstances, respectively: (1) The compensation for the employee for producing products or providing services shall be recorded as the product costs and service costs; (2) the compensation for the employee for any ongoing construction project or for any intangible asset shall be recorded as the costs of fixed asset or intangible assets; or (3) the compensation for the employee other than those as mentioned in Items (1) and (2) shall be recorded as profit or loss for the current period.

Article 5 During the accounting period of an employee's providing services to an enterprise, the enterprise shall calculate the medical and insurance, endowment insurance, unemployment insurance, work injury insurance, maternity insurance, and other social insurances, as well as the housing accumulation fund, which are paid by the enterprise to the employee, on the basis of a certain proportion in the total amount of wages, and treat them according to *Article 4* of these Standards.

Article 6 If an enterprise cancels the labor relationship with any employee prior to the expiration of the relevant labor contract or brings forward any compensation proposal for the purpose of encouraging the employee to accept a layoff, and the following conditions are met concurrently, the enterprise shall recognize the expected liabilities incurred due to the compensation for the cancelation of the labor relationship with the employee, and shall simultaneously record them into the profit or loss for the current period: (1) where the enterprise has formulated a formal plan on the cancelation of labor relationship or has brought forward a proposal on voluntary layoff and will execute it soon. This plan or proposal shall include the department at which the employee to be laid off works, the post of the employee and the number of the employees to be laid off, the amount of compensation for the cancelation of labor relationship or for layoff as determined on the basis of the job category or post according to the relevant provisions, and the planned time for the cancelation of labor relationship or layoff. (2) The enterprise is unable to unilaterally withdraw the plan on the cancelation of labor relationship or the layoff proposal.

13.3 Chapter III: Disclosure

Article 7 An enterprise shall disclose the following information related to the employee compensation in the annotation: (1) the wages, bonuses, allowances, and subsidies, which shall be paid to the employees, and the amounts payable at the end of period; (2) the medical insurance, endowment insurance, unemployment insurance, work injury insurance, maternity insurance, and other social insurances, which shall be paid by the enterprise for the employees, as well as the amounts payable at the end of period; (3) the housing accumulation fund that shall be paid for the employees, as well as the amounts payable at the end of period; (4) the non-monetary welfare provided for the employees, as well as the calculation basis; (5) the compensation that shall be paid for the cancelation of the labor relationship with the employees, as well as the amounts payable at the end of period; and (6) other employee compensations.

Article 8 The contingent liabilities incurred due to the uncertainty of the number of the employees who offer to accept the layoff proposal and the compensation standards shall be disclosed according to the Accounting Standard for Business Enterprises No. 13—Contingencies.

13.4 Comments

The term "employee compensation" refers to all kinds of payments and other relevant expenditures given by enterprise in exchange of the services offered by the employees (*Article 2*). The employee compensation shall include the following: (1) wages, bonuses, allowances, and subsidies for the employees; (2) welfare expenses for the employees; (3) medical insurance, endowment insurance, unemployment insurance, work injury insurance, maternity insurance, and other social insurances; (4) housing accumulation fund; (5) labor union expenditure and employee education expenses; (6) non-monetary welfare; (7) compensations for the cancelation of the labor relationship with the employees; and (8) other relevant expenditures of services offered by the employees.

Article 4 states that company shall treat all compensation expenses as liabilities. In particular, the cost for producing goods and providing services should be computed as good/service cost; the cost for ongoing construction projects or intangible assets recorded as the assets cost; and for those employee compensations not related to previous examples, the cost shall be recorded in profit or loss. The year-end disclosure shall contain the following: all payments due to the employee, the insurance expenses (in accordance with *Article 5*), all non-monetary welfare, the housing accumulation fund, the compensation that shall be paid for the cancelation of the labor relationship, and other employee compensation.

ASBE No. 9 changes the previous PRC GAAP as now following items are recognized within the scope of employees benefits: (1) salaries, bonuses, allowances, and subsidies, (2) staff welfare, (3) union running costs and employee education costs, (4) various social security contributions, (5) non-monetary benefits, (6) housing funds, and (7) other related expenses incurred in exchange for service rendered by employees. ASBE No. 9 places under the roof of employee benefits, compensation to employees for termination of the employment relationship.

Furthermore, it is established that an enterprise should recognize a liability in the period the services are provided at the amount of employee benefits payable for that service. The major introduction refers to the fact that under past regulation, a liability is only recognized for salaries, bonuses, allowances and subsidies, staff welfare, union running costs, and employee education costs. Other employee benefit-related expenses accrued at their payment. A similar treatment is expected when an enterprise is required to recognize a liability for compensation for employee's termination of employment relationship if the enterprise has a formal plan and it cannot unilaterally withdraw from that plan. In past version of PRC GAAP, such compensation was expensed when paid.

Under ASBE No. 9, no particular treatment is disposed for accounting requirements of defined benefit plans. At the same time, IAS 19 requires the recognition of a defined benefit liability and an expense throughout the expected service period of the related employee.

13.5 Examples

Company X produces safe systems and security devices to be sold to final customers. Actually, Company X employs a workforce of 10 people for daily production, earning an average compensation of 70,000 CNY per annum each. Three of them are subsequently assigned to the setting up of the internal security system to be used in next years. Furthermore, two company supervisors are charged to administration and overview procedures. They are paid 100,000 CNY per annum each.

Let us figure out the partition of these costs.

- 70,000 × 7 = 490,000 CNY will be referred to the cost of goods;
- 70,000 × 3 = 210,000 CNY will be recorded as the cost of an internally built asset;
- 100,000 × 2 = 200,000 CNY is the amount to be carried in profit or loss as it cannot be defined in first two classes.

Chapter 14
Accounting Standards for Business Enterprises No. 10—Enterprise Annuity Fund

14.1 Chapter I: General Provisions

Article 1 To standardize the confirmation and measurement of enterprise annuity fund and the presentation of financial statements, these standards are formulated in accordance with the Accounting Standard for Business Enterprises—Basic Standards.

Article 2 The term "enterprise annuity fund" refers to funds raised by an enterprise in light of the enterprise annuity plan and the supplementary endowment insurance fund raised by its operating income of investment.

Article 3 The enterprise annuity funds shall be confirmed, measured, and presented as independent accounting subjects. The entrusting party, entrusted party, trustee, account manager, investment manager, and other subjects providing services for the management of enterprise annuity fund shall strictly distinguish the enterprise annuity fund and its fixed assets from other assets so as to ensure the safety of the enterprise annuity fund.

14.2 Chapter II: Confirmation and Measurement

Article 4 The enterprise annuity fund shall be confirmed and measured, respectively, on the basis of assets, liabilities, incomes, expenses, and net assets.

Article 5 The assets formed by payments for the enterprise annuity fund and by the operation of the annuity fund shall include the monetary funds, settlement accounts receivable of securities, interests receivable, purchases of resale securities, other receivables, bond investments, fund investments, stock investments, and other investments.

Article 6 During the operation of the enterprise annuity fund, the initial acquisition values and subsequent values of the national debt gained under the state

L. Riccardi, *China Accounting Standards*,
DOI 10.1007/978-981-10-0006-5_14

investment scope, the financial debentures, and enterprise obligations with the credit rating at the investment grade or above, convertible obligations, investment insurance products, securities investment funds, stocks, and other financial products with good liquidity shall be measured as the fair value: (1) The transaction price paid on the transaction date shall be measured as the fair value when an initial investment is obtained. The transaction fee shall be directly recorded as profit or loss for the current period and (2) when estimating the value of an investment on the estimate day, the original carrying value of the investment shall be adjusted according to its fair value, and the difference between its fair value and its original carrying value shall be recorded as profit or loss for the current period. The determination of the fair value of an investment shall be subject to the Accounting Standard for Business Enterprises No. 22—Recognition and Measurement of Financial Instruments.

Article 7 The liabilities formed during the operation of the enterprise annuity fund include the settlement accounts receivable of securities, beneficiaries' treatments payable, the management fees payable to the entrusted, the management fees payable to the custodian, the management fees payable to the investment manager, the taxes payable, the sale accounts of repurchased bonds, the interests payable, the commissions payable, and other accounts payables.

Article 8 The incomes formed by the operations of the enterprise annuity fund include the interest incomes on deposits, interests, from the buying of resold bonds, gains on the changes in the fair value, incomes of investment disposal, and other incomes.

Article 9 The incomes shall be confirmed and measured according to the following provisions: (1) The interest income on deposits shall be determined according to the principal and applicable interest rate; (2) the incomes from buying resold bonds shall, within the time limit of securities loan, be determined according to the purchase price of the resold bonds and the interest rate as stipulated in the agreement; (3) the gains on the changes in the fair value, on the estimate date, are determined according to the difference between the fair value of the investment on the current date and the original carrying value (namely the fair value of the investment on the previous estimate date); (4) the incomes of investment disposal shall be determined according to the difference between the price obtained from the sale of investment and the carrying value of the investment; and (5) other incomes such as risk reserves shall be determined according to the amount actually incurred.

Article 10 The expenses incurred during the operation of the enterprise annuity fund include the transaction expenses, management fees of the entrusted party the trustee, and the investment manager, the disbursements for the sale of repurchased bonds, and other expenses.

Article 11 The expenses shall be confirmed and measured according to the provisions as follows: (1) The transaction expenses, including the commission charge, commissions and other necessary disbursements paid to the commissioned agents, consultation agents and broker—the amount of which shall be determined in accordance with the actually incurred amount; (2) the management fees payable to the entrusted party, trustee, and investment manager shall be determined according to the actual amount of provisions; (3) the disbursements for the sale of repurchased bonds shall, within the time limit for financing, be determined in accordance with the sales price of the repurchased bonds and the interest rate as stipulated in the agreement; and (4) other expenses shall be determined in accordance with the actually incurred amount.

Article 12 The net assets of the enterprise annuity fund refers to the balance of the assets of the enterprise annuity fund minus liabilities. The date of balance sheet shall carry forward the incomes and expenses of the current period into the net assets. Different accounts shall be created for the net assets of an enterprise in view of the enterprise itself and the individual employees, and the distributed operating proceeds shall timely be recorded in each of the aforesaid accounts in accordance with the plan of the enterprise annuity fund.

Article 13 The net assets shall be confirmed and measured in accordance with the provisions as follows: (1) For the payments collected from the enterprise and employees, the net assets shall be increased according to the amount received; (2) for the treatments paid to the beneficiaries, the net assets shall be reduced in accordance with the amount payable; (3) as the transfer-in amount of an individual account incurred due to an employee's transfer into the enterprise, the net assets shall be increased; and (4) as the transfer-out amount of an individual account incurred due to an employee's transfer out of the enterprise, the net assets shall be reduced.

14.3 Chapter III: Disclosure

Article 14 The financial statements for the enterprise annuity fund include the balance sheet, net assets change statements, and annotations.

Article 15 The balance sheet shall reflect the financial status of the enterprise annuity fund on a specific date. It shall be presented and sorted by the assets, liabilities, and net assets.

Article 16 The items of the assets shall at least present the information as follows: (1) the monetary fund; (2) the settlement accounts receivable of bonds; (3) the receivable interests; (4) the purchases of resold securities; (5) other accounts receivable; (6) the bond investments; (7) the fund investments; (8) the stock investments; (9) other investments; and (10) other assets.

Article 17 The items of the liabilities shall at least present the information as follows: (1) the settlement accounts payable of bolds; (2) the beneficiaries' treatments payable; (3) the management fees payable to the entrusted; (4) the management fees payable to the trustee; (5) the management fees payable to the investment manager; (6) the taxes payable; (7) the amounts from the sale of repurchased bonds; (8) the payable interests; (9) the commissions payable; and (10) other payables.

Article 18 The items of the net assets shall present the net value of the enterprise annuity fund.

Article 19 The net assets change statements shall reflect the increases and reductions of the net assets of the enterprise annuity fund and present the information as follows: (1) the opening net assets; (2) the current amount of increase of the net assets, including the current incomes, payments collected from the enterprise, payments collected from the employees, and transfer-in amount of individual accounts; (3) the current amount of reduction of net assets, including the current expenses, treatments paid to the beneficiaries, and transfer-out amount of individual account; and (4) the closing net assets.

Article 20 The annotations shall disclose the information as follows: (1) the main contents and important changes of the annuity fund plan of an enterprise; (2) the sorts of investments, amounts, and methods for the confirmation of the fair value; (3) the proportion of each kind of investments to the total amount of investments; and (4) any other item that is likely to cause important influence on the investment value.

14.4 Comments

New ASBE No. 10 introduces the concept of enterprise annuity funds and recognizes them as a supplementary retirement insurance fund (set up in accordance with related laws as a defined contribution plan) which is formed from the amounts raised under an enterprise annuity fund plan and the investment and operation earnings of the fund. According to this, an enterprise annuity fund shall be regarded as an individual entity for accounting purposes (i.e., recognition, measurement, and presentation). To this extent, *Article 3* prescribes that all subject providing management services for the enterprise annuity fund shall strictly distinguish the enterprise annuity fund and its fixed assets from other assets so as to ensure the safety of the enterprise annuity fund.

With regard to disclosure, *Article 14* recognizes that the financial statements of the enterprise annuity fund include the balance sheet, net assets change statements, and annotations. All financial assets obtained by an enterprise annuity fund should be measured at fair value with changes between the carrying amount and the fair value recognized in profit or loss. The items of the net assets shall present the net value of the enterprise annuity fund (*Article 18*). All components of assets and liabilities are, respectively, stated in *Article 16* and *Article 17*.

The net assets change statements described in *Article 19* shall reflect the increases and reductions of the net assets of the enterprise annuity fund. It must show: the opening net assets, the current amount of increase or decrease of the net assets—including the current incomes or expenses and payments collected or cashed-out—and the closing net assets. The annotation shall disclose the main changes occurred to the annuity fund plan, qualitative and quantitative information about the carrying pattern of investment, and any other information that is likely to influence the investment value.

While IAS 26 applies to all retirement benefit plans and prescribes the accounting and reporting by defined contribution and benefit plans, ASBE No. 10 does not deal with the accounting by defined benefit plans because they are not allowed under the existing PRC rules.

14.5 Examples

Company X records for its enterprise annuity fund the following entries:

- Initial amount of net assets 1,500,000 CNY;
- Payments collected from enterprise 450,000 CNY;
- Positive difference in fair value of assets held during the entire year 100,000 CNY;
- Interest accrued and retained on securities 15,000 CNY;
- Capital gains on disposal of financial assets 40,000 CNY with a carrying value of 200,000 CNY;
- Payment of treatments to beneficiaries: 300,000 CNY.

For the sake of ease, let us assume no other events occur.

The new income for the financial year is 100,000 + 15,000 + 40,000 = 155,000 CNY.

Change in the net assets: 305,000 CNY.

Opening net assets: 1,500,000 CNY.

Current account of increase in net assets: 155,000 CNY + 450,000 CNY.

Current reduction of net assets: 300,000 CNY.

Closing net assets: 1,805,000 CNY.

Chapter 15
Accounting Standards for Business Enterprises No. 11—Share-Based Payments

15.1 Chapter I: General Provisions

Article 1 These Standards are formulated in accordance with the Accounting Standards for Enterprises—Basic Standards for the purpose of regulating the recognition, and measurement of share-based payments, and the disclosure of relevant information.

Article 2 The term "share-based payment" refers to a transaction in which an enterprise grants equity instruments or undertakes equity-instrument-based liabilities in return for services from employee or other parties. The share-based payments shall consist of equity-settled share-based payments and cash-settled share-based payments. The term "equity-settled share-based payment" refers to a transaction in which an enterprise grants shares or other equity instruments as a consideration in return for services. The term "cash-settled share-based payment" refers to a transaction of payment of cash or any other asset obligation calculated and determined on the basis of shares or other equity instruments undertaken by the enterprise in return for services. The term "equity instrument" as mentioned in these Standards refers to the equity instruments of the enterprise's own.

Article 3 The following items shall be governed by other accounting standards: (1) The Accounting Standards for Enterprises No. 20—Business Combination shall apply to a transaction in which an enterprise issues the equity instrument and obtains the net assets of another enterprise in a business combination. (2) The Accounting Standards for Enterprises No. 22—Recognition and Measurement of Financial Instruments shall apply to a transaction in which equity instruments are granted as a consideration for other financial instruments.

L. Riccardi, *China Accounting Standards*,
DOI 10.1007/978-981-10-0006-5_15

15.2 Chapter II: The Equity-Settled Share-Based Payments

Article 4 The equity-settled share-based payment in return for employee services shall be measured at the fair value of the equity instruments granted to the employees. The fair value of the equity instruments shall be confirmed in accordance with Accounting Standards for Enterprises No. 22—Recognition and Measurement of Financial Instruments.

Article 5 As to an equity-settled share-based payment in return for services of employees, if the right may be exercised immediately after the grant, the fair value of the equity instruments shall, on the date of the grant, be included in the relevant cost or expense and the capital reserves shall be increased accordingly. The "grant date" refers to the date on which the share-based payment agreement is approved.

Article 6 As to an equity-settled share-based payment in return for employee services, if the right cannot be exercised until the vesting period comes to an end or until the prescribed performance conditions are met, then on each balance sheet date within the vesting period, the services obtained in the current period shall, based on the best estimate of the number of vested equity instruments, be included in the relevant costs or expenses and the capital reserves at the fair value of the equities instruments on the date of the grant. If, on the balance sheet date, the subsequent information indicates that the number of vested equity instruments is different from the previous estimate, an adjustment shall be made and on the vesting date, the estimate shall be adjusted to equal the number of the actually vested equity instruments. The "vesting period" refers to the period during which the specified vesting conditions are to be satisfied. As to a share-based payment with a specified service period as the vesting condition, the vesting period shall be from the grant date to the vesting date. As to a share-based payment with specified performances as the vesting condition, the length of the vesting period shall be estimated in accordance with the most likely performance outcome. The "vesting date" refers to the date on which the vesting conditions are met and the employees and other parties have the right to obtain the equity instruments or cash from an enterprise.

Article 7 An enterprise shall, after the vesting date, make no adjustment to the relevant costs or expenses as well as the total amount of the owner's equities which have been confirmed.

Article 8 An equity-settled share-based payment in return for the service of any other party shall be conducted in accordance with the following circumstances, respectively: (1) If the fair value of the service of any other party can be measured in a reliable way, the fair value of the service on the acquisition date by any other service party shall be included in the relevant costs or expenses, and the owner's equities shall be increased accordingly. (2) If the fair value of the service of any other party cannot be measured in a reliable way, but the fair value of the equity instruments can be measured in a reliable way, the fair value of the equity instruments on date of the service acquisition shall be included in the relevant costs or expenses, and the owner's equities shall be increased accordingly.

Article 9 On the vesting date, an enterprise shall, based on the number of the equity instruments of which the right is actually exercised, calculate and confirm the amount of the paid-in capital or capital stock to be transferred in, and transfer it in the paid-in capital or stock capital. The "vesting date" refers to the date on which the employees and other parties exercise the right, acquire cash or equity instruments.

15.3 Chapter III: The Cash-Settled Share-Based Payments

Article 10 A cash-settled share-based payment shall be measured in accordance with the fair value of liability calculated and confirmed based on the shares or other equity instruments undertaken by an enterprise.

Article 11 As to a cash-settled share-based payment instruments, if the right may be exercised immediately after the grant, the fair value of the liability undertaken by the enterprise shall, on the date of the grant, be included in the relevant costs or expenses, and the liabilities shall be increased accordingly.

Article 12 As to a cash-settled share-based payment, if the right may not be exercised until the vesting period comes to an end or until the specified performance conditions are met, on each balance sheet date within the vesting period, the services obtained in the current period shall, based on the best estimate of the information about the exercisable right, be included in the relevant costs or expenses and the corresponding liabilities at the fair value of the liability undertaken by the enterprise. If, on the balance sheet date, the subsequent information indicates that fair value of the current liability undertaken by the enterprise are different from the previous estimates, an adjustment shall be made and on the vesting date the estimate shall be adjusted to equal the actually exercisable right.

Article 13 An enterprise shall, on each balance sheet date and on each account date prior to the settlement of the relevant liabilities, remeasure the fair values of the liabilities and include the changes in the current profits and losses.

15.4 Chapter IV: Disclosure

Article 14 An enterprise shall, in the notes, disclose the information related to the cash-settled share-based payments as follows: (1) the total amounts of the equity instruments that are granted, exercised, and invalidated in the current period; (2) the range of the vesting prices for the share options or other equity instruments issued outward at the end of period, and the remainder of the contractual period; (3) the weighted average prices of the share options or other equity instruments exercised in the current period which are calculated based on the vesting date prices; and

(4) the measures for the confirmation of the fair value of the equity instruments. The enterprise may disclose the information of homogeneous share-based payments on a consolidated basis.

Article 15 An enterprise shall, in the notes, disclose the effects of the share-based payment transactions on the current financial status and operating outcomes, which shall at least include the information as follows: (1) the total amount of the expenses as a result of equity-settled share-based payments, which is recognized in the current period; (2) the total amount of the expenses as a result of cash-settled share-based payments, which is recognized in the current period; and (3) the total amount of the employee services and other party services as a result of the share-based payments in the current period.

15.5 Comments

Article 2 introduces "share-based payment" as a transaction in which an enterprise grants equity instruments or undertakes equity-instrument-based liabilities in return for services from employees or other parties. Transactions embedded in "share-based payments" are both to "equity-settled shared-based payments" (transactions in which an enterprise grants shares or other equity instruments as a consideration in return for services) and "cash-settled share-based payment" (transactions of payment of cash or any other asset obligation calculated and determined on the basis of shares or other equity instruments undertaken by the enterprise in return for services). Cash-settled share-based payments are initially recorded as liability. In both circumstances, the fair value approach shall be adapted to measure payments, and its recognition methods are required to be disclosed.

For the first time, new ASBE No. 11 requires an enterprise to recognize share-based payment transactions for services provided by employees and other parties. The period-end financial statements shall give evidence to show all share-based payments done during the accounting period, the number, and financial instruments granted, exercised, or invalidated during the period, the price range of these financial instruments and the weighted average price of share-based payment occurred.

Some key differences arise from the comparison to the equivalent IFRS 2. The latter disposes an entity to recognize share-based payment transactions (in which the entity receives goods or services) in its financial statements, including transactions with employees or other parties. Instead, ASBE No. 11 refers only to share-based transactions for which services are received. Furthermore, under ASBE No. 11, there is no provision about with cash alternatives.

15.6 Examples

Company X grants 100 share options to each of its 500 employees, and the vesting is limited to this financial year. The estimated fair value price of each option is 15 CNY. Furthermore, Company X grants other 50 cash-settled awards to its 500 employees on condition they remain in its job for next year. It is expected 10 % of current employees will leave.

The share-settled share-based payment is 100 × 500 × 15 = 750,000 CNY.

The cash-settled share-based payment is 50 × 500 × 90 % × 15 + 337,500 CNY.

The total expense for the period will be 1,087,500 CNY, whereas the liability 337,500 CNY.

Chapter 16
Accounting Standards for Business Enterprises No. 12—Debt Restructuring

16.1 Chapter I: General Provisions

Article 1 These Standards are formulated in accordance with the Accounting Standards for Enterprises—Basic Standards for the purpose of regulating the recognition and measurement of debt restructuring and disclosing of the relevant information.

Article 2 The term "debt restructuring" refers to an event in which the terms of a debt are given in as a result of a mutual agreement between a debtor and a creditor or a judgment of a court when the debtor gets into a financial problem.

Article 3 The manners of debt restructuring mainly include the following: (1) the liquidation of a debt by asset; (2) the conversion of a debt into capital; (3) the modification of other terms of a debt such as deduction of principal or interest of a debt, excluding the two manners aforesaid; and (4) a combination of the three aforesaid manners.

16.2 Chapter II: Accounting Treatment of Debtors

Article 4 When a debt is liquidated by cash, the debtor shall include the difference between the book value of the debt to be restructured and the actual cash payment into the current profits and losses.

Article 5 When a debt is liquidated by a non-cash asset, the debtor shall include the difference between the book value of the debt to be restructured and the fair value of the non-cash asset transferred into the current profits and losses. The difference between fair value of the non-cash asset transferred and its book value shall be included in the current profits and losses.

Article 6 When a debt is converted into capital, the debtor shall recognize the total par value of shares, to which the creditor becomes entitled for waiver of the

L. Riccardi, *China Accounting Standards*,
DOI 10.1007/978-981-10-0006-5_16

credit, as stock of capital (or paid-in capital), and shall recognize the difference between the total amount of the fair value of the shares and the stock of capital (or paid-in capital) as capital reserve. The difference between the book value of the debt to be restructured and total amount of the fair value of the shares shall be included in the current profits and losses.

Article 7 Where other terms of a debt are modified, the debtor shall regard the post-modification fair value of the debt as the entry value of the restructured debt and shall include the difference between the book value of the debt to be restructured and the entry value of the restructured debt in the current profits and losses. If the post-modification terms of a debt concern any contingent payment and if the contingent payment meets the conditions for the recognition of expected liabilities as prescribed in the Accounting Standards for Enterprises No. 13—Contingencies, the debtor shall recognize the contingent sum payable as expected liability, and shall include the difference between the book value of the debt to be restructured and the aggregate amount of the entry value of the restructured debt and the expected amount of liability in the current profits and losses. The term "contingent sum payable" refers to the payable sum in light of the occurrence of a future event that is uncertain.

Article 8 Where a debt restructuring is made by a combination of the liquidation of a debt by assets, the liquidation of a debt by non-cash asset, the conversion of a debt into capital, and the modification of other terms of a debt, the debtor shall offset, one by one, the cash paid, the fair value of the non-cash asset transferred, and the fair value of the shares to which the creditor becomes entitled, against the book value of the debt to be restructured, and then handle it in accordance with *Article 7* of these Standards.

16.3 Chapter III: Accounting Treatments of the Creditor

Article 9 When a debt is liquidated by cash, the creditor shall include the difference between the book balance of the debt to be restructured and the cash received in the current profits and losses. If the creditor has made provision for the impairment of the credit, he shall first offset the aforesaid difference against the impairment provision and then include the shortfall in the current profits and losses.

Article 10 When a debt is liquidated by non-cash asset, the creditor shall recognize the fair value of the non-cash asset received as the entry value and shall handle the difference between the book balance of the debt to be restructured and the fair value of the non-cash asset received in accordance with *Article 9* of these Standards.

Article 11 When a debt is converted into capital, the creditor shall recognize the fair value of the shares to which it becomes entitled as investment to the debtor and shall handle the difference between the book balance of the debt to be restructured and the fair value of the shares in accordance with *Article 9* of these Standards.

Article 12 When other terms of a debt are modified, the creditor shall recognize the fair value of the credit after the modification of other terms of the debt as the book value of the restructured debt and shall handle the book balance of the debt to be restructured and the book value of the restructured debt in accordance with *Article 9* of these Standards. If the post-modification terms of the debt concern any contingent sum receivable, the creditor shall not recognize the contingent sum receivable, nor he include it in the book value of the restructured debt. The term "contingent sum receivable" refers to the receivable sum in light of the occurrence of a future event that is uncertain.

Article 13 Where a debt restructuring is made by a combination of the liquidation of a debt by assets, the liquidation of a debt by non-cash asset, the conversion of a debt into capital and the modification of other terms of a debt, the creditor shall offset, one by one, the cash received, the fair value of the non-cash asset received, and the fair value of the shares to which the creditor becomes entitled, against the book balance of the debt to be restructured, and then handle it in accordance with *Article 12* of these Standards.

16.4 Chapter IV: Disclosure

Article 14 The debtor shall, in its notes, disclose the information concerning debt restructuring as follows: (1) the manners of debt restructuring; (2) the total amount of the gains of debt restructuring, which is confirmed; (3) the increment amount of stock capital (or paid-in capital) due to debt-to-capital conversion; (4) the contingent sum payable; and (5) the methods and basis for the ascertainment of the fair value of the non-cash asset transferred in a debt restructuring, the fair value of the shares converted by the debt, and the fair value of the debt after the modification of other terms of the debt.

Article 15 A creditor shall, in its notes, disclose the information concerning debt restructuring as follows: (1) the manners of debt restructuring; (2) the total amount of the loss of debt restructuring, which is recognized; (3) the increment amount of investment and the proportion to the total shares of the debtor due to credit-to-share conversion; (4) the contingent sum receivable; and (5) the methods and basis for the confirmation of the fair value of the non-cash asset received in a debt restructuring, the fair value of the shares converted by the credit, and the fair value of the credit after the modification of other terms of the debt.

16.5 Comments

Debt restructuring is defined in *Article 2* as an event in which a debtor is in financial difficulty and a creditor grants a concession to the debtor in accordance with a mutual agreement or a court judgment. Previous PRC GAAP recognized as debt restructuring all arrangements that resulted in modification of the original terms of debt obligation.

Article 3 states all possible patterns to undertake a debt restructuring. They are as follows: "(1) the liquidation of a debt by asset; (2) the conversion of a debt into capital; (3) the modification of other terms of a debt such as deduction of principal or interest of a debt, excluding the two manners aforesaid; and (4) a combination of the three aforesaid manners."

Articles 4–8 fix dispositions for a debt restructuring to be carried out. In case of debt liquidation by cash, the difference between the book value of debt to be restructured and the cash collected shall be recorded in profit and loss. In case of liquidation by non-monetary assets, the difference between the fair value of the assets and the book value of the debt to be restructured shall be recorded in profit and loss. The debtor should record the difference between the fair value and the book value of the assets. In case of conversion into capital, the difference between the cash collected and share price shall be recorded as capital reserve and the debtor shall recognize the par value of new shares, through the creditor is now entitled of shareholder's rights. Blended solutions shall separately account for each of previous measurements. These records relate both to debtor and to creditor involved in debt restructuring.

They have to disclose also the manners of debt restructuring; the total amount of the gains of debt restructuring, which is confirmed; the increment amount of stock capital due to debt-to-capital conversion; the contingent sum payable; and all the methods used to determine the fair value.

Also, it is disposed that assets or equity interests received or surrendered by debtor or creditor to be measured at fair value. The following gains or losses should be recognized in profit and loss. This is a second introduction, as before 2007, the capital gain accounted for "capital reserve." Finally, new ASBE No. 12 does not cover principles for derecognition of debts.

16.6 Examples

Company X claims an outstanding credit on Company Y for 800,000 CNY due within the financial year. Since Company Y is experiencing financial distress, boards agree a debt restructuring. In particular, the terms dispose that half of outstanding debt will be paid up though a property held by Company Y and worth 450,000 CNY at fair value, while the remaining part will be subject to a conversion into capital of Company Y. At the time of facts, the fair value of Company Y's shares is 10 CNY each.

With regard to fixed assets, Company X will recognize the property at its fair value and account for a positive income item of 50,000 CNY (the opposite will happen for the debtor).

With regard to conversion into capital, the par value is established to be in line with the fair value (10 CNY), so no other differences shall be recorded in respective profits and losses.

Chapter 17
Accounting Standards for Business Enterprises No. 13—Contingencies

17.1 Chapter I: General Provisions

Article 1 These Standards are formulated in accordance with the Accounting Standards for Enterprises—Basic Standards for the purpose of regulating the recognition and measurement of Contingencies, and the disclosure of relevant information.

Article 2 The term "Contingencies" refers to the conditions that formed by past transactions or events, and the outcome of which will be confirmed only by the occurrence or non-occurrence of future events.

Article 3 Other accounting standards shall apply to the contingencies formed by events such as employee wages and salaries, construction contracts, income taxes, business combination, leases, original insurance contracts, and reinsurance contracts.

17.2 Chapter II: Recognition and Measurement

Article 4 The obligation pertinent to a contingency shall be recognized as an estimated debts when the following conditions are satisfied simultaneously: (1) That obligation is a current obligation of the enterprise; (2) it is likely to cause any economic benefit to flow out of the enterprise as a result of performance of the obligation; and (3) the amount of the obligation can be measured in a reliable way.

Article 5 The estimated debts shall be initially measured in accordance with the best estimate of the necessary expenses for the performance of the current obligation. If there is a sequent range for the necessary expenses and if all the outcomes within this range are equally likely to occur, the best estimate shall be determined in accordance with the middle estimate within the range. In other cases, the best estimate shall be conducted in accordance with the following situations, respectively: (1) If the Contingencies concern a single item, it shall be determined in light

L. Riccardi, *China Accounting Standards*,
DOI 10.1007/978-981-10-0006-5_17

of the most likely outcome. (2) If the Contingencies concern two or more items, the best estimate should be calculated and determined in accordance with all possible outcomes and the relevant probabilities.

Article 6 To determine the best estimate, an enterprise shall take into consideration the full risk of uncertainty, time value of money, and other factors pertinent to the Contingencies. If the time value of money is of great significance, the best estimate shall be determined after discounting the relevant future outflow of cash.

Article 7 When all or some of the expenses necessary for the liquidation of the estimated debts of an enterprise are expected to be compensated by a third party, the compensation should be separately recognized as an asset only when it is virtually certain that the reimbursement will be obtained. The amount recognized for the reimbursement should not exceed the book value of the estimated debts.

Article 8 Where an executive contract turns to be a loss contract, the obligation generated from the loss contract which meets the provisions of *Article 4* of these Standards shall be recognized as an estimated debt. The term "executive contract" refers to a contract, the contractual obligations of which fail to be performed by the relevant contracting parties, or some of the equal obligations have been performed. The term "loss contract" refers to a contract whose performance of the contractual obligations will inevitably incur costs in excess of the expected economic benefits.

Article 9 The future operating losses of an enterprise shall not be recognized as estimated debts.

Article 10 If a restructuring obligations undertaken by an enterprise meets the provisions of *Article 4* of these Standards, it shall be recognized as an estimated debts. The simultaneous existence of the following situations indicates that the enterprise has undertaken the restructuring obligation: (1) Having a detailed and formal restructuring plan, which consists of the businesses concerning restructuring, the main places, the number of employees to be compensated and the nature of their posts, the expected expenditure for the recombination, the execution time of the plan; and (2) the restructuring plan has been proclaimed to the general public. The term "restructuring" refers to the act of implementing a plan made and controlled by an enterprise, which may substantially change the organizational form, business scope, or operating manner of the enterprise.

Article 11 The enterprise shall determine the amount of estimated debts in light of the direct expenditure pertinent to the restructuring. The direct expenditure excludes the expenses for the pre–post training of the employees who stay on to work, market promotion, new systems, marketing network, etc.

Article 12 An enterprise shall check the book value of the estimated debts on the balance sheet date. If there is any exact evidence indicating that the book value cannot really reflect the current best estimate, the enterprise shall adjust the book value in accordance with the current best estimate.

Article 13 Any enterprise may not recognize any contingent debts or contingent asset. The term "contingent debts" refers to a potential obligation caused by past transactions or events and whose existence will be confirmed only by the occurrence or non-occurrence of uncertain future events, or refers to a current obligation caused by a past transaction or event, but is not recognized because the performance of the obligation is not likely to incur an outflow of economic benefits from the enterprise or because the amount of the obligation cannot be measured in a reliable way. The term "contingent asset" refers to a potential asset caused by a past transaction or event and whose existence will be confirmed only by the occurrence or non-occurrence of uncertain future events.

17.3 Chapter III: Disclosure

Article 14 An enterprise shall, in its notes, disclose the information pertinent to the Contingencies as follows: (1) estimated debts (a) the types and causes of the estimated debts, as well as an explanation for the uncertainty of the outflow of economic benefits; (b) the changes at the beginning and the end of the period, and the current changes in the estimated debts; and (c) the amount of expected compensations pertinent to the estimated debts, and the amount of excepted compensation that has been recognized in the current period. (2) Contingent debts (excluding those contingent liabilities that caused little possibility of any outflow of economic benefits) (a) the types and causes of the contingent debts, consisting of the contingent debts arising from discounted commercial acceptance bills of exchange, pending litigations, pending arbitrations, and guarantees provided for the debts of other enterprises; (b) an explanation for the uncertainty of the outflow of the economic benefits; and (c) an estimate of the expected financial effect of the contingent debts and the possibility of any expenditure. If it is unable to make an estimate, the reasons shall be explained. (3) In general, no enterprise may disclose the contingent assets. However, if a contingent asset will probably give rise to an inflow of economic benefits to the enterprise, the enterprise shall disclose the cause, the expected financial effect, etc.

Article 15 In the case of a pending litigation or arbitration, if the disclosure of some or all information in accordance with the provisions as prescribed in *Article 14* of these Standards can be expected to produce great unfavorable impact upon the enterprise, the enterprise shall not need to disclose the information, but shall disclose the nature of the pending litigation or arbitration as well as the truth and reasons for the failure to disclose the information.

17.4 Comments

ASBE No. 13 disposes guidance on how to recognize and measure onerous contracts restructuring. Previous PRC GAAP did not address these areas. Contingencies are defined in *Article 2* as the conditions that formed by past transactions or events, and the outcome of which will be confirmed only by the occurrence or non-occurrence of future events.

Three conditions shall be satisfied simultaneously for the obligations referred to Contingencies to be recognized as debt: That obligation is a current obligation of the enterprise; it is likely to cause any economic benefit to flow out of the enterprise as a result of performance of the obligation; and the amount of the obligation can be measured in a reliable way. In accordance with *Article 5*, the estimated debts shall be initially measured in line with "the best estimate of the necessary expenses for the performance of the current obligation."

The best estimate shall be calculated according to the middle value in the range of occurrence of expense. Otherwise, respectively, if the Contingencies concern a single item, it shall be determined in light of the most likely outcome; if the Contingencies concern two or more items, the best estimate should be calculated and determined in accordance with all possible outcomes and the relevant probabilities. *Article 14* divides disclosure of contingencies in estimated debts, contingent debts, and contingent assets. For each of these categories, financial statements shall contain amount, and changes occurred during the period and the assessment of uncertainty. Generally speaking, ASBE No. 13 follows guidelines provisioned in the equivalent IAS 37.

17.5 Examples

Company X during financial year gives warranties on its products. According to previous experience, about 5 % of sales lead to a warranty claim. During the year, Company X has sold 1,000,000 CNY. For this reason, Company X must recognize a liability of 50,000 CNY as a contingency.

Chapter 18
Accounting Standards for Business Enterprises No. 14—Revenue

18.1 Chapter I

Article 1 These standards are formulated in accordance with the Accounting Standards for Enterprises—Basic Standards for the purpose of regulating the recognition and measurement of the revenues, and the disclosure of the relevant information.

Article 2 The term "revenue" refers to the gross inflow of economic benefits formed during the course of the ordinary activities of an enterprise, which may increase the owner's equities and is irrelevant to the invested capital of the owner. The revenues as mentioned in these Standards consist of those from selling goods, providing labor services, and abalienating the right to use assets. The collection charged by an enterprise for third parties shall be treated as debts rather than revenues.

Article 3 Other relevant accounting standards shall apply to the revenue formed by long-term equity investments, construction contracts, leases, original insurance contracts, reinsurance contracts, etc.

18.2 Chapter II: Revenue from Selling Goods

Article 4 No revenue from selling goods may be recognized unless the following conditions are met simultaneously:

1. The significant risks and rewards of ownership of the goods have been transferred to the buyer by the enterprise;
2. The enterprise retains neither continuous management right that usually keeps relation with the ownership nor effective control over the sold goods;
3. The relevant amount of revenue can be measured in a reliable way;
4. The relevant economic benefits may flow into the enterprise; and
5. The relevant costs incurred or to be incurred can be measured in a reliable way.

L. Riccardi, *China Accounting Standards*,
DOI 10.1007/978-981-10-0006-5_18

Article 5 An enterprise shall ascertain the revenue incurred by selling goods in accordance with the received or receivable price stipulated in the contract or agreement signed between the enterprise and the buyer, unless the received or receivable amount as stipulated in the contract or agreement is unfair. If the collection of the price as stipulated in the contract or agreement is delayed and if it has the financing nature, the revenue incurred by selling goods shall be ascertained in accordance with the fair value of the receivable price as stipulated in the contract or agreement. The difference between the price stipulated in the contract or agreement and its fair value shall be amortized within the period of the contract or agreement employing the real interest method and shall be included in the current profits and losses.

Article 6 If the sale of goods concerns any cash discount, the revenue incurred by selling goods shall be ascertained in accordance with the amount prior to the deduction of the cash discount. The cash discount shall be included in the current profits and losses when it is actually incurred. The term "cash discount" refers to the amount of reduction of a debt offered by a creditor to a debtor for the purpose of encouraging the debtor to make payment within a prescribed period.

Article 7 If any trade discount in selling goods is concerned, the revenue incurred by selling goods shall be ascertained in accordance with the amount after the deduction of the trade discount. The term "trade discount" refers to a discount on the listed price granted by an enterprise for the purpose of sales promotion of goods.

Article 8 As to any sales discounts and allowance arising from any sold goods and of which the revenue from the sale has been recognized by the enterprise, the current revenue incurred by selling goods shall be offset against. The Accounting Standards for Enterprises No. 29—Events Occurring after the Balance Sheet Date, shall apply to the sales discounts and allowances that belong to the scope of the events occurring after the date of the balance sheet. The term "sales discounts and allowance" refers to the amount of reduction in the sales price as a result of the unqualified quality of the goods to be sold by an enterprise, or for other reasons.

Article 9 As to any sales return arising from any sold goods and of which the revenue from the sale has been recognized by the enterprise, the current revenue incurred by selling goods shall be offset against. The Accounting Standards for Enterprises No. 29—Events Occurring after the Balance Sheet Date shall apply to the sales returns that belong to the scope of events occurring after the date of the balance sheet. The term "sales return" refers to the return of goods sold by an enterprise as a result of the unqualified quality of the goods or inconformity with the required variety, or for other reasons.

18.3 Chapter III: Revenue from Providing Labor Services

Article 10 If an enterprise can, on the date of the balance sheet, reliably estimate the outcome of a transaction concerning the labor services it provides, it shall recognize the revenue from providing services employing the percentage-of-completion method. The term "percentage-of-completion method" refers to a method to recognize the revenues and expenses in light of the stage of completion under a transaction concerning the providing of labor services.

Article 11 The outcome of a transaction concerning the providing of labor services can be measured in a reliable way, means that the following conditions shall be met simultaneously:

1. The amount of revenue can be measured in a reliable way;
2. The relevant economic benefits are likely to flow into the enterprise;
3. The schedule of completion under the transaction can be confirmed in a reliable way;
4. The costs incurred or to be incurred in the transaction can be measured in a reliable way.

Article 12 An enterprise may adopt the following methods to ascertain the schedule of completion under the transaction concerning the providing of labor services:

1. The measurement of the work completed;
2. The proportion of the labor services provided against the total labor services to be provided; and
3. The proportion of the costs incurred against the estimated total costs.

Article 13 An enterprise shall ascertain the total revenue from the providing of labor services in accordance with the received or to-be-received price of the party that receives the labor services as stipulated in the contract or agreement, unless the received or to-be-received price as stipulated in the contract or agreement is unfair. An enterprise shall, on the date of the balance sheet, ascertain the current revenue from providing labor services in accordance with the amount of multiplying the total amount of revenues from providing labor services by the schedule of completion then deducting the accumulative revenues from the providing of labor services that have been recognized in the previous accounting periods. At the same time, the enterprise shall carry forward the current cost of labor services in accordance with the sum of multiplying the total amount of revenues arising from the providing of labor services by the schedule of completion and then deducting the accumulative revenues from the providing of labor services.

Article 14 If an enterprise cannot, on the date of the balance sheet, measure the result of a transaction concerning the providing of labor services in a reliable way, it shall be conducted in accordance with the following circumstances, respectively:

1. If the cost of labor services incurred is expected to be compensated, the revenue from the providing of labor services shall be recognized in accordance with the amount of the cost of labor services incurred, and the cost of labor services shall be carried forward at the same amount; or
2. If the cost of labor services incurred is not expected to compensate, the cost incurred should be included in the current profits and losses, and no revenue from the providing of labor services may be recognized.

Article 15 Where a contract or agreement signed between enterprises concerns selling goods and providing of labor services, if the part of sale of goods and the part of providing labor services can be distinguished from each other and can be measured, respectively, the part of sale of goods shall be conducted as selling goods and the part of providing labor services shall be conducted as providing labor services. If the part of selling goods and the part of providing labor services cannot be distinguished from each other, or if the part of sale of goods and the part of providing labor services can be distinguished from each other but cannot be measured, respectively, both parts shall be conducted as selling goods.

18.4 Chapter IV: Revenue from Abalienating the Right to Use Assets

Article 16 The revenue from abalienating of right to use assets consists of interest revenue and royalty revenue.

Article 17 No revenue from abalienating of right to use assets may be recognized unless the following conditions are met simultaneously:

1. The relevant economic benefits are likely to flow into the enterprise; and
2. The amount of revenues can be measured in a reliable way.

Article 18 An enterprise shall ascertain the amount of revenues from the abalienating of right to use assets based on the following circumstances, respectively:

1. The amount of interest revenue should be measured and confirmed in accordance with the length of time for which the enterprise's cash is used by others and the actual interest rate; or
2. The amount of royalty revenue should be measured and confirmed in accordance with the period and method of charging as stipulated in the relevant contract or agreement.

18.5 Chapter V: Disclosure

Article 19 An enterprise shall, in its notes, disclose the information concerning the revenue as follows:

1. The accounting policies adopted for the recognition of revenues, consisting of the methods for the ascertainment of the schedule of completion under the transaction concerning the providing of labor services;
2. The amount of revenues from selling goods, providing labor services, interest, and royalty recognized in the current period.

18.6 Comments

The principle specifies the actual condition to recognize revenues. In particular, the term "revenue" shall be featured by the following: "inflows of economic benefits derived from the course of the ordinary activities of the enterprise; inflows resulting in increases in owner's equity, other than those relating to capital contributions from owners; Inflows are to be reported gross in the financial statements." At the same time, it is clarified that revenue does not contain inflows from economic benefits resulting from equity contribution.

Revenue is measured at the fair value of the consideration after considering the effect of discounting any deferred payments. This last effect was not considered under past version of PRC GAAP. Revenue shall be recognized only when it is earned and it is realized or realizable. The revenue is accounted according to the fair value stipulated in the contract or agreement, except where this value is clearly not fair.

The principle deepens revenue from sales of goods. It is prescribed that revenue from the sale of goods shall be recognized when all the following conditions have been satisfied: (1) the enterprise has transferred to the buyer the significant risks and rewards of ownership of the goods; (2) the enterprise retains neither continuing managerial involvement to the degree usually associated with ownership nor effective control over the goods sold; (3) the amount of revenue can be measured reliably; (4) it is probable that the economic benefits associated with the transaction will flow to the entity; and (5) the costs incurred or to be incurred in respect of the transaction can be measured reliably.

The ASBE No. 14 embraces revenue from rendering services. When the outcome of a transaction involving the rendering of services can be estimated reliably, revenue associated with the transaction shall be recognized at the balance sheet date by adopting the percentage-of-completion method, namely according to the state in the completion process.

Revenue arising from the utilization of enterprise's asset: the main categories refer to yield of interest and royalties. It is disposed the "accretion" approach, meaning that revenue arise during the production process. Both interests and royalties can be recognized as revenue if the economic benefits inflows into the company and their value can be reliably estimated.

If a contract or an agreement comprises both the sale of goods and the rendering of services and these two components cannot be separately identified, or the components are separately identifiable but not separately measurable, the entire contract or agreement shall be accounted for as a sale of goods. No relevant differences are recognizable upon respective IAS 11.

18.7 Examples

Company X operates both in trading goods and services. During this month, it sells to Company Y different batches of merchandise for a total amount of 1,500,000 CNY. Also it is recognized a combined sale of 500,000 CNY consisting of goods and rendering-related service. It is not possible to divide or measure separate components. Finally, Company X allows Company Y to use its assets for a royalty of 1.5 CNY per piece on a total amount of 100,000 pieces. During this month, Company Y turns 50 % of the established production.

Assuming that all the conditions that recognize revenue occur, let us show the calculation of total revenue for this month:

- 1,500,000 CNY: sale of goods;
- 500,000 CNY: combined amount of services and goods, however, as their single value is not identifiable the total amount refers to goods;
- 75,000 CNY: total amount of royalties (1.5 × 100,000 × 50 %).

Total revenue = 2,075,000 CNY.

Chapter 19
Accounting Standards for Business Enterprises No. 15—Construction Contracts

19.1 Chapter I: General Provisions

Article 1 In order to regulate the recognition, measure construction contracts of enterprises (construction contractors, the same below), and disclose the relevant information, these Standards are formulated according to the Accounting Standards for Enterprises—Basic Standards.

Article 2 The term "construction contract" means the contract signed for the construction of an asset or several assets that are closely interrelated in the matter of their design, technology, and function or their ultimate purpose or use.

Article 3 Construction contracts consist of fixed price contracts and cost-plus contracts. A fixed price contract means a construction contract in which the construction price is ascertained on the basis of a fixed contract price or a fixed unit price. A cost-plus contract means a construction contract in which the construction price is ascertained on the basis of the costs stipulated in the contract or costs negotiated otherwise plus a proportion of these costs or a fixed fee.

19.2 Chapter II: The Split Up and Combination of Contracts

Article 4 Generally, an enterprise shall have accounting treatment in accordance with each construction contract. However, in some cases, it is necessary to split up a single contract or combine several contracts in order to reflect the essence of a single contract or a group of contracts.

L. Riccardi, *China Accounting Standards*,
DOI 10.1007/978-981-10-0006-5_19

Article 5 For a construction contract including several assets, the construction of each asset shall be treated as a single construction contract when the conditions as follows are met simultaneously:

1. Independent construction plan of each asset;
2. Each asset needs a separate negotiation with the customer, and the parties have been able to accept or reject the contract terms pertinent to each asset; and
3. The revenue and costs of each asset can be identified separately.

Article 6 The construction of each additional asset shall be accounted for as a separate contract if either of the conditions is met as follows:

1. There is great difference between the additional asset and the original asset under the original contract in terms of design, technology, or function; or
2. It is not necessary to take into account of the original contract price when the price of the additional asset is separately negotiated.

Article 7 A group of contracts, whether with a single customer or with several customers, shall be treated as a single construction contract when all of the conditions are met as follows:

1. The group of contracts is signed as a package deal;
2. The contracts are so closely related that they are, in fact, parts of a single project with an overall profit margin; and
3. The contracts are carried out concurrently or in a sequential manner.

19.3 Chapter III: Contract Revenue

Article 8 The contract revenue shall consist of:

1. The initial amount of revenue stipulated in the contract; and
2. Revenue incurred by alterations in contract, claims for compensation, and incentive payments.

Article 9 An alteration in a contract is an adjustment by the customer for a change in the range of the work to be performed under the contract. Revenues incurred by alterations in the contract shall be recognized when both of the conditions as follows are met simultaneously:

1. The customer will approve the amount of revenues incurred by the variation; and
2. The amount of revenues can be measured in a reliable way.

Article 10 A claim for compensation is an amount that is not included in the contract price and which the contractor seeks to charge from the customer or a third party as a compensation for costs that caused by the customer or a third party.

Revenue incurred by claims should be recognized when both of the conditions as follows are met simultaneously:

1. The customer is expected to accept the claims for compensation in accordance with the situations of negotiations; and
2. The amount that is accepted by the other party can be measured in a reliable way.

Article 11 Incentive payments refer to the additional amounts agreed to pay to the contractor by the customer if the specified performance standards are met or exceeded. Revenue incurred by incentive payments should be recognized when both of the conditions as follows are met simultaneously:

1. The contract has reached a stage of completion so that it can be deduced that the schedule and quality of the contract will meet or exceed the specified performance standards; and
2. The amount of incentive payments can be measured in a reliable way.

19.4 Chapter IV: Contract Costs

Article 12 The contract costs shall consist of the direct and indirect costs incurred and related to a contract during the period from the date of the contract signed to the date of the contract completed.

Article 13 The direct costs under a contract shall consist of the items as follows:

1. Costs of materials;
2. Labor costs;
3. Utilization expenses of equipment; and
4. Other direct costs, referring to other expenses that may be directly included in the contract costs.

Article 14 The indirect costs refer to the costs incurred by organizing and managing operating activities for construction entity or production entity subordinate to an enterprise.

Article 15 The direct costs shall be directly included as part of the contract costs when they are incurred. The indirect costs shall be allocated to the contract costs in light of a systematic and reasonable method on the date of the balance sheet.

Article 16 The contract costs may be offset against by any incidental income pertinent to the contract, such as the income from the disposal of surplus materials at the end of the contract.

Article 17 The contract costs do not include the costs that shall be included in the current profits and losses, such as the administration costs, the selling costs, and the financial costs. The relevant expenses incurred by the sign of a contract shall be directly included in the current profits and losses.

19.5 Chapter V: Recognition of Contract Revenue and Contract Costs

Article 18 If the outcome of a construction contract can be estimated in a reliable way, the contract revenue and contract costs shall be recognized in light of the percentage-of-completion method on the date of the balance sheet. The term "percentage-of-completion method" means a method by which the contractor recognizes its revenues and costs in light of the schedule of the contracted project.

Article 19 The outcome of a fixed price contract can be estimated in a reliable way when all of the conditions as follows are met simultaneously:

1. The total contract revenue can be measured in a reliable way;
2. The economic benefits pertinent to the contract will flow into the enterprise;
3. The actual contract costs incurred can be clearly distinguished and can be measured in a reliable way; and
4. Both the schedule of the contracted project and the contract costs to complete the contract can be measured in a reliable way.

Article 20 The outcome of a cost-plus contract can be estimated in a reliable way when the conditions as follows are met simultaneously:

1. The economic benefits pertinent to the contract will flow into the enterprise; and
2. The actual contract costs incurred can be clearly distinguished and measured in a reliable way.

Article 21 The schedule of a contracted project may be ascertained by employing the methods as follows:

1. The proportion of accumulative actual contract costs incurred against the expected total contract costs;
2. The proportion of the completed contract work against the expected total contract work; and
3. Surveys of the work performed.

Article 22 When the schedule of the project is ascertained on the basis of the proportion of accumulative actual contract costs incurred against the expected total contract costs, the items as follows are excluded from the actual contract costs incurred:

1. The construction costs pertinent to future activity under the contract, such as costs of materials that are not installed or used during the construction; and
2. The advance payments made to the subcontractors prior to the completion of the subcontract works.

Article 23 The current contract revenues in the current period shall, on the balance sheet date, be recognized in accordance with the balance of the total contract revenues times the schedule of completion then deducting the accumulated revenue recognized in previous accounting periods. At the same time, the current contract expenses in the current period shall be recognized in accordance with the balance of the expected total contract costs times the schedule of completion then deducting the accumulated expenses recognized in previous accounting periods.

Article 24 For a construction contract completed in the current period, the balance of the total actual contract revenues deducting the accumulated revenue recognized in previous accounting periods should be acknowledged as contract revenues in the current period. Meanwhile, the balance of the accumulated contract costs incurred deducting the accumulated contract costs recognized in previous accounting periods should be acknowledged as contract expenses in the current period.

Article 25 If the outcome of a construction contract can not be estimated in a reliable way, it shall be treated in accordance with the circumstances as follows, respectively:

1. If the contract costs can be recovered, the contract revenue shall be acknowledged in accordance with contract costs that can be recovered and the contract costs shall be acknowledged as contract expenses in the current period they are incurred; and
2. If the contract costs cannot be recovered, these costs shall be acknowledged as contract expenses immediately when incurred and no contract revenue shall be acknowledged.

Article 26 If the uncertainties, which cause that the outcome of a construction contract cannot be measured in a reliable way, have passed out of existence, the revenues and expenses pertinent to the construction contract shall be acknowledged in light of the provisions as prescribed in *Article 18* of these Standards.

Article 27 If the total expected contract costs exceed the total expected contract revenue, the expected loss shall be recognized as the current expenses.

19.6 Chapter VI: Disclosure

Article 28 An enterprise shall disclose the information concerning the construction contracts in its notes as follows:

1. The total contract amount and the methods used to ascertain the schedule of each contract project;
2. The aggregate amount of costs incurred and aggregate gross profits (or loss) acknowledged for each contract;
3. The settlement amount of each contract; and
4. The reasons and the amount of the expected loss in the current period.

19.7 Comments

Construction contract is a contract specifically negotiated for the construction of an asset or a combination of assets that are closely interrelated or interdependent in terms of their design, technology, and function or their ultimate purpose or use. There are two separate methods to negotiate the contract price: fixed price and cost plus (either markup or fixed fee).

Revenue arising from construction contract refers to the initial amount of revenue agreed in the contract; and variations in contract work, claims, and incentive payments. In particular, a variation is an instruction by the customer for a change in the scope of the work to be performed under the contract changing the total revenue. A variation shall be recognized when it is probable that the customer will approve the variation and the amount of revenue arising from the variation, and the amount of revenue can be reliably measured.

The direct costs computed to construction cost are as follows: labor costs, costs of materials used in construction, depreciation of plant and equipment used on the contract, and other costs that are directly related to the contract. New provisions introduced in ASBE No. 15 allow borrowing costs to be capitalized, in line with general disposition in ASBE No. 17 (borrowing costs) and accordingly included as part of contract costs. Previously, these items were year-referred expenses.

A major difference with construction contracts under IAS 11 regards the costs for securing a contract. IAS 11 allows direct costs incurred in securing a construction contract to be included as part of the contract costs if they can be separately identified and measured reliably and it is possible that the contract will be obtained. On the contrary, ASBE No. 15 requires such costs to be expensed as incurred.

When the outcome of a construction contract can be estimated reliably, contract revenue and contract costs associated with the construction contract shall be recognized as revenue and expenses, respectively, by reference to the stage of completion of the contract activity at the balance sheet date (percentage-of-completion method). Under this method, contract revenue is matched with the contract costs incurred in reaching the stage of completion, resulting in the reporting of revenue, expenses, and profit which can be attributed to the proportion of work completed.

Three methods may be used to reliably determine the effective stage of completion, depending on the nature of the contract. The methods are as follows: the proportion that contract costs incurred for work performed to date bear to the estimated total contract costs, surveys of work performed and the proportion of completion of a physical proportion of the contract work to date bear to the estimated total contract costs.

End-year disclosure shall contain following elements: total amount of contracts and the methods used to determine the stage of completion of contracts in progress; aggregate amount of costs incurred and aggregate recognized gross profit/(loss) to date; amount of progress billings to date; and reasons for expected loss and amount of loss in the period.

19.8 Examples

Company X stipulates a construction contract with its best client, and Company Y concerning following features:

- Fixed agreed price of 1,800,000 CNY;
- Costs occurred: labor costs 120,000 CNY, costs of materials 330,000 CNY, depreciation of machinery entirely devoted to construction 80,000 CNY;
- Borrowing costs 20,000 CNY;
- Initial costs to secure the contract 10,000 CNY;
- According to an on-purpose survey, the end-year stage of completion is 50 %.

The items that shall be recognized to the construction are as follows:

$$\text{Revenue: } 1{,}800{,}000 \times 50\,\% = 900,000 \text{ CNY}$$
$$\text{Cost: } (120{,}000 + 330{,}000 + 80{,}000 + 20{,}000) \times 50\,\% = 275{,}000 \text{ CNY}$$

Instead, the initial cost incurred to secure the contract shall be accounted in profit and loss.

Chapter 20
Accounting Standards for Business Enterprises No. 16—Government Subsidies

20.1 Chapter I: General Provisions

Article 1 In order to regulate the recognition, measure government subsidies, and disclose the relevant information, these Standards are formulated in light of the Accounting Standards for Enterprises—Basic Standards.

Article 2 A government subsidy means the monetary or non-monetary assets obtained free by an enterprise from the government, but excluding the capital invested by the government as the owner of the enterprise.

Article 3 Government subsidies consist of the government subsidies pertinent to assets and government subsidies pertinent to income. The government subsidies pertinent to assets mean the government assets that are obtained by enterprises used for purchase or construction, or forming the long-term assets by other ways. The government subsidies pertinent to income refer to all the government subsides except those pertinent to assets.

Article 4 Other related accounting standards shall apply to the items as follows:

1. The Accounting Standards for Enterprises No. 12—Debt Recombination shall apply to the debt exemptions; and
2. The Accounting Standards for Enterprises No. 18—Income Tax shall apply to the deductions and exemptions of income tax.

20.2 Chapter II: Recognition and Measurement

Article 5 No government subsidy may be recognized unless the following conditions are met simultaneously as follows:

1. The enterprise can meet the conditions for the government subsidies; and
2. The enterprise can obtain the government subsidies.

L. Riccardi, *China Accounting Standards*,
DOI 10.1007/978-981-10-0006-5_20

Article 6 If a government subsidy is a monetary asset, it shall be measured in light of the received or receivable amount. If a government subsidy is a non-monetary asset, it shall be measured at its fair value. If its fair value cannot be obtained in a reliable way, it shall be measured at its nominal amount.

Article 7 The government subsidies pertinent to assets shall be recognized as deferred income, equally distributed within the useful lives of the relevant assets, and included in the current profits and losses. But the government subsidies measured at their nominal amounts shall be directly included in the current profits and losses.

Article 8 The government subsidies pertinent to incomes shall be treated, respectively, in accordance with the circumstances as follows:

1. Those subsidies used for compensating the related future expenses or losses of the enterprise shall be recognized as deferred income and shall included in the current profits and losses during the period when the relevant expenses are recognized; or
2. Those subsidies used for compensating the related expenses or losses incurred to the enterprise shall be directly included in the current profits and losses.

Article 9 If it is necessary to refund any government subsidy which has been recognized, it shall be treated, respectively, in accordance with the circumstances as follows:

1. If there is the deferred income concerned, the book balance of the deferred income shall be offset against, but the excessive part shall be included in the current profits and losses; and
2. If there is no deferred income concerned to the government subsidy, it shall be directly included in the current profits and losses.

20.3 Chapter III: Disclosure

Article 10 In its notes, an enterprise shall disclose the information concerning the government subsidies as follows:

1. The type and amount of the government subsidies;
2. The amount of the government subsidies which are included in the current profits and losses; and
3. The amount of the government subsidies refunded in the current period as well as the reasons.

20.4 Comments

Government grants are described as the assistance by government in the form of transfers of resources to an enterprise in return for compliance with certain conditions. Are excluded other forms of capital contributions as an owner of an enterprise that is accounted for as a capital surplus. This principle divides between asset-related grants from all other not asset-related.

Government grants shall be recognized when the entity complies with all requirements and when they are received.

New ASBE No. 16 changes the recognition principle of government grants from the cash basis to the accrual basis. These grants are recognized as income when the enterprise can comply with the conditions (if any), and it is entitled to receive the grants.

Government grants in the form of non-monetary assets shall be measured at the fair value. Asset-related grants shall be presented as deferred income and recognized as income evenly over the useful life of the related asset. If fair value cannot be obtained, the asset should be measured at nominal value. The nominal value and its amount shall be directly recognized as income for the current period.

Previous disposition of PRC GAAP provided that the whole amount of an asset-related grant should have been credited to the "capital reserve" upon completion of construction of the related asset. Rather, government subsidies were recognized as income on a cash basis.

Comparing ASBE No. 16 with equivalent dispositions under IAS/IFRS, two major differences arise. First, IAS 20 allows either the presentation of asset-related grants as deferred income (and their recognition as income on a systematic and rational basis over the useful life of the asset) or the deduction of the grant from the carrying amount of the asset (i.e., reducing the depreciation charge). Only the latter model is allowed under ASBE No.16.

Second, referring to biological assets, IAS 41 requires a conditional government grant related to a biological asset measured at its fair value less estimated point-of-sale costs to be recognized as income when the conditions attaching to the grant are met. No specific requirements are disposed in ASBE No. 16 in relation to biological assets.

20.5 Examples

Company X receives a government grant for 250,000 CNY at the beginning of financial year. This grant is related to an already existent asset with a carrying value of 1500,000 CNY with an expected useful life of 5 years (annual deprecation of 300,000 CNY according a straight-line pattern).

As Company X complies with all requirements need, and actually receives the grant, it shall proceed to recognize the value of 250,000 CNY in the form of deferred income.

As it is asset-related, the government grant shall act reducing the asset's annual depreciation. Accordingly, the annual amount should be 250,000/5 = 50,000 CNY and the final depreciation 250,000 CNY (from the initial 300,000 CNY).

Chapter 21
Accounting Standards for Business Enterprises No. 17—Borrowing Costs

21.1 Chapter I: General Provisions

Article 1 With a view to regulating the recognition and measurement of borrowing costs, and the disclosure of relevant information, the present Standards are formulated according to the Accounting Standards for Enterprises—Basic Standard.

Article 2 The term "borrowing costs" refer to the interest and other relevant costs, which are incurred by an enterprise in the borrowing of loans. The borrowing costs shall include interest on borrowings, amortization of discounts or premiums on borrowings, ancillary expenses, and exchange balance on foreign currency borrowings.

Article 3 The financing costs related to the financing leases shall be subject to the Accounting Standards for Enterprises No. 21—Leases.

21.2 Chapter II: Recognition and Measurement

Article 4 Where the borrowing costs incurred to an enterprise can be directly attributable to the acquisition and construction or production of assets eligible for capitalization, it shall be capitalized and recorded into the costs of relevant assets. Other borrowing costs shall be recognized as expenses on the basis of the actual amount incurred and shall be recorded into the current profits and losses. The term "assets eligible for capitalization" shall refer to the fixed assets, investment real estate, inventories, and other assets, of which the acquisition and construction or production may take quite a long time to get ready for its intended use or for sale.

Article 5 The borrowing costs shall not be capitalized unless they simultaneously meet the following requirements:

L. Riccardi, *China Accounting Standards*,
DOI 10.1007/978-981-10-0006-5_21

1. The asset disbursements have already incurred, which shall include the cash, transferred non-cash assets, or interest-bearing debts paid for the acquisition and construction or production activities for preparing assets eligible for capitalization;
2. The borrowing costs have already incurred; and
3. The acquisition and construction or production activities which are necessary to prepare the asset for its intended use or sale have already started.

Article 6 During the period of capitalization, the to-be-capitalized amount of interests (including the amortization of discounts or premiums) in each accounting period shall be determined according to the following provisions:

1. As for specifically borrowed loans for the acquisition and construction or production of assets eligible for capitalization, the to-be-capitalized amount of interests shall be determined in light of the actual cost incurred of the specially borrowed loan at the present period minus the income of interests earned on the unused borrowing loans as a deposit in the bank or as a temporary investment. The term "specifically borrowed loan" shall refer to a fund which is borrowed specifically for the acquisition and construction or production activities of assets eligible for capitalization.
2. Where a general borrowing is used for the acquisition and construction or production of assets eligible for capitalization, the enterprise shall calculate and determine the to-be-capitalized amount of interests on the general borrowing by multiplying the weighted average asset disbursement of the part of the accumulative asset disbursements minus the general borrowing by the capitalization rate of the general borrowing used. The capitalization rate shall be calculated and determined in light of the weighted average interest rate of the general borrowing. The capitalization period shall refer to the period from the commencement to the cessation of capitalization of the borrowing costs, excluding the period of suspension of capitalization of the borrowing costs.

Article 7 Where there is any discount or premium, the amount of discounts or premiums that shall be amortized during each accounting period shall be determined by the real interest rate method, and an adjustment shall be made to the amount of interests in each period.

Article 8 During the period of capitalization, the amount of interest capitalized during each accounting period shall not exceed the amount of interest actually incurred to the relevant borrowings in the current period.

Article 9 During the period of capitalization, the exchange balance on foreign currency borrowings shall be capitalized and shall be recorded into the cost of assets eligible for capitalization.

Article 10 For the ancillary expense incurred to a specifically borrowed loan, those incurred before a qualified asset under acquisition, construction, or production is ready for the intended use or sale shall be capitalized at the incurred amount when they are incurred and shall be recorded into the costs of the asset eligible for capitalization; those incurred after a qualified asset under acquisition and construction or production is ready for the intended use or sale shall be recognized as expenses on the basis of the incurred amount when they are incurred and shall be recorded into the profits and losses of the current period. The ancillary expenses arising from a general borrowing shall be recognized as expenses at their incurred amount when they are incurred and shall be recorded into the profits and losses of the current period.

Article 11 Where the acquisition and construction or production of a qualified asset is interrupted abnormally and the interruption period lasts for more than 3 months, the capitalization of the borrowing costs shall be suspended. The borrowing costs incurred during such period shall be recognized as expenses and shall be recorded into the profits and losses of the current period, till the acquisition and construction or production of the asset restarts. If the interruption is a necessary step for making the qualified asset under acquisition and construction or production ready for the intended use or sale, the capitalization of the borrowing costs shall continue.

Article 12 When the qualified asset under acquisition and construction or production is ready for the intended use or sale, the capitalization of the borrowing costs shall be ceased. The borrowing costs incurred after the qualified asset under acquisition and construction or production are ready for the intended use or sale shall be recognized as expenses at the incurred amount when they are incurred and shall be recorded into the profits and losses of the current period.

Article 13 The qualified assets under acquisition and construction or production, which have been ready for the intended use or sale, shall be judged from the following aspects:

1. The substantial construction (including installation), or the production of the qualified assets, has been finished completely or substantially;
2. The qualified assets under acquisition and construction or production meet or basically meet the design requirements, contractual provisions, or production requirements, even if there is any specific discrepancy between it and the design, contractual, or production requirements, and its normal use or sale is not affected;
3. The amount of continuing disbursements for the qualified assets under acquisition and construction or production is very small, or nearly no such disbursement incurs. Where a qualified asset under acquisition and construction or production needs trial production or trial operation, it shall be deemed to be ready for the intended use or sale, when the result of the trial production indicates that the asset is able to normally produce qualified products, or when the trial operation result indicates that the asset is able to run or operate normally.

Article 14 Where each part of a qualified asset under acquisition and construction or production is completed separately and is ready for use or sale during the continuing construction of other parts, and if the acquisition and construction or production activities which are necessary to prepare this part of the asset for the intended use or sale have already been completed substantially, the capitalization of the borrowing costs in relation to this part of asset shall be ceased. Where each part of a asset under acquisition and construction or production is completed separately and is ready for use or sale during the continuing construction of other parts, but it cannot be used or sold until the asset is entirely completed, the capitalization of the borrowing costs shall be ceased when the asset is completed entirely.

21.3 Chapter III: Disclosure

Article 15 An enterprise shall, in its notes, disclose the following information related to the borrowing costs:

1. the amount of the borrowing costs which is capitalized in the current period; and
2. the capitalization rate, which is used for calculating and determining the amount of the borrowing costs to be capitalized in the current period.

21.4 Comments

Borrowing costs are defined as interest and other costs an enterprise incurs in connection with the borrowing of funds. The principle allows borrowing costs on specific borrowings in relation to a qualifying asset form part of the cost of that asset. Other borrowing costs are recognized as an expense in the period in which they are incurred. ASBE No. 17 requires capitalization of borrowing costs for a broader scope of assets, introducing inventories and intangible assets besides fixed assets. The broader character of new provisions embraces also the generality of borrowing costs instead of specific borrowings. The principle disposes "an enterprise shall capitalize borrowing costs that are directly attributable to the acquisition, construction, or production of a qualifying asset as part of the cost of that asset." It is also stated that expenditures on a qualifying asset include only those expenditures that have resulted in payments of cash, transfers of non-cash assets, or the assumption of interest-bearing liabilities.

The amount of interest to be capitalized in each accounting period should be determined according to two methods. If funds are specifically borrowed for the purpose of obtaining a qualifying asset, then "the enterprise shall determine the amount of borrowing costs eligible for capitalization as the actual borrowing costs incurred on that borrowing during the period less any interest income earned from undrawn borrowings and any investment income on the temporary investment of those borrowings." Alternatively, if funds are generally borrowed and enterprise uses them for the purpose of obtaining a qualifying asset, "the entity shall determine the amount of borrowing costs eligible for capitalization by applying a capitalization rate to the excess of weighted average of accumulated expenditures on that asset over the specific borrowings. The capitalization rate shall be determined based on the weighted average interest rates of the general borrowings."

The formula for calculating the weighted average amount of accumulated expenditures (WAAE) is the following one:

$$\text{WAAE} = \sum \text{Amount of expenditures on an asset} \times (\text{Number of days the expenditure period had been incurred during the period/Number of days in the period})$$

The capitalization rate should be the one used for borrowing, or if more than one borrowing rate is used, the capitalization rate is the weighted average interest rate on those borrowings. The formula for calculating the weighted average interest rate (WAIR) is as follows:

$$\text{WAIR} = (\text{Total interest incurred during the period/Weighted average amount of carrying amount of the principals of borrowings}) \times 100\,\%$$

where the weighted amount of carrying amount of borrowing is defined as follows:

$$\text{WAP} = \sum \text{Principal of each borrowing} \times (\text{Number of days each borrowing incurred in the period/Number of days in the period})$$

Borrowing costs that can be capitalized are actual borrowing costs incurred on specific borrowing less any interest income earned from undrawn borrowings and income on the temporary investment of those borrowings. For funds that are borrowed generally, the amount to be capitalized shall be determined by applying a capitalization rate to the related expenditure on the asset. Previous dispositions under PRC GAAP allowed only the amount determined by applying a capitalization rate of specific borrowings to cumulative expenditures were capitalized. Moreover, temporary income earned from undrawn borrowings was not allowed to be deducted from the capitalized amount.

ASBE No. 17 provides the capitalization approach when capitalization criteria need to be satisfied. Under Correspondent IAS 23, borrowing costs are either expensed as incurred or capitalized when capitalization criteria are met. Furthermore, borrowing costs under IAS 23 include also finance charges in respect of financial leases. ASBE No. 17 does not deal with this issue and postpones it in ASBE No. 21.

21.5 Examples

Company X on July 1 borrows 1,500,000 CNY completely referred to the construction of a self-built asset, the interest rate is 7 %. In addition, there are outstanding borrowings for 3,000,000 CNY, some of these are devoted to the assets. Average interest rate of general borrowings is 8 %, the amount of 1,000,000 is allocated to the asset. These borrowings are supposed to be recorded from January 1.

The borrowing costs referred to the asset is 132,500 CNY

$$1{,}500{,}000 \times 7\,\% \times 6/12 = 52{,}500 \text{ CNY}$$
$$3{,}000{,}000 \times 8\,\% \times 1/3 = 80{,}000 \text{ CNY}.$$

Chapter 22
Accounting Standards for Business Enterprises No. 18—Income Taxes

22.1 Chapter I: General Provisions

Article 1 With a view to regulating the recognition and measurement of enterprise income taxes and the presentation of relevant information, the present Standards are formulated according to the Accounting Standards for Enterprises—Basic Standards.

Article 2 The "income taxes" as mentioned in the present Standards shall include all types of domestic and oversea tax amounts based on the amounts of taxable income of enterprises.

Article 3 The present Standards shall not cover the recognition and measurement of government subsidies. But the temporary difference of income tax arising from government subsidies shall be recognized and measured according to the present Standard.

22.2 Chapter II: Tax Base

Article 4 Where an enterprise obtains assets or liabilities, it shall determine its tax base. Where there is difference between the carrying amount of the assets or liabilities and its tax base, the deferred income tax assets or the deferred income tax liabilities shall be determined according to the present Standards.

Article 5 The "tax base of an asset" shall refer to the amount which may be deducted from the taxable benefits when the amount of taxable income is calculated according to the tax law provisions during the course of the enterprise recovering the carrying amount of the asset.

Article 6 The "tax base of an liability" shall refer to the carrying amount of a liability minus the amount that can be deducted according to the tax law when the amount of taxable income is calculated in the future period.

L. Riccardi, *China Accounting Standards*,
DOI 10.1007/978-981-10-0006-5_22

22.3 Chapter III: Temporary Difference

Article 7 The "temporary difference" shall refer to the difference between the carrying amount of an asset or liability and its tax base. As for an item that has not been recognized as an asset or liability, if its tax base can be determined in light of the tax law, the difference between the tax base and its carrying amount shall also be a temporary difference. Pursuant to the effect of temporary differences on taxable amounts during future periods, they can be classified into taxable temporary differences and deductible temporary differences.

Article 8 The term "taxable temporary difference" shall refer to temporary differences that will result in taxable amounts in the future when the carrying amount of the asset is recovered or the liability is settled.

Article 9 The term "deductible temporary difference" shall refer to temporary differences that will result in amounts that are deductible in the future when the carrying amount of the asset is recovered or the liability is settled.

22.4 Chapter IV: Recognition

Article 10 An enterprise shall recognize the accrued income tax of the current period and prior periods as a liability and shall recognize the part of the income tax already paid minus the payable amount as an asset. Where there is any taxable temporary difference or deductible temporary difference, it shall be recognized as a deferred income tax liability or deferred income tax asset according to the present Standards.

Article 11 Except for the deferred income tax liabilities arising from the following transactions, an enterprise shall recognize the deferred income tax liabilities arising from all taxable temporary differences:

1. the initial recognition of business reputation;
2. the initial recognition of assets or liabilities arising from the following transactions which are simultaneously featured by the following:

   (a) The transaction is not business combination;
   (b) At the time of transaction, the accounting profits will not be affected, nor will the taxable amount (or the deductible loss) be affected. The deferred income tax liabilities arising from the taxable temporary differences related to the investments of subsidiary companies, associated enterprises, and contractual enterprises shall be recognized according to *Article 12* of the present Standard.

Article 12 The taxable temporary differences related to the investments of subsidiary companies, associated enterprises, and joint enterprises shall recognize corresponding deferred income tax liabilities. However, those that can simultaneously meet the following conditions shall be excluded:

1. The investing enterprise can control the time of the reverse of temporary differences;
2. The temporary differences are unlikely to be reversed in the excepted future.

Article 13 An enterprise shall recognize the deferred income tax liabilities arising from a deductible temporary difference to the extent of the amount of the taxable income which it is most likely to obtain and which can be deducted from the deductible temporary difference. However, the deferred income tax assets, which are arising from the initial recognition of assets or liabilities during a transaction which is simultaneously featured by the following, shall not be recognized:

1. This transaction is not business combination;
2. At the time of transaction, the accounting profits will not be affected, nor will the taxable amount (or the deductible loss) be affected. On the balance sheet date, where there is any exact evidence showing that it is likely to acquire sufficient amount of taxable income tax in a future period to offset against the deductible temporary difference, the deferred income tax assets unrecognized in prior periods shall be recognized.

Article 14 Where the deductible temporary difference related to the investments of the subsidiary companies, associated enterprises, and joint enterprises can meet the following requirements simultaneously, the enterprise shall recognize the corresponding deferred income tax assets:

1. The temporary differences are likely to be reversed in the expected future;
2. It is likely to acquire any amount of taxable income tax that may be used for making up the deductible temporary differences.

Article 15 As for any deductible loss or tax deduction that can be carried forward to the next year, the corresponding deferred income tax assets shall be determined to the extent that the amount of future taxable income to be offset by the deductible loss or tax deduction to be likely obtained.

22.5 Chapter V: Measurement

Article 16 On the balance sheet day, the current income tax liabilities (or assets) incurred in the current period or prior periods shall be measured in light of the expected payable (refundable) amount of income taxes according to the tax law.

Article 17 On the balance sheet day, the deferred income tax assets and deferred income tax liabilities shall be measured at the tax rate applicable to the period during which the assets are expected to be recovered or the liabilities are expected to be settled. In case the applicable tax rate changes, the deferred income tax assets and deferred income tax liabilities which have been recognized shall be remeasured, excluding the deferred income tax assets and deferred income tax liabilities arising from any transaction or event directly recognized as the owners' rights and interests, and the amount affected by them shall be recorded into the income tax expenses of the current period during which the change occurs.

Article 18 The measurement of deferred income tax assets and deferred income tax liabilities shall reflect the effect of the expected asset recovery or liability settlement method on the balance sheet day on the income taxes, i.e., the tax rate and tax base, which is adopted at the time of measurement of the deferred income tax assets and deferred income tax liabilities and shall be identical with those of expected asset recovery or liability settlement method.

Article 19 An enterprise shall not discount any deferred income tax asset or deferred income tax liability.

Article 20 The carrying amount of deferred income tax assets shall be reexamined on balance sheet day. If it is unlikely to obtain sufficient taxable income taxes to offset the benefit of the deferred income tax assets, the carrying amount of the deferred income tax assets shall be written down. When it is probable to obtain sufficient taxable income taxes, such write-down amount shall be subsequently reversed.

Article 21 The income taxes of the current period and deferred income tax of an enterprise shall be treated as income tax expenses or incomes and shall be recorded into the current profits and losses, excluding the income taxes incurred under the following circumstances:

1. the business combination;
2. the transactions or events directly recognized as the owner's rights and interests.

Article 22 The income taxes of the current period and deferred income tax related to the transactions or events directly recorded in the owner's rights and interests shall be recorded into the owner's rights and interests.

22.6 Chapter VI: Presentation

Article 23 The deferred income tax assets and deferred income tax liabilities shall be, respectively, presented as the non-current assets and non-current liabilities in the balance sheet.

Article 24 The income tax expenses shall be presented separately in the profit statement.

Article 25 An enterprise shall, in its notes, disclose the following information related to the income taxes:

1. the main constituent parts of the income tax expenses (incomes);
2. a statement of the relationship between the income tax expenses (incomes) and the accounting profits;
3. the amounts of deductible temporary difference or deductible loss of unrecognized deferred income tax assets (if there is a date due, it shall disclose the date due);

4. every category of temporary difference and deductible loss, the amount of the deferred income tax assets or deferred income tax liabilities which are recognized during the presentation period, and the basis for the recognition of the deferred income tax assets;
5. as for any deferred income tax liabilities which have not been recognized, the amounts of temporary differences related to the investments of the subsidiary companies, associated enterprises, and joint enterprise.

22.7 Comments

"The tax base of an asset is the amount that will be deductible for tax purposes against any taxable economic benefits that will flow to an entity when it recovers the carrying amount of the asset. If those economic benefits will not be taxable, the tax base of the asset is equal to its carrying amount." At the same time, there is a dispose for liabilities that "the tax base is the carrying amount, less any amount that will be deductible for tax purposes in respect of that liability in future periods."

Most notably, new ASBE No. 18 disallows tax payable method. To this extent, the balance sheet method is allowed to determine deferred tax of temporary differences. Under previous PRC GAAP, both methods coexisted, and deferred tax were recognized for timing differences. In principle, ASBE No. 18 completely refers to the same dispositions under equivalent IAS 12.

The principle explains the method of tax recognition. Specifically, it disposes that current tax for current and prior periods shall, to the extent unpaid, be recognized as a liability. If the amount already paid in respect of current and prior periods exceeds the amount due for those periods, the excess shall be recognized as a credit. Deferred tax credit shall be recognized for the carryforward of deductible tax losses and tax deductions to the extent that it is probable that future taxable profit will be available against which the deductible tax losses and tax deductions can be utilized.

Finally, items related to deferred tax assets or deferred tax liabilities shall be presented in non-current assets or liabilities.

22.8 Examples

Company X shows for this financial year a pre-tax income of 2,500,000 CNY. The average tax rate borne by Company X is 30 %. During the same financial year, Company X expensed 500,000 CNY referred to research activities.

The current tax burden for Company X in this year is referred to 3,000,000 × 30 % = 900,000 CNY instead of 750,000 CNY (2,500,000 × 30 %). In fact, the amount of 500,000 CNY according to tax principles is not taxable in the current financial year. For these reasons, there will be a deferred tax credit of 500,000 × 30 % = 150,000 CNY to be discounted in next years.

Let us suppose it will be evenly distributed in 5 years, we will have an annual lower tax burden for 30,000 CNY.

Chapter 23
Accounting Standards for Business Enterprises No. 19—Foreign Currency Translation

23.1 Chapter I: General Provisions

Article 1 With a view to regulating the accounting treatment for the foreign currency transactions, conversion of foreign currency financial statements, and disclosure of relevant information, the present Standards are formulated according to the Accounting Standards for Enterprises—Basic Standards.

Article 2 The "foreign currency transaction" refers to transactions which are valuated and settled in foreign currency. The "foreign currency" refers to a currency other than the functional currency of an enterprise. The foreign currency transactions include the following:

1. the purchase or sale of goods or services valuated in foreign currency;
2. foreign currency funds that are borrowed or lent; and
3. other transactions that are valuated or settled in foreign currency.

Article 3 The following items shall be subjected to other relevant accounting standards:

1. The balance of exchange arising from foreign currency borrowings for the purchase and construction or production of qualified assets shall be subject to the Accounting Standards for Business Enterprises No. 17—Borrowing Costs;
2. The hedge of foreign currency items shall be subject to the Accounting Standards for Enterprise No. 24—Hedging; and
3. The translation of foreign currency in the cash flow statement shall be subject to the Accounting Standards for Business Enterprises No. 31—Cash Flow Statement.

L. Riccardi, *China Accounting Standards*,
DOI 10.1007/978-981-10-0006-5_23

23.2 Chapter II: Determination of Functional Currency

Article 4 The "functional currency" refers to the currency of the primary economic environment in which the enterprise is operated. An enterprise shall, in general, choose RMB as its functional currency. For an enterprise of which the incomes and expenses are mainly valuated in the currency other than RMB, it may choose a currency as its functional currency according to *Article 5* of the present Standards. However, the financial statements shall be translated into the ones RMB.

Article 5 When an enterprise chooses a functional currency, it shall take account of the following factors:

1. This currency mainly affects the selling prices of goods and services, and generally, the goods and services are valuated and settled in this currency;
2. This currency mainly affects the labor, materials, and other costs for the goods and services, and generally, the goods and services are valuated and settled in this currency; and
3. The currency acquired in financing activities as well as the currency utilized to preserve the money charged in the business operation.

Article 6 When an enterprise chooses the functional currency for its overseas business, it shall take account of the following factors as well:

1. Whether or not the overseas businesses are quite independent from the activities in which it is engaged;
2. Whether or not the transactions with the enterprise in overseas business operations account for a relatively large proportion in oversea business operations;
3. Whether or not the cash flow incurred in overseas business operations directly affects the cash flow of the enterprise, and whether or not the cash may be remitted back at any time; and
4. Whether or not the cash flow incurred in overseas business operations is sufficient to settle its current liabilities and predictable liabilities.

Article 7 The "overseas business operation" refers to the enterprise' overseas subsidiary companies, joint ventures, associated enterprises, and branches. Where the domestic subsidiary company, joint enterprise, associated enterprise, or a branch of an enterprise adopts a functional currency which is different from that of the enterprise, it shall be deemed as overseas business.

Article 8 Once the functional currency of an enterprise is determined, it shall not be modified at will, unless the main economic environment in which the enterprise is operated has greatly changed. Where it is really necessary to modify the functional currency because the primary economic environment in which the enterprise is operated has greatly changed, the enterprise shall translate all items into the post-change functional currency at the spot exchange rate of the current date of the change.

23.3 Chapter III: Accounting Treatment for Foreign Currency Transactions

Article 9 As for a foreign currency transaction, the enterprise shall translate the amount in a foreign currency into amount in its functional currency.

Article 10 At the time of initial recognition of a foreign currency transaction, the amount in the foreign currency shall be translated into the amount in the functional currency at the spot exchange rate of the transaction date, or at an exchange rate which is determined through a systematic and reasonable method and is approximate to the spot exchange rate of the transaction date.

Article 11 An enterprise shall, on the balance sheet date, treat the foreign currency monetary items and foreign currency non-monetary items in accordance with the following provisions:

1. The foreign currency monetary items shall be translated at the spot exchange rate on the balance sheet date. The balance of exchange arising from the difference between the spot exchange rate on the balance sheet date and the spot exchange rate at the time of initial recognition or prior to the balance sheet date shall be recorded into the profits and losses at the current period.
2. The foreign currency non-monetary items measured at the historical cost shall still be translated at the spot exchange rate on the transaction date, of which the amount of functional currency shall not be changed. The "monetary item" shall refer to the money held by an enterprise and the assets and liabilities to be received or paid in fixed or determinable amounts of money. The "non-monetary item" shall refer to the items other than the monetary ones.

23.4 Chapter IV: Translation of Foreign Currency Financial Statements

Article 12 When translating the financial statements on the overseas businesses, an enterprise shall comply with the following provisions:

1. The asset and liability items in the balance sheets shall be translated at a spot exchange rate on the balance sheet date. Among the owner's equity items, except the ones as "undistributed profits," others shall be translated at the spot exchange rate at the time when they are incurred.
2. The income and expense items in the profit statements shall be translated at the spot exchange rate of the transaction date, or at a spot exchange rate which is determined through a systematic and reasonable method and is approximate to the spot exchange rate of the transaction date. The balance arisen from the

translation of foreign currency financial statements in compliance with the aforesaid Items (1) and (2) shall be presented separately under the owner's equity item of the balance sheets. The translation of comparable financial statements shall be subject to the aforesaid provisions.

Article 13 An enterprise shall translate the financial statements of overseas business as situated in a hyperinflationary economy in accordance with the following provisions: It shall restate the balance sheet items by adopting the general price index, restate the items of the profit statement by adopting the changes of the general price index, and then translate them at the spot exchange rate on the recent balance sheet date. If an overseas business is no longer situated in the hyperinflationary economy, it shall stop the restatement and shall translate the restated financial statements at the price of the cessation date.

Article 14 When disposing an overseas business, an enterprise shall shift the balance, which is presented under the items of the owner's equities in the balance sheet and arises from the translation of foreign currency financial statements related to this oversea business, into the disposal profits and losses of the current period. If the overseas business is disposed of partially, the enterprise shall calculate the balance arising from the translation of foreign currency statements of the part of disposal based on the disposal rate and shall shift them into the profits and losses of the current period.

Article 15 Where an enterprise does not choose RMB as its functional currency, it shall translate its financial statements into RMB financial statements according to *Article 12* of the present Standard.

23.5 Chapter V: Disclosure

Article 16 An enterprise shall, in its notes, disclose the following information related to the translation of foreign currencies:

1. The functional currency chosen by an enterprise and its overseas businesses and the reasons for such choice; if the functional currency is changed, the grounds for the change shall be given;
2. If an approximate exchange rate is adopted, the method for the determination of the approximate exchange rate shall be given;
3. The balance of exchange which shall be recorded into the profits and losses of the current period; and
4. The effects of disposal of any overseas business on the balance arising from the translation of foreign currency financial statements.

23.6 Comments

A foreign currency is defined as a currency other than the functional currency of the enterprise. Any transaction that occurs in a foreign currency is a transaction that is denominated or requires settlement in a foreign currency. Transactions involving foreign currency might be the following: buys or sells goods or services whose price is denominated in a foreign currency, borrows or lends funds when the amounts payable or receivable are denominated in a foreign currency, or otherwise engages in other transactions denominated in a foreign currency.

New dispositions contained in ASBE No. 19 redefine the meaning of recording currency, now more in line with the term of "functional currency" used in correspondent IAS 21. Each enterprise shall determine its own recording currency according to the primary economic environment in which the enterprise operates.

Foreign currency transactions shall be translated at the spot exchange rate between the functional currency and the foreign currency at the date of the transaction. At the end of each reporting period, foreign currency monetary items shall be translated into the functional currency using the closing rate. Exchange differences arising on the settlement of monetary items or on translating monetary items at rates different from those at which they were translated on initial recognition during the period or in previous financial statements should be recognized in profit or loss in the period in which they arise.

Financial statements of an enterprise whose functional currency is not the presentation currency or the financial statements of an enterprise's foreign operation should be translated according to different procedures. The closing rate is used for assets and liabilities for each financial statement. The rate on the date of transaction is used for owner's equity items (except for undistributed profit) and income and expenses for each income statement. For latter two categories, an approximation of the exchange rates at the dates of the transaction is allowed as well. Finally, all resulting exchange differences shall be presented separately under owner's equity.

Although no specific disposition is prescribed, enterprises operating in People's Republic of China are required to present their financial statements in RMB as recording currency, in accordance with PRC laws and regulations. On this point, IAS 21 rules that a reporting entity might present its financial statements in any currency.

The principle prescribes specific translation requirements of financial statements of a foreign operation which is operating in a hyperinflationary economy. At the same time, IAS 29 is completely dedicated to this issue. More specifically, it applies to the financial statements of any entity whose functional currency of a hyperinflationary economy. In this case, whether the financial statements are based on a historical cost approach or a current cost approach, they shall be stated in terms of the measuring unit current at the balance sheet date. In addition, upon disposal of a foreign operation, the cumulative amount of exchange differences deferred in a separate component of equity (related to the foreign operation) is recognized in profit or loss when the gain or loss on disposal is recognized.

23.7 Examples

Company X, operating in China with RMB as functional currency, buys raw materials from Company Y established in a foreign country and running operation under foreign currency for 300,000 YFC (Y Functional Currency) on November. On the date of transaction, the spot exchange rate is 1 RMB = 1.20 YFC (Y Functional Currency). The value of account payable in November is 250,000 RMB.

As on December 31 the operation has not been settled yet, and the spot rate prevailing *t* that date is 1 RMB = 1.25 YFC, Company X shall recognize the new value of the account payable is 240,000 RMB. Accordingly, Company X should recognize on profit and loss an income item of 10,000 RMB due to the exchange difference.

Chapter 24
Accounting Standards for Business Enterprises No. 20—Business Combinations

24.1 Chapter I: General Provisions

Article 1 With a view to regulating the recognition and measurement of leases, as well as the presentation of relevant information, the present Standards are formulated according to the Accounting Standards for Enterprises—Basic Standard.

Article 2 The term "lease" refers to an agreement under which the lessor conveys to the lessee in return for rent the right to use an asset for an agreed period of time.

Article 3 The following items shall be subject to other accounting standard:

1. The land use right and buildings rented out by a lessor by way of operating lease shall be subject to the Accounting Standards for Enterprises No. 3—Investment Real Estates;
2. The licensing agreements for the use of items such as films, video recordings, plays, manuscripts, patents, and copyrights shall be subject to the Accounting Standards for Enterprises No. 6—Intangible Assets; and
3. The impairment of long-term credits formed by the financing leases of a lessor shall be subject to the Accounting Standards for Enterprises No. 22—Recognition and Measurement of Financial Instruments.

24.2 Chapter II: Classification of Leases

Article 4 A lessee and a lessor shall classify a lease as a financing lease or an operating lease on the lease beginning date. The lease beginning date shall refer to the earlier one of the dates of lease agreement or the date on which the parties to the lease make commitments on the key terms of lease.

L. Riccardi, *China Accounting Standards*,
DOI 10.1007/978-981-10-0006-5_24

Article 5 The "finance lease" shall refer to a lease that has transferred in substance all the risks and rewards related to the ownership of an asset. The ownership of it may or may not eventually be transferred.

Article 6 Where a lease satisfies one or more of the following criteria, it shall be recognized as a finance lease:

1. The ownership of the leased asset is transferred to the lessee when the term of lease expires;
2. The lessee has the option to buy the leased asset at a price which is expected to be far lower than the fair value of the leased asset at the date when the option becomes exercisable. Thus, on the lease beginning date, it can be reasonably determined that the option will be exercised;
3. Even if the ownership of the asset is not transferred, the lease term covers the major part of the use life of the leased asset;
4. In the case of the lessee, the present value of the minimum lease payments on the lease beginning date amounts to substantially all of the fair value of the leased asset on the lease beginning date; in the case of the lessor, the present value of the minimum lease receipts on the lease beginning date amounts to substantially all of the fair value of the leased asset on the lease beginning date; and
5. The leased assets are of a specialized nature that only the lessee can use them without making major modifications.

Article 7 The "lease term" shall refer to the period as specified in the lease agreement, during which the lease may not be canceled. Once a lease contract is signed, generally it may not be canceled except for the following circumstances:

1. With the consent of the lessor;
2. Where the lessee enters into a new lease for the same asset or asset of the same kind with the same lessor;
3. Where the lessee makes an additional payment of a sufficiently large amount;
4. Upon the occurrence of some remote contingency. If the lessee has the option to continue to lease the asset for any further period, and it is reasonably certain on the lease beginning date that the lessee will exercise the option, the renewed period shall be included in the lease term, no matter whether rents will be paid again or not.

Article 8 The term "minimum lease payment" shall refer to the payments (excluding contingent rents and execution costs) that the lessee shall, or may be required to make, for the term of lease, plus the residual values guaranteed by the lessee or a party related to the lessee. Where the lessee has an option to buy the leased asset at a price which is expected to be far lower than the fair value on the date when the option becomes exercisable, and thus, it is reasonably certain that the lessee will exercise the option on the lease beginning date; the payment required to exercise this purchase option shall be included in the minimum lease payments. The term "contingent rent" shall refer to the rent which is not fixed in amount and calculated on the basis of factors other than the length of time, such as the sale quantity, amount of usage, price indices. The term "execution cost" shall refer to costs incurred during the lease term for using the leased asset, such as the fees for technical consultation and services, training, maintenance, and insurance.

Article 9 The term "minimum lease receipt" shall refer to the minimum lease payments plus the residual values guaranteed to the lessor by a third party independent from the lessor or the lessee.

Article 10 The term "operating lease" shall refer to a lease other than a financing lease.

24.3 Chapter III: Accounting Treatments of Lessees in Finance Leases

Article 11 On the lease beginning date, a lessee shall record the lower one of the fair value of the leased asset and the present value of the minimum lease payments on the lease beginning date as the entering value in an account, recognize the amount of the minimum lease payments as the entering value in an account of long-term account payable, and treat the balance between the recorded amount of the leased asset and the long-term account payable as unrecognized financing charges. The initial direct costs such as commissions, attorney's fees and traveling expenses, stamp duties directly attributable to the leased item incurred during the process of lease negotiating, and signing the leasing agreement shall be recorded in the asset value of the current period. The lease beginning date shall refer to the date on which the lessee begins to have the right to use the leased asset.

Article 12 When a lessee calculates the present value of the minimum lease payments, if it can obtain the lessor's interest rate implicit in the lease, it shall adopt the interest rate implicit in the lease as the discount rate. Otherwise, it shall adopt the interest rate provided in the lease agreement as the discount rate. In case the lessee cannot obtain the lessor's interest rate implicit in the lease and no interest rate is provided in the lease agreement, the lessee shall adopt the borrowing interest rate of the bank for the same period as the discount rate.

Article 13 The expression "interest rate implicit in the lease" shall refer to the discount rate that, on the lease beginning date, makes the aggregate present value of the minimum lease payments and the unguaranteed residual values equal to the sum of the fair value of the leased asset and the initial direct costs of the lessor.

Article 14 The term "guaranteed residue value" shall refer to, in the case of a lessee, the residual value of the asset which is guaranteed by the lessee or by a third party related to the lessee; and in the case of a lessor, the guaranteed residual value from the standpoint of the lessee plus the residual value of the asset which is guaranteed by a third party independent from both the lessor and the lessee. The term "residual value of the asset" shall refer to the fair value of the leased asset when the term of lease expires as estimated on the lease beginning date. The term "unguaranteed residue value" shall refer to the residual value of the leased asset minus the guaranteed residual value of the lessor.

Article 15 The unrecognized financing charge shall be amortized to each period during the lease term. The lessee shall adopt the effective interest rate method to calculate and recognize the financing charge in the current period.

Article 16 In calculating the depreciation of a leased asset, the lessee should adopt a depreciation policy for leased assets consistent with that for depreciable assets which are owned by the lessee. If it is reasonable to be certain that the lessee will obtain the ownership of the leased asset when the lease term expires, the leased asset shall be fully depreciated over its useful life. If it is not reasonable to be certain that the lessee will obtain the ownership of the leased asset at the expiry of the lease term, the leased asset shall be fully depreciated over the shorter one of the lease term or its useful life.

Article 17 Contingent rents shall be recognized as an expense in the period in which they are actually incurred.

24.4 Chapter IV: Accounting Treatments of Lessors in Finance Leases

Article 18 On the beginning date of the lease term, a lessor shall recognize the sum of the minimum lease receipts on the lease beginning date and the initial direct costs as the entering value in an account of the financing lease values receivable, and record the unguaranteed residual value at the same time. The balance between the sums of the minimum lease receipts, the initial direct costs and the unguaranteed residual value, and the sum of their present values shall be recognized as unrealized financing income.

Article 19 The unrealized financing income shall be allocated to each period during the lease term. The lessor shall calculate the financing income at the current period by adopting the effective interest rate method.

Article 20 The lessor shall, at least at the end of each year, reexamine the unguaranteed residual values. No adjustment may be made if the unguaranteed residual value increases. Where there is evidence showing a reduction in the unguaranteed residual value, the interest rate implicit in the lease shall be recalculated and the associated reduction of the net investment in the lease shall be recognized as a loss for the current period. The financing incomes for subsequent periods shall be recognized on the basis of the revised net investment in the lease and the recalculated implicit interest rate. The net investment in the lease shall be the difference between the sum of the minimum lease receipts and the unguaranteed residual value in a finance lease and unrealized financing incomes. Where the unguaranteed residual value for which a loss has been recognized previously is subsequently recovered, the reversal of the loss shall be limited to the amount of the loss recognized, and the interest rate implicit in the lease shall be recalculated.

The financing incomes for subsequent periods shall be determined based on the revised net investment in the lease and the recalculated implicit interest rate.

Article 21 Contingent rents shall be recorded into the profits and losses of the period in which they actually arise.

24.5 Chapter V: Accounting Treatments of Lessees in Operating Leases

Article 22 The rents from operating leases shall be recorded by the lessee in the relevant asset costs or the profits and losses of the current period by using the straight-line method over each period of the lease term, unless there are other more reasonable methods.

Article 23 The initial direct costs incurred by a lessee shall be recognized as the profits and losses of the current period.

Article 24 The contingent rents shall be recorded into the profits and losses of the current period in which they actually arise.

24.6 Chapter VI: Accounting Treatments of Lessors in Operating Leases

Article 25 A lessor shall include the assets subject to operating leases in relevant items of its balance sheets in light of the nature of the asset.

Article 26 The rents from operating leases shall be recorded in the profits and losses of the current period by using the straight-line method over each period of the lease term, unless there are other more reasonable methods.

Article 27 The initial direct costs incurred to a lessor shall be recorded into the profits and losses of the current period.

Article 28 As for the fixed assets subject to operating leases, the lessor shall calculate the depreciation of it by adopting depreciation policy for similar assets. As for other leased assets, systematic and reasonable methods shall be adopted for its amortization.

Article 29 The contingent rents shall be recorded in the profits and losses of the period in which they actually arise.

24.7 Chapter VII: Sale and Leaseback Transactions

Article 30 A lessor and a lessee shall recognize a sale and leaseback transaction as a financing lease or an operating lease according to Chapter II of the present Standard.

Article 31 Where a sale and leaseback transaction is determined as a financing lease, any balance between the sales proceeds and the carrying amount of the asset shall be deferred and amortized as an adjustment to depreciation in light of the depreciation pattern of the leased asset.

Article 32 Where a sale and leaseback transaction is determined as an operating lease, any balance between the sales proceeds and the carrying amount of the asset shall be deferred and amortized as an adjustment to the lease payments in light of the proportion of the lease payments during the lease term. However, in case any evidence shows that the sale and leaseback transaction is based on the fair value, the balance between the sales proceeds and the carrying amount of the asset shall be recorded in the profits and losses of the current period.

24.8 Chapter VIII: Presentation

Article 33 A lessee shall, in its balance sheet, present the balances between the long-term accounts payable minus the unrecognized financing charges related to the financing leases, long-term liabilities and long-term liabilities due within 1 year, respectively.

Article 34 A lessee shall, in its notes, disclose the following information related to the financing leases:

1. the originally recorded carrying amounts at the beginning and the end of the period of each class of leased fixed assets, and the accumulated depreciation amount;
2. the minimum lease payment for each of the next 3 accounting years subsequent to the balance sheet date and the aggregate minimum lease payment thereafter; and
3. the unamortized balance of unrecognized financing charges and the method used to allocate the unrecognized financing charges.

Article 35 A lessor shall, in its balance sheet, present the balances between the financing lease accounts receivable minus the unrealized finance incomes as long-term liabilities.

Article 36 A lessor shall, in its notes, disclose the following information related to the financing leases:

1. the minimum lease receipt for each of the next 3 accounting years subsequent to the balance sheet date and the aggregate minimum lease receipt thereafter; and

2. the unamortized balance of unrealized financing income and the method used to allocate the unrealized financing income.

Article 37 As for an important operating lease, the lessee shall, in its notes, disclose the following information:

1. the minimum lease payment for the irrevocable operating lease for each of the next 3 accounting years subsequent to the balance sheet date; and
2. the aggregate minimum lease payment thereafter for the irrevocable operating lease.

Article 38 A lessor shall disclose the carrying amount of each class of leased assets in the operating leases.

Article 39 A lessee and a lessor shall disclose each sale and leaseback transaction as well as the significant items in the contract on the sale and leaseback transaction.

24.9 Comments

The business combinations are defines as transaction through which two or more entities are brought together into one reporting entity. In addition, the principle distinguishes between business combinations arising from companies under the same control or different control.

A business combination involving enterprises under common control is a business combination in which all of the combining enterprises are ultimately controlled by the same party or parties both before and after the business combination, and that control is not transitory. Any adjustment resulting from the difference between the carrying amount paid and carrying amount of controlled assets shall be reflected in the shareholders' equity. In case of negative difference, the difference, arising from the combination, shall reduce existing earnings. For business combinations involving entities under common control are now required to use the "pooling of interest method."

A business combination not involving enterprises under common control "a business combination in which all of the combining enterprises are not ultimately controlled by the same party or parties both before and after the business combination." In this case, the acquisition method is disposed. Accordingly, the acquisition method requires the following elements: (1) Identifying the acquirer; (2) Determining the acquisition date; (3) Measuring the costs of the business combination; and (4) Allocating the cost of the business combination to the assets acquired and liabilities and contingent liabilities assumed. It is important to underline how to gain control of the acquiree's net assets and operations it is not necessary for the acquirer to acquire the 100 % of the acquiree's paid-in capital, as long as he acquires more than 50 %. In such circumstances, the balance belongs to the outside stockholders that are called "minority stockholders interests."

Goodwill is defined as "an asset representing the future economic benefits arising from other assets acquired in a business combination that are not individually identified and separately recognized." Still accounting for treatment of Goodwill, when the acquirer's interest in the fair value of the identifiable assets, liabilities, and contingent liabilities of the acquiree exceeds the cost of the combination (i.e., negative goodwill), the acquirer should reassess the measurement of the fair value of the identifiable assets, liabilities, and contingent liabilities. Any accounting of Goodwill shall be recorded on provisional basis. What is more, within 12 months of the acquisition date and from the acquisition date any adjustment to those provisional values should be recognized as a result of completing the initial accounting.

In case of goodwill/discount on acquisition is the difference between the cost of the acquisition and the acquirer's share in the fair value (rather than their carrying amounts under current PRC GAAP) of the identifiable assets and liabilities acquired. Goodwill cannot be amortized, while discount on acquisition shall be immediately recorded as an income item.

The acquirer is now required to allocate part of the cost of a business combination to the acquiree's contingent liabilities at fair value (if it can be reliably measured) at the acquisition date. Furthermore, new disclosure requirements are introduced. A particular case is the reverse acquisition, occurring when the entity that issues securities (the legal acquirer) is identified as the acquiree for accounting purposes. The entity whose equity interests are acquired (the legal acquiree) must be the acquirer for accounting purposes for the transaction to be considered a reverse acquisition.

Comparing ASBE No. 20 with the equivalent IFRS 3, we notice that only the former embraces business combinations under common control, whereas the latter covers reverse acquisition, not addressed under ASBE No. 20.

24.10 Examples

Let us assume Company X and Company Y are entities not under common control. At the beginning of current financial year, Company X acquires control for 60 % of capital of Company Y for 1,800,000 CNY. Carrying value of Company Y's total assets is 2,000,000 while their fair value amounts to 2,500,000 CNY. The payment expensed by Company X also contains transaction costs incurred to carry out the operation.

The business combination shall be carried at its cost of 1,800,000 CNY in Company X balance sheet. At the same time, the minority stockholders' interest shall be measured as 40 % × 2,500,000 = 1,000,000 CNY, in accordance with the requirements of ASBE No. 20.

Chapter 25
Accounting Standards for Business Enterprises No. 21—Leases

25.1 Chapter I: General Provisions

Article 1 With a view to regulating the recognition and measurement of leases, as well as the presentation of relevant information, the present Standards are formulated according to the Accounting Standards for Enterprises—Basic Standards.

Article 2 The term "lease" refers to an agreement under which the lessor conveys to the lessee in return for rent the right to use an asset for an agreed period of time.

Article 3 The following items shall be subject to other accounting standard:

1. The land-use right and buildings rented out by a lessor by way of operating lease shall be subject to the Accounting Standards for Enterprises No. 3—Investment Real Estates;
2. The licensing agreements for the use of items such as films, video recordings, plays, manuscripts, patents, and copyrights shall be subject to the Accounting Standards for Enterprises No. 6—Intangible Assets; and
3. the impairment of long-term credits formed by the financing leases of a lessor shall be subject to the Accounting Standards for Enterprises No. 22—Recognition and Measurement of Financial Instruments.

25.2 Chapter II: Classification of Leases

Article 4 A lessee and a lessor shall classify a lease as a financing lease or an operating lease on the lease beginning date. The lease beginning date shall refer to the earlier one of the date of lease agreement or the date on which the parties to the lease make commitments on the key terms of lease.

L. Riccardi, *China Accounting Standards*,
DOI 10.1007/978-981-10-0006-5_25

Article 5 The "finance lease" shall refer to a lease that has transferred in substance all the risks and rewards related to the ownership of an asset. The ownership of it may or may not eventually be transferred.

Article 6 Where a lease satisfies one or more of the following criteria, it shall be recognized as a finance lease:

1. The ownership of the leased asset is transferred to the lessee when the term of lease expires;
2. The lessee has the option to buy the leased asset at a price which is expected to be far lower than the fair value of the leased asset at the date when the option becomes exercisable. Thus, on the lease beginning date, it can be reasonably determined that the option will be exercised;
3. Even if the ownership of the asset is not transferred, the lease term covers the major part of the use life of the leased asset;
4. In the case of the lessee, the present value of the minimum lease payments on the lease beginning date amounts to substantially all of the fair value of the leased asset on the lease beginning date; in the case of the lessor, the present value of the minimum lease receipts on the lease beginning date amounts to substantially all of the fair value of the leased asset on the lease beginning date; and
5. The leased assets are of a specialized nature that only the lessee can use them without making major modifications.

Article 7 The "lease term" shall refer to the period as specified in the lease agreement, during which the lease may not be canceled. Once a lease contract is signed, generally it may not be canceled except for the following circumstances:

1. With the consent of the lessor;
2. Where the lessee enters into a new lease for the same asset or asset of the same kind with the same lessor;
3. Where the lessee makes an additional payment of a sufficiently large amount;
4. Upon the occurrence of some remote contingency. If the lessee has the option to continue to lease the asset for any further period, and it is reasonably certain on the lease beginning date that the lessee will exercise the option, the renewed period shall be included in the lease term, no matter whether rents will be paid again or not.

Article 8 The term "minimum lease payment" shall refer to the payments (excluding contingent rents and execution costs) that the lessee shall, or may be required to make, for the term of lease, plus the residual values guaranteed by the lessee or a party related to the lessee. Where the lessee has an option to buy the leased asset at a price which is expected to be far lower than the fair value on the date when the option becomes exercisable, and thus, it is reasonably certain that the lessee will exercise the option on the lease beginning date, the payment required to exercise this purchase option shall be included in the minimum lease payments. The term "contingent rent" shall refer to the rent which is not fixed in amount and calculated on the basis of factors other than the length of time, such as the sale quantity, amount of usage, price indices. The term "execution cost" shall refer to costs incurred during the lease term for using the leased asset, such as the fees for technical consultation and services, training, maintenance, and insurance.

Article 9 The term "minimum lease receipt" shall refer to the minimum lease payments plus the residual values guaranteed to the lessor by a third party independent from the lessor or the lessee.

Article 10 The term "operating lease" shall refer to a lease other than a financing lease.

25.3 Chapter III: Accounting Treatments of Lessees in Finance Leases

Article 11 On the lease beginning date, a lessee shall record the lower one of the fair value of the leased asset and the present value of the minimum lease payments on the lease beginning date as the entering value in an account, recognize the amount of the minimum lease payments as the entering value in an account of long-term account payable, and treat the balance between the recorded amount of the leased asset and the long-term account payable as unrecognized financing charges. The initial direct costs such as commissions, attorney's fees, traveling expenses, and stamp duties directly attributable to the leased item incurred during the process of lease negotiating and signing the leasing agreement shall be recorded in the asset value of the current period. The lease beginning date shall refer to the date on which the lessee begins to have the right to use the leased asset.

Article 12 When a lessee calculates the present value of the minimum lease payments, if it can obtain the lessor's interest rate implicit in the lease, it shall adopt the interest rate implicit in the lease as the discount rate. Otherwise, it shall adopt the interest rate provided in the lease agreement as the discount rate. In case the lessee cannot obtain the lessor's interest rate implicit in the lease and no interest rate is provided in the lease agreement, the lessee shall adopt the borrowing interest rate of the bank for the same period as the discount rate.

Article 13 The expression "interest rate implicit in the lease" shall refer to the discount rate that, on the lease beginning date, makes the aggregate present value of the minimum lease payments and the unguaranteed residual values equal to the sum of the fair value of the leased asset and the initial direct costs of the lessor.

Article 14 The term "guaranteed residue value" shall refer to, in the case of a lessee, the residual value of the asset which is guaranteed by the lessee or by a third party related to the lessee; and in the case of a lessor, the guaranteed residual value from the standpoint of the lessee plus the residual value of the asset which is guaranteed by a third party independent from both the lessor and the lessee. The term "residual value of the asset" shall refer to the fair value of the leased asset when the term of lease expires as estimated on the lease beginning date. The term "unguaranteed residue value" shall refer to the residual value of the leased asset minus the guaranteed residual value of the lessor.

Article 15 The unrecognized financing charge shall be amortized to each period during the lease term. The lessee shall adopt the effective interest rate method to calculate and recognize the financing charge in the current period.

Article 16 In calculating the depreciation of a leased asset, the lessee should adopt a depreciation policy for leased assets consistent with that for depreciable assets which are owned by the lessee. If it is reasonable to be certain that the lessee will obtain the ownership of the leased asset when the lease term expires, the leased asset shall be fully depreciated over its useful life. If it is not reasonable to be certain that the lessee will obtain the ownership of the leased asset at the expiry of the lease term, the leased asset shall be fully depreciated over the shorter one of the lease term or its useful life.

Article 17 Contingent rents shall be recognized as an expense in the period in which they are actually incurred.

25.4 Chapter IV: Accounting Treatments of Lessors in Finance Leases

Article 18 On the beginning date of the lease term, a lessor shall recognize the sum of the minimum lease receipts on the lease beginning date and the initial direct costs as the entering value in an account of the financing lease values receivable, and record the unguaranteed residual value at the same time. The balance between the sums of the minimum lease receipts, the initial direct costs and the unguaranteed residual value, and the sum of their present values shall be recognized as unrealized financing income.

Article 19 The unrealized financing income shall be allocated to each period during the lease term. The lessor shall calculate the financing income at the current period by adopting the effective interest rate method.

Article 20 The lessor shall, at least at the end of each year, reexamine the unguaranteed residual values. No adjustment may be made if the unguaranteed residual value increases. Where there is evidence showing a reduction in the unguaranteed residual value, the interest rate implicit in the lease shall be recalculated and the associated reduction of the net investment in the lease shall be recognized as a loss for the current period. The financing incomes for subsequent periods shall be recognized on the basis of the revised net investment in the lease and the recalculated implicit interest rate. The net investment in the lease shall be the difference between the sum of the minimum lease receipts and the unguaranteed residual value in a finance lease and unrealized financing incomes. Where the unguaranteed residual value for which a loss has been recognized previously is subsequently recovered, the reversal of the loss shall be limited to the amount of the loss recognized, and the interest rate implicit in the lease shall be recalculated.

The financing incomes for subsequent periods shall be determined based on the revised net investment in the lease and the recalculated implicit interest rate.

Article 21 Contingent rents shall be recorded into the profits and losses of the period in which they actually arise.

25.5 Chapter V: Accounting Treatments of Lessees in Operating Leases

Article 22 The rents from operating leases shall be recorded by the lessee in the relevant asset costs or the profits and losses of the current period by using the straight-line method over each period of the lease term, unless there are other more reasonable methods.

Article 23 The initial direct costs incurred by a lessee shall be recognized as the profits and losses of the current period.

Article 24 The contingent rents shall be recorded into the profits and losses of the current period in which they actually arise.

25.6 Chapter VI: Accounting Treatments of Lessors in Operating Leases

Article 25 A lessor shall include the assets subject to operating leases in relevant items of its balance sheets in light of the nature of the asset.

Article 26 The rents from operating leases shall be recorded in the profits and losses of the current period by using the straight-line method over each period of the lease term, unless there are other more reasonable methods.

Article 27 The initial direct costs incurred to a lessor shall be recorded into the profits and losses of the current period.

Article 28 As for the fixed assets subject to operating leases, the lessor shall calculate the depreciation of it by adopting depreciation policy for similar assets. As for other leased assets, systematic and reasonable methods shall be adopted for its amortization.

Article 29 The contingent rents shall be recorded in the profits and losses of the period in which they actually arise.

25.7 Chapter VII: Sale and Leaseback Transactions

Article 30 A lessor and a lessee shall recognize a sale and leaseback transaction as a financing lease or an operating lease according to Chapter II of the present Standard.

Article 31 Where a sale and leaseback transaction is determined as a financing lease, any balance between the sales proceeds and the carrying amount of the asset shall be deferred and amortized as an adjustment to depreciation in light of the depreciation pattern of the leased asset.

Article 32 Where a sale and leaseback transaction is determined as an operating lease, any balance between the sales proceeds and the carrying amount of the asset shall be deferred and amortized as an adjustment to the lease payments in light of the proportion of the lease payments during the lease term. However, in case any evidence shows that the sale and leaseback transaction is based on the fair value, the balance between the sales proceeds and the carrying amount of the asset shall be recorded in the profits and losses of the current period.

25.8 Chapter VIII: Presentation

Article 33 A lessee shall, in its balance sheet, present the balances between the long-term accounts payable minus the unrecognized financing charges related to the financing leases, long-term liabilities, and long-term liabilities due within 1 year, respectively.

Article 34 A lessee shall, in its notes, disclose the following information related to the financing leases:

1. the originally recorded carrying amounts at the beginning and the end of the period of each class of leased fixed assets, and the accumulated depreciation amount;
2. the minimum lease payment for each of the next 3 accounting years subsequent to the balance sheet date and the aggregate minimum lease payment thereafter; and
3. the unamortized balance of unrecognized financing charges and the method used to allocate the unrecognized financing charges.

Article 35 A lessor shall, in its balance sheet, present the balances between the financing lease accounts receivable minus the unrealized finance incomes as long-term liabilities.

Article 36 A lessor shall, in its notes, disclose the following information related to the financing leases:

1. the minimum lease receipt for each of the next 3 accounting years subsequent to the balance sheet date and the aggregate minimum lease receipt thereafter; and
2. the unamortized balance of unrealized financing income and the method used to allocate the unrealized financing income.

Article 37 As for an important operating lease, the lessee shall, in its notes, disclose the following information:

1. the minimum lease payment for the irrevocable operating lease for each of the next 3 accounting years subsequent to the balance sheet date; and
2. the aggregate minimum lease payment thereafter for the irrevocable operating lease.

Article 38 A lessor shall disclose the carrying amount of each class of leased assets in the operating leases.

Article 39 A lessee and a lessor shall disclose each sale and leaseback transaction as well as the significant items in the contract on the sale and leaseback transaction.

25.9 Comments

"A finance lease is an operation that transfers substantially all the risks and rewards incidental to ownership of an asset." In defining the circumstances of guaranteed residual value, for the lessee is the residual value guaranteed from the lessee or other lessee-related party, whereas for the lessor it is the residual value guaranteed from the lessee or other parties unrelated to either the lessee or the lessor. The remaining portion of residual value is deemed as unguaranteed, and its realization for the lessor is not assured.

At the beginning of the lease term, a lessee shall recognize a finance lease asset in its balance sheet at an amount equal to the fair value of the leased asset or, if lower, the present value of the minimum lease payments. These provisions change previous PRC GAAP, which required a financial lease asset to be recorded at the lower of the original carrying amount of the asset and the present value of the minimum lease payments. Any initial direct cost that can be identified as attributable to the process of negotiating and securing the leasing agreement for a finance lease shall be added to the amount recognized as an asset. The superseded standard, referring to "Leases," required the initial direct costs to be recognized as an expense in the period when they are incurred.

The principle defines the significance of risk, including the possibilities of losses from idle capacity or technological obsolescence and of variations in return because of changing economic conditions. In addition, rewards may be represented by the expectation of profitable operation over the asset's economic life and of gain from appreciation in value or realization of a residual value.

An operating lease depends on the substance of the transaction rather than the form of the contract. Elements leading to operating leases are the following: (1) The lease transfers ownership of the asset to the lessee by the end of the lease term; (2) The lessee has the option to purchase the asset at a price that is expected to be sufficiently lower than the fair value at the date the option becomes exercisable for it to be reasonably certain, at the inception of the lease, that the option will be exercised (bargain purchase option); (3) The lease term is for the major part of the useful life of the asset even if title is not transferred; (4) At the inception of the lease, the present value of the minimum lease payments amounts to at least substantially all of the fair value of the leased asset; and (5) The leased assets are of such a specialized nature that only the lessee can use them without major modifications.

In the case of finance lease, at the commencement of the lease term, lessees shall recognize finance leases as a fixed asset in their statement of financial positions at amounts equal to the fair value of the leased property or, if lower, the present value of the minimum lease payments, each determined at the inception of the lease. Any initial direct costs of the lessee are added to the amount recognized as an asset if they are attributable to the process of negotiating and securing the leasing agreement. The discount rate to be used in calculating the present value of the minimum lease payments is the interest rate implicit in the lease, if it is known to the lessee; if not, the discount rate is the interest rate specified in the lease agreement.

The principle analyses sale and leaseback transactions involving the sale of an asset and the leasing back of the same asset. The lease payment and the sale price are usually interdependent because they are negotiated as a package. The accounting treatment of a sale and leaseback transaction depends upon the type of lease involved. Particular attention is paid toward finance lease. If a sale and leaseback transaction results in a finance lease, any excess of sales proceeds over the carrying amount shall not be immediately recognized as income by a seller–lessee. Instead, it shall be deferred and amortized over the lease term as an adjustment to depreciation expense according to the depreciation pattern of the leased asset. Moreover, if the leaseback is a finance lease, the transaction is a means whereby the lessor provides finance to the lessee, with the asset as security. For this reason, it is not appropriate to regard an excess of sales proceeds over the carrying amount as income. Such excess is deferred and amortized over the lease term.

New ASBE No. 21 also introduces that in the case of evidence that a sale and leaseback transaction resulting in an operating lease is established at fair value, the difference between the sales proceeds and the carrying amount of the asset shall be recognized as profit or loss in the current period. Otherwise, the difference between the sales proceeds and the carrying amount of the asset shall be deferred and amortized over the lease term as an adjustment to rental expenses. Past PRC GAAP allowed only the second model.

Referring to leases, the equivalent IAS 17 disposes leasehold interest in land shall be classified as an operating lease unless it meets certain criteria and is accounted for as an investment property under the fair value model. This issue is addressed in ASBE No. 6, among the intangible assets, whereas if criteria referred to land-use rights are met, the provisions under ASBE No. 3 shall be applied.

25.10 Examples

Company Y leases machinery from Company X for 5 years. There is no expected residual value for the machinery at the end of the lease and its current-carrying value is 250,000 CNY. The leasing agreement consists of rental expenses for

15,000 CNY on a quarterly basis. According to the leasing features, this transaction shall be classified as an operating lease.

Company X (the lessor) shall account for the annual depreciation of the asset according to the depreciation method already used for that machinery, let us suppose 50,000 CNY (under straight-line method and residual life of five years).

Company Y (the lessee) shall account for the quarterly lease payments of 15,000 CNY.

Chapter 26
Accounting Standards for Business Enterprises No. 22—Recognition and Measurement of Financial Instruments

26.1 Chapter I: General Principles

Article 1 With a view to regulating the recognition and measurement of financial instruments, the present Standards are formulated according to the Accounting Standards for Enterprises—Basic Principles.

Article 2 The term "financial instruments" refers to the contracts under which the financial assets of an enterprise are formed and the financial liability or right instruments of any other entity are formed.

Article 3 The term "derivative instruments" refers to the financial instruments or other contracts which are involved in the present Standards and are characterized by the following:

1. The values thereof varies with particular interest rates, prices of financial instruments, prices of commodities, foreign exchange rates, price indexes, premium rate indexes, credit ratings, credit indexes, and other similar variables; if the variable is a non-financial variable, there shall not exist any special relationship between such variable and any party to the contract;
2. No initial net investment is required, or as compared to contracts of other types that have similar responses to the market changes, very little initial net investment is required;
3. It is settled on a certain future date. Derivative instruments shall include forward contracts, future contracts, exchanges and options, as well as the instruments that contain one or more of the characters of a forward contract, future contract, exchange, or option.

Article 4 The following items shall be subject to other relevant accounting standards:

1. The long-term equity investments as regulated by the Accounting Standards for Enterprises No. 2—Long-term Equity Investment shall be subject to the Accounting Standards for Enterprises No. 2—Long-term Equity Investments;

L. Riccardi, *China Accounting Standards*,
DOI 10.1007/978-981-10-0006-5_26

2. The share-based payments as regulated by the Accounting Standards for Enterprises No. 11—Share-based Payments shall be subject to the Accounting Standards for Enterprises No. 11—Share-based Payments;
3. The recombination of debts shall be subject to the Accounting Standards for Enterprises No. 12—Debt Recombination;
4. The rights available from the settlement of anticipated debts shall be subject to the Accounting Standards for Enterprises No. 13—Contingencies;
5. The contingent consideration contracts of the combining parties in business combinations shall be subject to the Accounting Standards for Enterprises No. 2—Business Combination;
6. The rights and obligations involved in a lease shall be subject to the Accounting Standards for Enterprises No. 21—Leases;
7. The transfer of financial assets shall be subject to the Accounting Standards for Enterprises No. 23—Transfer of Financial Assets;
8. Hedges shall be subject to the Accounting Standards for Enterprises No. 24—Hedging;
9. The rights and obligations involved in the original insurance contracts shall be subject to the Accounting Standards for Enterprises No. 25—Original Insurance Contracts;
10. The rights and obligations involved in a reinsurance contract shall be subject to the Accounting Standards for Enterprises No. 26—Reinsurance Contracts;
11. The equity instruments as issued by an enterprise shall be subject to the Accounting Standards for Enterprises No. 37—Presentation of Financial Instruments.

Article 5 The present Standards do not regulate the irrevocable credit commitments as made by enterprises (i.e., commitments to grant loans), with the exception of the following:

1. the designated commitments to grant loans made to the financial liabilities which are measured at their fair values, of which the variation is recorded into the profits and losses of the current period;
2. the commitments to grant loans which can be settled with the net amount of cash or by way of exchange or by issuing any other financial instrument; and
3. the commitments to grant loans at an interest rate which is lower than the market interest rate. For the commitments to grant loans not regulated by the present Standards, the Accounting Standards for Enterprises No. 13—Contingencies shall apply.

Article 6 The present Standards do not regulate the contracts, which are concluded for the stipulated purchase, sale, or use, and when the time becomes mature, non-financial items are bought or sold as a performance of the contract. However, the contracts which can be settled with cash or the net amount of other financial instruments or can be bought or sold and settled by exchanging financial instruments shall be subject to the present Standards.

26.2 Chapter II: Classification of Financial Assets and Financial Liabilities

Article 7 Financial assets shall be classified into the following four categories when they are initially recognized:

1. the financial assets which are measured at their fair values and the variation of which is recorded into the profits and losses of the current period, including transactional financial assets and the financial assets which are measured at their fair values and of which the variation is included in the current profits and losses;
2. the investments which will be held to their maturity;
3. loans and the account receivables; and
4. financial assets available for sale.

Article 8 Financial liabilities shall be classified into the following two categories when they are initially recognized:

1. the financial liabilities which are measured at their fair values and of which the variation is included in the current profits and losses, including transactional financial liabilities and the designated financial liabilities which are measured at their fair values and of which the variation is included in the current profits and losses; and
2. other financial liabilities.

Article 9 The financial assets or liabilities meeting any of the following requirements shall be classified as transactional financial assets or financial liabilities:

1. The purpose to acquire the said financial assets or undertake the financial liabilities is mainly for selling or repurchasing of them in the near future;
2. Forming a part of the identifiable combination of financial instruments which are managed in a centralized way and for which there are objective evidences proving that the enterprise may manage the combination by way of short-term profit making in the near future;
3. Being a derivative instrument, excluding the designated derivative instruments which are effective hedging instruments, or derivative instruments to financial guarantee contracts, and the derivative instruments which are connected with the equity instrument investments for which there is no quoted price in the active market, whose fair value cannot be reliably measured, and which shall be settled by delivering the said equity instruments.

Article 10 Besides the provisions of *Articles 21* and *22* of the present Standards, only the financial assets or financial liabilities meeting any of the following requirements can be designated, when they are initially recognized, as financial assets or financial liabilities as measured at its fair value and of which the variation is included in the current profits and losses:

1. The designation is able to eliminate or obviously reduce the discrepancies in the recognition or measurement of relevant gains or losses arisen from the different basis of measurement of the financial assets or financial liabilities;
2. The official written documents on risk management or investment strategies of the enterprise concerned have recorded that the combination of said financial assets, the combination of said financial liabilities, or the combination of said financial assets and said financial liabilities will be managed and evaluated on the basis of their fair values and be reported to the key management personnel. The equity investment instruments, for which there is no quoted price in the active market and whose fair value cannot be reliably measured, shall not be designated as a financial asset which is measured at its fair value and of which the variation is recorded into the profits and losses of the current period. The active market refers to the markets which are concurrently featured by the following:

    1. The objects of transaction in the market are homogeneous;
    2. Buyers and sellers are available at any time to undertake the transaction at their own free will; and
    3. The pricing information of the market is open.

Article 11 The term "held-to-maturity investment" refers to a non-derivative financial asset with a fixed date of maturity, a fixed or determinable amount of repo price and which the enterprise holds for a definite purpose or the enterprise is able to hold until its maturity. The following non-derivative financial assets shall not be classified as investments held to their maturity:

1. the designated non-derivative financial assets which, at their initial recognition, are measured at their fair values and of which the variation is included in the current profits and losses;
2. the non-derivative financial assets which are designated as sellable at their initial recognition; and
3. loans and account receivables. An enterprise shall, on the balance sheet date, make an appraisal on its purpose of holding and ability to hold. Where there is any change, it shall be dealt with according to the present Standards.

Article 12 Under any of the following circumstances, it shows that the enterprise concerned does not have a clear intention to hold the financial asset investment until its maturity:

1. The term for holding the financial assets is not definite;
2. It will sell the financial assets when any of the following changes: the market interest rate, the fluid demand, the substitutive investment opportunity or the investment returns ratio, the source and condition of financing, or foreign exchange risk, etc., with the exception of the sale of the financial assets which is caused by any uncontrollable and independent event which is anticipated not to repeat and is difficult to be reasonably predicted;

3. The issuer of the financial assets can settle it with a sum which is obviously lower than the post-amortization cost;
4. Any other circumstance which shows that the enterprise concerned does not have the clear intention to hold the financial assets until its maturity.

Article 13 The post-amortization cost of a financial asset or financial liability refers to the following result after adjustment of the initially recognized amount of the financial asset or financial liability:

1. after deducting the already paid principal;
2. after plus or minus the accumulative amount of amortization incurred from amortizing the balance between the initially recognized amount and the amount of the maturity date by adopting the actual interest rate method; and
3. after deducting the impairment losses that have actually incurred (only applicable to financial assets).

Article 14 The actual interest rate method refers to the method by which the post-amortization costs and the interest incomes of different installments or interest expenses are calculated in light of the actual interest rates of the financial assets or financial liabilities (including a set of financial assets or financial liabilities). The actual interest rate refers to the interest rate adopted to cash the future cash flow of a financial asset or financial liability within the predicted term of existence or within a shorter applicable term into the current carrying amount of the financial asset or financial liability. When the actual interest rate is determined, the future cash flow shall be predicted on the basis of taking into account all the contractual provisions concerning the financial asset or financial liability (including the right to repay the loan ahead of schedule, call options, and similar options), and the future credit losses shall not be taken into account. The various fee charges, trading expenses, premiums, or reduced values, etc., which are paid or collected by the parties to a financial asset or financial liability contract and which form a part of the actual interest rate, shall be taken into account in the determination of the actual interest rate. Where the future cash flow or term of existence of a financial asset or financial liability cannot be predicted reliably, the contractual cash flow of the financial asset or financial liability for the whole term of the contract shall be taken into account.

Article 15 Under any of the following circumstances, it shows that the enterprise concerned is not able to hold the fixed term financial asset investment until its maturity:

1. Having no available financial resources to continuously provide funds to the financial asset investment so as to hold the financial asset investment until its maturity;
2. Being subject to the restriction of any law or administrative regulation so that it is hard for the enterprise concerned to hold the financial asset investment until its maturity;
3. Any other circumstance showing that the enterprise concerned is not able to hold the fixed term financial asset investment until its maturity.

Article 16 Where an enterprise sells its outstanding held-to-maturity investment within the current accounting year or reclassifies it as the amount of sellable financial asset, and such amount is considerably large as compared with the amount before such investment is sold or reclassified, the surplus of such investment shall be reclassified as a sellable financial asset which shall not be classified as a held-to-maturity investment within the current accounting year and the following two complete accounting years. However, the following circumstances shall be excluded:

1. The date of sale or reclassification is quite near to the maturity date or the repo date of the said investment (e.g., within 3 months prior to maturity) that any change of the market interest rate will produce little impact on the fair value of the said investment;
2. After almost all the initial principal of the investment has been drawn back by way of repayment at fixed intervals or repayment ahead of schedule according to the provisions of the contract, the remaining part of the investment will be sold or reclassified;
3. The sale or reclassification is caused by any independent event that the enterprise cannot control, is predicted not to occur again, and is hard to be reasonably predicted. Such events mainly include the following:

   (i) The held-to-maturity investment is sold due to the serious worsening of the credit situation of the investee;
   (ii) The held-to-maturity investment is sold due to the fact that the relevant tax provisions have canceled the relevant policies on the pre-tax credit of interest taxes against the held-to-maturity investment or have remarkably reduced the pre-tax creditable amount;
   (iii) The held-to-maturity investment is sold due to any important business enterprise combination or serious disposal so as to maintain the prevailing interest risk position or maintain the prevailing credit risk policies;
   (iv) The held-to-maturity investment is sold due to any significant readjustment of laws or administrative regulations on the scope of permitted investment or the amount of investment of any particular investment product;
   (v) The held-to-maturity investment is sold due to the regulatory department's demands for significantly enhancing the fluidity of assets or significantly enhancing the risk weight of the held-to-maturity investment in the calculation of capital adequacy ratio.

Article 17 "Loans and accounts receivable" refers to the non-derivative financial assets for which there is no quoted price in the active market and of which the repo amount is fixed or determinable. An enterprise shall not classify any of the following non-derivative financial assets as a loans or accounts receivable:

1. the non-derivative financial assets which are to be sold immediately or in the near future;
2. the non-derivative financial assets which are designated to be measured at their fair value when they are initially recognized and of which the variation is recorded into the profits and losses of the current period;

3. the non-derivative financial assets which are designated as sellable when they are initially recognized;
4. the non-derivative financial assets whose holder finds it hard to take back almost all of the initial investment due to any reason other than the worsening of the credit of the debtor. The funds for securities investment and other similar funds as held by an enterprise shall not be classified as a loans or accounts receivable.

Article 18 The "sellable financial assets" refers to the non-derivative financial assets which are designated as sellable when they are initially recognized as well as the financial assets other than those as described below:

1. loans and accounts receivables;
2. investments held until their maturity; and
3. financial assets measured at their fair values and of which the variation is recorded into the profits and losses of the current period.

Article 19 An enterprise shall not, after classifying a financial asset or financial liability as a financial asset or financial liability measured at its fair value and of which the variation is recorded into the profits and losses of the current period when it is initially recognized, reclassify it as any other type of financial assets or financial liabilities, nor may it reclassify any other type of financial assets or financial liabilities as a financial asset or financial liability measured at its fair value and of which the variation is recorded into the profits and losses of the current period.

26.3 Chapter III: Embedded Derivative Instruments

Article 20 An embedded derivative instrument shall refer to a derivative instrument which is embedded into a non-derivative instrument (namely, the principal contract) so that some or all of the cash flow of the mixed instrument changes with the change of particular interest rates, prices of the financial instrument, prices of commodities, foreign exchange rates, pricing indexes, premium rate indexes, credit ratings, credit indexes, or other similar variables. The embedded derivative instruments and the principal contract jointly form into a mixed instrument, e.g., the convertible company bonds.

Article 21 An enterprise may designate a mixed instrument as a financial asset or financial liability measured at its fair value and of which the variation is recorded into the profits and losses of the current period, excepting those under the following circumstances:

1. Where the embedded derivative instrument does not significantly change the cash flow of the mixed instrument;
2. Where the derivative instruments embedded in similar mixed instruments shall obviously not be separated from the relevant mixed instruments.

Article 22 Where a mixed instrument related to an embedded derivative instrument fails to be designated as a financial asset or financial liability measured at its fair value and of which the variation is included in the current profits and losses, and it can simultaneously meet the following conditions, the embedded derivative instrument shall be separated from the mixed instrument and treated as an independent derivative instrument:

1. Where there is no close relationship between it and the principal contract in terms of economic features and risks; and
2. Where it shares the same conditions with those of the embedded derivative instrument, and the independent instrument meets the requirements of the definition of derivative instrument. Where it is impossible to make an independent measurement when it is obtained or subsequently on the balance sheet date, the mixed instrument shall be designated entirely as a financial asset or financial liability measured at its fair value and of which the variation is included in the current profits and losses.

Article 23 Where the principal contract is a financial instrument after the embedded derivative instrument is separated from the mixed instrument according to the present Standard, it shall be dealt with according to the present Standard; if the principal contract is a non-financial instrument, it shall be dealt with according to other accounting standards.

26.4 Chapter IV: Recognition of Financial Instruments

Article 24 When an enterprise becomes a party to a financial instrument, it shall recognize a financial asset or financial liability.

Article 25 Where a financial asset satisfies any of the following requirements, the recognition of it shall be terminated:

1. Where the contractual rights for collecting the cash flow of the said financial asset are terminated; or
2. Where the said financial asset has been transferred and meets the conditions for recognizing the termination of financial assets as provided for in Accounting Standards for Enterprises No. 23—Transfer of Financial Assets. The "termination of recognition" shall refer to the writing off the financial asset or financial liability from the account or balance sheet of the enterprise concerned.

Article 26 Only when the prevailing obligations of a financial liability are relieved in all or in part may the recognition of the financial liability be terminated in all or partly. Where an enterprise transfers any of its assets used for repaying its financial liabilities into any institution or to establish a trust, and the prevailing obligations to repay the liabilities remain to exist, it shall not terminate the recognition of the said financial liability and the transferred asset.

Article 27 Where an enterprise (debtor) enters into an agreement with a creditor so as to substitute the existing financial liabilities by way of any new financial liability, and if the contractual stipulations regarding the new financial liability are substantially different from those regarding the existing financial liability, it shall terminate the recognition of the existing financial liability and shall at the same time recognize the new financial liability. Where an enterprise makes substantial revisions to some or all of the contractual stipulations of the existing financial liability, it shall terminate the recognition of the existing financial liability or part of it and at the same time recognize the financial liability after revising the contractual stipulations as a new financial liability.

Article 28 Where the recognition of a financial liability is totally or partially terminated, the enterprise concerned shall include into the profits and losses of the current period the gap between the carrying amount which has been terminated from recognition and the considerations it has paid (including the non-cash assets it has transferred out and the new financial liabilities it has assumed).

Article 29 Where an enterprise buys back part of its financial liabilities, it shall distribute, on the repo day, the carrying amount of the whole financial liabilities in light of the comparatively fair value of the part that continues to be recognized and the part whose recognition has already been terminated. The gap between the carrying amount which is distributed to the part whose recognition has terminated and the considerations it has paid (including the non-cash assets it has transferred out and the new financial liabilities it has assumed) shall be recorded into the profits and losses of the current period.

26.5 Chapter V: Measurement of Financial Instruments

Article 30 The financial assets and financial liabilities initially recognized by an enterprise shall be measured at their fair values. For the financial assets and liabilities measured at their fair values and of which the variation is recorded into the profits and losses of the current period, the transaction expenses thereof shall be directly recorded into the profits and losses of the current period; for other categories of financial assets and financial liabilities, the transaction expenses thereof shall be included into the initially recognized amount.

Article 31 The "transaction expenses" refers to the newly added external expenses attributable to the purchase, distribution, or disposal of a financial instrument. The newly added external expenses refer to the expenses that will occur only when the enterprise concerned purchase, distribution, or disposal of any financial instrument. The transaction expenses include handing charges and commissions as well as other necessary expenditures an enterprise pays to its agency institutions, consultation companies, and securities dealers, but exclude the bond premiums, reduced values, financing expenses, internal management costs, and other expenses that are not directly related to the transaction.

Article 32 An enterprise shall make subsequent measurement on its financial assets according to their fair values and may not deduct the transaction expenses that may occur when it disposes the said financial asset in the future. However, those under the following circumstances shall be excluded:

1. The investments held until their maturity and loans and accounts receivable shall be measured on the basis of the post-amortization costs by adopting the actual interest rate method;
2. The equity instrument investments for which there is no quotation in the active market and whose fair value cannot be measured reliably and the derivative financial assets which are connected with the said equity instrument and must be settled by delivering the said equity instrument shall be measured on the basis of their costs.

Article 33 An enterprise shall make subsequent measurement on its financial liabilities on the basis of the post-amortization costs by adopting the actual interest rate method, with the exception of those under the following circumstances:

1. For the financial liabilities measured at their fair values and of which the variation is recorded into the profits and losses of the current period, they shall be measured at their fair values, and none of the transaction expenses may be deducted, which may occur when the financial liabilities are settled in the future;
2. For the derivative financial liabilities, which are connected to the equity instrument for which there is no quotation in the active market and whose fair value cannot be reliably measured, and which must be settled by delivering the equity instrument, they shall be measured on the basis of their costs;
3. For the financial guarantee contracts which are not designated as a financial liability measured at its fair value and the variation thereof is recorded into the profits and losses of the current period, and for the commitments to grant loans which are not designated to be measured at the fair value and of which the variation is recorded into the profits and losses of the current period and which will enjoy an interest rate lower than that of the market, a subsequent measurement shall be made after they are initially recognized according to the higher one of the following:

   (i) the amount as determined according to the Accounting Standards for Enterprises No. 13—Contingencies; or
   (ii) the surplus after accumulative amortization as determined according to the principles of the Accounting Standards for Enterprises No. 14—Revenues is subtracted from the initially recognized amount.

Article 34 Where an enterprise has the intention of holding or the ability to make changes so that an investment is no longer suitable to be classified as a held-to-maturity investment, the investment shall be reclassified as a sellable financial asset, and a subsequent measurement shall be made according to its fair value. The balance between the carrying amount of the said investment at the reclassification day and the fair value shall be computed into the owner's equity, and when the said sellable financial asset is impaired or transferred out when it is terminated from recognizing, it shall be recorded into the profits and losses of the current period.

Article 35 Where part of the held-to-maturity investment is sold or the reclassified amount thereof is considerably large, and if it does not fall within any of the exceptions as described in *Article 16*, so that the remainder of the said investment is no longer suitable to be classified as a held-to-maturity investment, the enterprise shall reclassify the remainder of the said investment as a sellable financial asset and shall make subsequent measurement on it according to its fair value. The gap between the carrying amount of the said remnant part of the investment at the reclassification day and the fair value shall be computed into the owner's equity. And when the said sellable financial asset is impaired or transferred out when it is terminated from recognition, it shall be recorded into the profits and losses of the current period.

Article 36 As for the financial assets and financial liabilities, which, according to the present Accounting Standards, shall be measured at their fair values, but of which the prior fair values cannot be measured reliably, the enterprise shall measure them at their fair values when their fair values can be reliably measured, and the gap between the relevant carrying amount and the fair value shall be dealt with according to *Article 38* of the present Accounting Standards herein.

Article 37 Where the intention of holding or the ability to hold changes, or the fair value can not be reliably measured any more, or the term of holding has exceeded "two complete accounting years" as described in *Article 16* of the present Accounting Standards herein, which makes it no longer suitable to measure the financial asset or financial liability at its fair value, the enterprise concerned may measure the said financial asset or financial liability on the basis of its cost or post-amortization cost. And such cost or post-amortization cost at the reclassification day shall be the fair value or carrying amount of the financial asset or financial liability. The gains or losses that are related to the said financial asset and that are directly included in the owner's equity shall be dealt with according to the following provisions: (1) Where such financial asset has a fixed date of maturity, it shall be amortized within the remaining period of the said financial asset by adopting the actual interest rate method and be recorded into the profits and losses of the current period. The gap between the post-amortization cost of the financial asset and the amount on the maturity date shall also be amortized within the remaining period of the said financial asset by adopting the actual interest rate method and be recorded into the profits and losses of the current period. If, during the subsequent accounting period, the financial asset is impaired, the relevant profits and losses that were included in the owner's equity shall be transferred out and be recorded into the current profits and losses. (2) Where such financial asset does not have a fixed date of maturity, it shall remain in the owner's equity. And when the said financial asset is transferred out at its disposal, it shall be recorded into the profits and losses of the current period. Where such financial asset is impaired during the remaining period of accounting that follows, the relevant profits and losses that were included in the owner's equity shall be transferred out and be recorded into the profits and losses of the current period.

Article 38 The profits and losses arising from the change in the fair value of a financial asset or financial liability shall be dealt with according to the following provisions, unless it is related to hedging:

1. The profits and losses, arising from the change in the fair value of the financial asset or financial liability which is measured at its fair value and of which the variation is recorded into the profits and losses of the current period, shall be recorded into the profits and losses of the current period;
2. The profits and losses arising from the change in the fair value of a sellable financial asset shall be included directly in the owner's equity with the exception of impairment losses and the gap arising from foreign exchange conversion of cash financial assets in any foreign currency, and when the said financial asset is stopped from recognition and is transferred out, it shall be recorded into the profits and losses of the current period. The gap arising from the foreign exchange conversion of a sellable cash financial asset in any foreign currency shall be recorded into the profits and losses of the current period. The interests of the sellable financial assets calculated according to the actual interest rate method shall be recorded into the profits and losses of the current period. The cash dividends of the sellable equity instrument investments shall be recorded into the profits and losses of the current period when the investee announces the distribution of dividends. The treatment of the profits and losses arising from the change in the fair value of a financial asset or financial liability related to hedging shall be subject to the Accounting Standards for Enterprises No. 24—Hedging.

Article 39 For the financial assets and financial liabilities measured at the post-amortization costs, the profits and losses that arise when such financial assets or financial liabilities are terminated from recognition, or are impaired or amortized, shall be recorded into the profits and losses of the current period. However, if a financial asset or financial liability is designated as an item of hedging, the treatment of the relevant profits and losses shall be subject to the Accounting Standards for Enterprises No. 24—Hedging.

26.6 Chapter VI: Impairment of Financial Assets

Article 40 An enterprise shall carry out an inspection, on the balance sheet day, on the carrying amount of the financial assets other than that measured at their fair values and of which the variation is recorded into the profits and losses of the current period. Where there is any objective evidence proving that such financial asset has been impaired, an impairment provision shall be made.

Article 41 The expression "objective evidence proving that the financial asset has been impaired" refers to the actually incurred events which, after the financial asset is initially recognized, have an impact on the predicted future cash flow of the said financial asset that can be reliably measured by the enterprise. The objective evidences that can prove the impairment of a financial asset shall include the following:

1. A serious financial difficulty occurs to the issuer or debtor;
2. The debtor breaches any of the contractual stipulations, for example, fails to pay or delays the payment of interests or the principal, etc.;
3. The creditor makes any concession to the debtor which is in financial difficulties due to economic or legal factors, etc.;
4. The debtor will probably become bankrupt or carry out other financial reorganizations;
5. The financial asset can no longer continue to be traded in the active market due to serious financial difficulties of the issuer;
6. It is impossible to identify whether the cash flow of a certain asset within a certain combination of financial assets has decreased or not. But after making an overall appraisal according to the public data available, it is found that the predicted future cash flow of the said combination of financial assets has indeed decreased since it was initially recognized and such decrease can be measured, for example, the ability of the debtor of the said combination of financial assets worsens gradually, the unemployment rate of the country or region where the debtor is situated increases, the prices of the region where the guaranty is situated are obviously dropping, or the industrial sector concerned is in slump;
7. Any seriously disadvantageous change has occurred to technical, market, economic, or legal environment, etc. wherein the debtor operates its business, which makes the investor of an equity instrument unable to take back its investment;
8. Where the fair value of the equity instrument investment drops significantly or not contemporarily;
9. Other objective evidences showing the impairment of the financial asset.

Article 42 Where a financial asset measured on the basis of post-amortization costs is impaired, the carrying amount of the said financial asset shall be written down to the current value of the predicted future cash flow (excluding the loss of future credits not yet occurred), and the amount as written down shall be recognized as loss of the impairment of the asset and shall be recorded into the profits and losses of the current period. The current value of the predicted future cash flow shall be determined according to the capitalization of the original actual interest rate of the said financial asset, taking into account the value of the relevant guarantee (but the expenses arising from the acquisition or sale of the guarantee shall be deducted). The original actual interest rate is the actual interest rate as determined when the financial asset was initially recognized. With regard to the floating interest rate loans, accounts receivable, and the investments held until their maturity, the current actual interest rate as stipulated in the contract shall be adopted as the capitalization rate in the calculation of current value of the cash flow. Where there is a very small gap between the predicted future cash flow of a short-term account receivable item and the current value thereof, the predicted future cash flow is not required to be capitalized when determining the relevant impairment-related losses.

Article 43 An impairment test shall be made on the financial assets with significant single amounts. If any objective evidence shows that it has been impaired, the impairment-related losses shall be recognized and shall be recorded into the profits and losses of the current period. With regard to the financial assets with insignificant single amounts, an independent impairment test may be carried out, or they may be included in a combination of financial assets with similar credit risk features so as to carry out an impairment-related test. Where, upon independent test, the financial asset (including those financial assets with significant single amounts and those with insignificant amounts) has not been impaired, it shall be included in a combination of financial assets with similar risk features so as to conduct another impairment test. The financial assets which have suffered from an impairment loss in any single amount shall not be included in any combination of financial assets with similar risk features for any impairment test.

Article 44 Where any financial asset measured on the basis of post-amortization costs is recognized as having suffered from any impairment loss, if there is any objective evidence proving that the value of the said financial asset has been restored, and it is objectively related to the events that occur after such loss is recognized (e.g., the credit rating of the debtor has been elevated), the impairment-related losses as originally recognized shall be reversed and be recorded into the profits and losses of the current period. However, the reversed carrying amount shall not be any more than the post-amortization costs of the said financial asset on the day of reverse under the assumption that no provision is made for the impairment.

Article 45 Where an equity instrument investment for which there is no quoted price in the active market and whose fair value cannot be reliably measured, or a derivative financial asset which is connected with the equity instrument and which must be settled by delivering the equity instrument, suffers from any impairment, the gap between the carrying amount of the equity instrument investment or the derivative financial asset and the current value of the future cash flow of similar financial assets capitalized according to the returns ratio of the market at the same time shall be recognized as impairment-related losses and be recorded into the profits and losses of the current period.

Article 46 Where a sellable financial asset is impaired, even if the recognition of the financial asset has not been terminated, the accumulative losses arising from the decrease of the fair value of the owner's equity which was directly included shall be transferred out and recorded into the profits and losses of the current period. The accumulative losses that are transferred out shall be the balance obtained from the initially obtained costs of the sold financial asset after deducting the principals as taken back, the current fair value, and the impairment-related losses as was recorded into the profits and losses of the current period.

Article 47 As for the sellable debt instruments whose impairment-related losses have been recognized, if, within the accounting period thereafter, the fair value has risen and are objectively related to the subsequent events that occur after the originally impairment-related losses were recognized, the originally recognized impairment-related losses shall be reversed and be recorded into the profits and losses of the current period.

Article 48 The impairment-related losses incurred to a sellable equity instrument investment shall not be reversed through profits and losses. However, the impairment-related losses incurred to an equity instrument investment for which there is no quoted price in the active market and whose fair value cannot be reliably measured, or incurred to a derivative financial asset which is connected with the said equity instrument and which shall be settled by delivering the said equity instrument, may not be reversed.

Article 49 After an impairment of a financial asset, the interest incomes shall be recognized at the interest rate which is used as the capitalization rate in the capitalization of the future cash flow when the impairment-related losses are determined.

26.7 Chapter VII: Determination of the Fair Value

Article 50 The "fair value" refers to the amount, at which both parties to a transaction who are familiar with the condition exchange their assets or clear off their debts under fair conditions. In a fair transaction, both parties to it shall be enterprises in continuous operation, and do not plan or do not need to carry out any liquidation, significantly reduce their operational scale or carry out transactions notwithstanding the unfavorable conditions they face.

Article 51 As for the financial assets or financial liabilities for which there is an active market, the quoted prices in the active market shall be used to determine the fair values thereof. The quoted prices in the active market refer to the prices, which are easily available from the stock exchanges, brokers, industry associations, pricing service institutions, etc., at a fixed term and which represent the prices at which actually occurred market transactions are made under fair conditions.

1. In the active market, the quoted prices of an enterprise for the financial assets it holds or the financial liabilities it plans to assume shall be the present actual offer, while the quoted prices of an enterprise for the financial assets it plans to acquire or the financial liabilities it has assumed shall be the available charge.
2. Where an enterprise holds the assets or liabilities that can be used to counteract the market risks, it may adopt the middle price of the market to determine the fair value of the positions that can counteract the risks of the market; meanwhile, the offer or charge shall be the basis for determining the fair value of net exposure.
3. Where there is no available offer or charge for a financial asset or financial liability, but there is no significant change to the economic environment after the latest transaction day, the enterprise shall adopt the market quoted price of the latest transaction to determine the fair value of the said financial asset or financial liability. Where there is any significant change to the economic

environment after the latest transaction day, the enterprise concerned shall adjust its market quoted price of the latest transaction by referring to the available prices or interest rates of similar financial assets or financial liabilities so as to determine the fair value of the said financial asset or financial liability. Where the enterprise has adequate evidences to prove that the market quoted price of the latest transaction is not a fair value, it shall make appropriate adjustment to the market quoted price of the latest transaction so as to determine the fair value of the said financial asset or financial liability.
4. The fair value of a combination of financial instruments shall be determined according to both the number of the single financial instruments within the combination and the unit quoted price of the market.
5. The fair value of a current deposit shall not be lower than the amount the depositor shall pay when it becomes drawable. The fair value of a deposit at notice shall not be lower than the current value of the payable amount as of the first day it becomes drawable upon the request of the depositor for draw.

Article 52 Where there is no active market for a financial instrument, the enterprise concerned shall adopt value appraisal techniques to determine its fair value. The result obtained by adopting value appraisal techniques shall be able to reflect the transaction prices that may be adopted in fair dealings on the value appraisal day. The value appraisal techniques mainly include the prices adopted by the parties, who are familiar with the condition, in the latest market transaction upon their own free will, the current fair value obtained by referring to other financial instruments of the same essential nature, the cash flow capitalization method, and the option pricing model. To determine the fair value of a financial asset, an enterprise shall choose those value appraisal techniques which are generally acknowledged by market participants and have been proved as reliable by past actual transaction prices of the market:

1. To determine the fair value of a financial asset by adopting value appraisal techniques, one shall adopt, if possible, all the market parameters that are taken into account by market participants in pricing financial instruments, including the risk-free interest rates, credit risks, foreign exchange rates, commodity prices, stock prices or stock indexes, the future fluctuation rate of financial instrument prices, risks of repayment ahead of schedule, and the service costs of financial assets or financial liabilities, and try its best to avoid adopting those parameters that relate to particular enterprises.
2. An enterprise shall regularly use the open transaction prices of the financial instruments that have never been revised or reorganized to rectify the value appraisal techniques it employs and test the effectiveness of the said value appraisal techniques.
3. The transaction price of a financial instrument shall be the best evidence for initially recognizing the fair value thereof. However, where there is any objective evidence showing that it is more fair to adopt the open transaction price of identical financial instrument or it is more fair to adopt the result determined by employing the value appraisal techniques that only take open

market parameters into account, it shall not take the transaction price as the fair value for its initial recognition. Instead, it shall employ a more fair transaction price or the value appraisal result to determine the fair value.

Article 53 As for the financial assets initially obtained or produced at source and the financial liabilities assumed, the fair value thereof shall be determined on the basis of the transaction price of the market. The fair value of a liability instrument shall be determined on the basis of the market situation of the day when it is acquired or issued and the current market situation, or the current market interest rates of other similar liability instruments (such as having a similar remaining period, mode of cash flow, pricing currency, credit risks, basis of guarantee and interest rate). Where the credit risks of the debtor and the applicable credit risk agios remain unchanged after the issuance of the liability instrument, the benchmark interest rate may be adopted to estimate the interest rate of the current market so as to determine the fair value of the liability instrument. If the credit risks of the debtor and the corresponding risk agios have undergone any change after the issuance of the liability instrument, the current prices or interest rates of similar liability instruments shall be referred to and the adjustment to the differences between different financial instruments shall be taken into consideration in the determination of the fair value of the liability instrument.

Article 54 Where an enterprise adopts the method of future cash flow capitalization to determine the fair value of a financial instrument, it shall use the market returns ratio of other financial instruments with essentially the same contractual stipulations and features as the rate of capitalization. The stipulations and features of a financial instrument shall include the credit quality of the financial instrument itself, the remaining period for calculating the interest at a fixed interest rate as described in the contract, the remaining period for repaying the principal, and the currency used at the time of payment . Where there is little difference between the current value of the short-term accounts receivable and accounts payable whose interest rate has not been indicated and the actual transaction price, it may be measured at the actual transaction price.

Article 55 As for the equity instrument investments for which there is no quoted price in the active market and the derivative instruments which are connected with the said equity instrument and shall be settled by delivering the said equity instrument, the satisfaction of any of the following circumstances will mean that the fair value thereof can be reliably measured:

1. Where there is a very small range for the variation of the reasonable fair value estimate of the said financial instrument;
2. Where, within the range of variation of the said financial instrument, the various probabilities adopted to determine the estimate of the fair values thereof can be reasonably determined.

26.8 Chapter VIII: Definition of Financial Assets, Financial Liabilities, and Equity Instruments

Article 56 The “financial assets” refers to the following assets of an enterprise:

1. cash;
2. the equity instruments of other entities it holds;
3. the cash it charged from other entities or the contractual rights to other financial assets it holds;
4. the contractual rights it has obtained through the exchange of financial assets or financial liabilities with other entities under potentially favorable conditions;
5. the contractual rights to non-derivative instruments which must be settled or may be settled by the enterprise with its own equity instruments in the future, whereby the enterprise will receive an unfixed amount of equity instruments of its own according to the said contract;
6. the contractual rights to non-derivative instruments which must be settled or may be settled by the enterprise with its own equity instruments in the future, excluding the contractual rights to the derivative instruments for which the enterprise will exchange for a fixed amount of its own equity instruments with a fixed amount of cash or any other type of financial assets. Particularly, the enterprise’s own equity instruments shall not include the contracts which are the basis for the enterprise to charge or pay the equity instruments of its own.

Article 57 The “financial liabilities” refers to the following liabilities of an enterprise:

1. the contractual obligations to deliver cash or other financial assets to any other entity;
2. the contractual obligations to exchange with other entity financial assets or financial liabilities under potentially unfavorable conditions;
3. the contractual obligations to non-derivative instruments which must be settled or may be settled by the enterprise with its own equity instruments in the future, whereby the enterprise will deliver an unfixed amount of equity instruments of its own according to the said contract;
4. the contractual obligations to non-derivative instruments which must be settled or may be settled by the enterprise with its own equity instruments in the future, excluding the contractual obligations to the derivative instruments for which the enterprise will exchange for a fixed amount of its own equity instruments with a fixed amount of cash or any other type of financial assets. Particularly, the enterprise’s own equity instruments shall not include the contracts that are the basis for the enterprise to charge or pay the equity instruments of its own.

Article 58 The “equity instruments” refers to the contracts which can prove that a certain enterprise holds the surplus equities of the assets after the deduction of all the debts.

26.9 Comments

ASBE N. 22 applies for the major part of all financial instruments. The following types of items are recognized as financial assets: cash; equity instruments of another entity; contractual rights; and contracts that will or may be settled in the entity's own equity instruments. This standard covers the recognition and measurement of financial instruments. It will potentially affect all enterprises, not only financial institutions. The new "investment" standard deals with all financial instruments, including equity and debt securities, payables, receivables, derivatives, cash/bank deposits, convertible bonds, and preference shares. PRC GAAP only covered investment in debt and equity securities.

Particular attention is devoted to derivatives. A derivative instrument is defined as a financial instrument or other contract within the scope of this Standard, embedding all of the following characteristics: (1) Its value changes in response to the change in a specified underlying instrument (interest rate, financial instrument price, commodity price, foreign exchange rate, index of prices or rates, credit rating or credit index, or other variables, provided in the case of a non-financial variable that the variable is not specific to a party from the contract); (2) it requires no initial net investment or an initial net investment that is smaller than that would be required for other types of contracts that would be expected to have a similar response to changes in market factors; and (3) it is settled at a future date.

New categories of financial instruments are introduced: financial assets (loans and receivables, held-to-maturity investments, financial assets measured at fair value through profit or loss, and available-for-sale investments) and financial liabilities (financial liabilities at fair value through profit or loss and other financial liabilities measured at amortized cost using the effective interest method). Finally, it is disposed for both financial instruments and derivatives to be recognized at fair value.

ASBE No. 22 completely follows the general principles under comparable IAS 39. If an issuer of financial guarantee contracts has previously asserted explicitly that it regards such contracts as insurance contracts and has used accounting applicable to insurance contracts, the issuer may elect to apply either IAS 39 Insurance Contracts to such financial guarantee contracts. The issuer may make that election contract by contract, but the election for each contract is irrevocable. Accounting by the holder is excluded from the scope of this standard (unless the contract is a reinsurance contract).

It is worth to recall how loan commitments are outside the scope of ASBE 22, if they cannot be settled net in cash or another financial instrument, they are not designated as financial liabilities at fair value through profit or loss, and the entity does not have a past practice of selling the loans that resulted from the commitment shortly after origination. An issuer of a commitment to provide a loan at a below-market interest rate is required initially to recognize the commitment at its fair value; subsequently, the issuer will remeasure it at the higher of (a) the amount recognized and (b) the amount initially recognized less, where appropriate, cumulative amortization.

Some contracts that themselves are not financial instruments may nonetheless have financial instruments embedded in them. For example, a contract to purchase a commodity at a fixed price for delivery at a future date has embedded in it a derivative that is indexed to the price of the commodity.

An embedded derivative is a feature within a contract, such that the cash flows associated with that feature behave in a similar fashion to a stand-alone derivative. In the same way that derivatives must be accounted for at fair value on the balance sheet with changes recognized in the income statement, so must some embedded derivatives. ASBE 22 requires that an embedded derivative be separated from its host contract and accounted for as a derivative when the economic risks and characteristics of the embedded derivative are not closely related to those of the host contract. If an embedded derivative is separated, the host contract is accounted for under the appropriate standard. Held-to-maturity investments are non-derivative financial assets with fixed or determinable payments that an entity intends and is able to hold to maturity and that do not meet the definition of loans and receivables and are not designated on initial recognition as assets at fair value through profit or loss or as available for sale. Held-to-maturity investments are measured at amortized cost. If an entity sells a held-to-maturity investment other than in insignificant amounts or as a consequence of a non-recurring, isolated event beyond its control that could not be reasonably anticipated, all of its other held-to-maturity investments must be reclassified as available-for-sale for the current and next two financial reporting years. Held-to-maturity investments are measured at amortized cost.

A financial liability should be removed from the balance sheet when, and only when, it is extinguished, that is, when the obligation specified in the contract is either discharged or canceled or expires. Where there has been an exchange between an existing borrower and lender of debt instruments with substantially different terms, or there has been a substantial modification of the terms of an existing financial liability, this transaction is accounted for as an extinguishment of the original financial liability and the recognition of a new financial liability. A gain or loss from extinguishment of the original financial liability is recognized in profit or loss.

A financial asset or group of assets is impaired, and impairment losses are recognized, only if there is objective evidence as a result of one or more events that occurred after the initial recognition of the asset. An entity is required to assess at each balance sheet date whether there is any objective evidence of impairment. If any such evidence exists, the entity is required to do a detailed impairment calculation to determine whether an impairment loss should be recognized. The amount of the loss is measured as the difference between the asset's carrying amount and the present value of estimated cash flows discounted at the financial asset's original effective interest rate.

Assets that are individually assessed and for which no impairment exists are grouped with financial assets with similar credit risk statistics and collectively assessed for impairment.

If, in a subsequent period, the amount of the impairment loss relating to a financial asset carried at amortized cost or a debt instrument carried as available-for-sale decreases due to an event occurring after the impairment was originally recognized, the previously recognized impairment loss is reversed through profit or loss. Impairments relating to investments in available-for-sale equity instruments are not reversed through profit or loss.

26.10 Examples

On December 15, Company X purchases securities in the Shenzhen Stock Exchange intended to be sold to grasp expected capital gains. In particular, Company X acquires 200,000 ordinary shares of Company Y at 3.50 CNY per share and 100,000 shares of Company Z at 5.00 CNY per share. Assuming that no transaction costs are borne, Company X shall record its investment in ordinary shares for 1,200,000 CNY (3.5 × 200,000 + 5.00 × 100,000).

At year-end date, it is found that per share price for Company Y is 4.20 CNY, whereas per share price for Company Z is 4.50 CNY. The value of the investment in ordinary shares to be recorded is 1,290,000 CNY (4.20 × 200,000 + 4.50 × 100,000).

Accordingly, Company X shall record on its year-end income statement a positive income item for 90,000 CNY.

Chapter 27
Accounting Standards for Business Enterprises No. 23—Transfer of Financial Assets

27.1 Chapter I: General Provisions

Article 1 These Standards are formulated in accordance with the Accounting Standards for Enterprises—Basic Standards for the purpose of regulating the recognition and measurement of the transfer of financial assets (including a single or a group of similar financial assets).

Article 2 The term "transfer of a financial asset" refers to an enterprise's (the transferor's) transferring or delivering a financial asset to a party other than the issuer of the financial asset (the transferee).

Article 3 If the enterprise has the control right over the transferee of the financial asset, it shall not only apply these Standards to its financial statements, but also include the transferee into its scope of consolidated financial statements according to the Accounting Standards for Enterprises No. 33—Consolidated Financial Statements.

27.2 Chapter II: Recognition of Transfer of Financial Assets

Article 4 The transfer of financial asset by an enterprise includes two circumstances as follows:

1. The enterprise transfers the right to another party for receiving the cash flow of the financial asset; and
2. The enterprise transfers the financial asset to another party, but maintains the right to receive the cash flow of the financial asset and undertakes the obligation to pay the cash flow it receives to the final recipient, and meets the conditions as follows at the same time:

L. Riccardi, *China Accounting Standards*,
DOI 10.1007/978-981-10-0006-5_27

(a) The enterprise is not obliged to make any payment to the final recipient until it receives the cash flow which is equivalent to the financial asset. For any short-term payment made by the enterprise on behalf of others, if the enterprise has the right to recover the full amount of the payment and charge interests according to the market bank loan interest rate of the same period, the conditions shall be deemed to have been satisfied.
(b) In accordance with the contractual stipulations, the enterprise cannot sell the financial asset or use it as a guaranty, but it may use it as a guarantee for paying the cash flow to the final recipient.
(c) The enterprise is obliged to pay the cash flow it receives to the final recipient in a timely manner.

The enterprise has no right to make a reinvestment with the cash flow, but in accordance with the contractual stipulations, it may make investment with cash or cash equivalent by using the cash flow it receives during the interval of between two consecutive payments.

If the enterprise makes a reinvestment in accordance with the contractual stipulations, it shall pay the proceeds by investment to the final recipient in accordance with the contractual stipulations.

Article 5 An enterprise shall differentiate the transfer of a financial asset into the entire transfer and the partial transfer of financial assets and deal with them, respectively, according to these Standards.

Article 6 The partial transfer of financial asset includes the circumstances as follows:

1. To transfer the specific or identifiable portion of the cash flow arising from the financial asset, for example, the enterprise transfers the receivable interests of a group of similar loans, etc.;
2. To transfer a certain proportion of the total cash flow arising from the financial asset, for example, the enterprise transfers a certain proportion of the principal and receivable interests of a group of similar loans, etc.; and
3. To transfer a certain proportion of the specific or identifiable portion of the cash flow arising from the financial asset, for example, the enterprise transfers a certain portion of the receivable interests of a group of the similar loans, etc.

Article 7 Where an enterprise has transferred nearly all of the risks and rewards related to the ownership of the financial asset to the transferee, it shall stop recognizing the financial asset. If it retained nearly all of the risks and rewards related to the ownership of the financial asset, it shall not stop recognizing the financial asset. The expression "to stop recognizing" shall refer to a financial asset or financial liability to be written off from the account and balance sheet of the enterprise.

Article 8 When an enterprise makes a judgment about whether nearly all of the risks and rewards related to the ownership of a financial asset are transferred to the transferee, it shall compare the pre- and post-transfer risks it faces due to the change of the net present value of the future cash flow of the financial asset and the time distribution. If the risks that the enterprise faces have changed substantially resulting from the transfer of a financial asset, it shows that the enterprise has transferred nearly all of the risks and rewards related to the ownership of financial asset to the transferee, for example, the sale of a financial asset without any additional term of guarantee. If the risks that the enterprise faces have not changed substantially resulting from the transfer of a financial asset, it shows that the enterprise still retains all the risks and rewards related to the ownership of the financial asset, for example, it transfers an entire loan and undertakes a full amount of compensation for the possible credit losses of the loan. Where an enterprise requires to judge, by calculation, whether it has transferred nearly all of the risks and rewards related to the ownership of financial asset to the transferee, when it calculates the net present value of the future cash flow of the financial asset, it shall take into consideration all the reasonable and possible fluctuating of the cash flow and shall adopt an appropriate present market interest rate as the discount rate.

Article 9 Where an enterprise does not transfer or retain nearly all of the risks and rewards related to the ownership of a financial asset (that is to say, it is not under a circumstance as mentioned in *Article 7* of these Standards), it shall deal with it according to the circumstances as follows, respectively:

1. If it gives up its control over the financial asset, it shall stop recognizing the financial asset;
2. If it does not give up its control over the financial asset, it shall, according to the extent of its continuous involvement in the transferred financial asset, recognize the related financial asset and recognize the relevant liability accordingly. The term "continuous involvement in the transferred financial asset" shall refer to the risk level that the enterprise faces resulting from the change of the value of the financial asset.

Article 10 When an enterprise judges whether its control over the transferred financial asset has been given up, the enterprise shall pay more attention to the transferee's actual ability of selling the financial asset. If the transferee is able to independently sell the entire transferred financial asset to a third party without any relationship with it as an associated party and there is no additional condition to limit the sale, it shows that the enterprise has given up its control over the financial asset.

Article 11 To judge whether the transfer of a financial asset can satisfy the conditions as prescribed in these Standards for stopping the recognition of a financial asset, the enterprise shall pay more attention to the essentials of the transfer of the financial asset.

1. For the sale of a financial asset with a repurchase agreement, if the asset to be repurchased by the transferor is identical with or substantially identical with the sold financial asset, and if the repurchase price is fixed or is the original sales price plus a reasonable return, the sold financial asset shall not be stopped to recognize, for example, selling any bonds through a buyout repo or a pledged repo transaction.

2. After the transfer of a financial asset, if the transferor only retains the priority to repurchase the right of financial asset at its fair value (when the transferee sells the financial asset), it shall stop recognizing the transferred financial asset.
3. For the transfer of a financial asset in which the secondary equitics are retained or a credit guaranty is given for upgrading the level of credit, if the transferor only retains partial (not nearly all of) the risks and rewards related to the ownership of the transferred financial asset and may control the transferred financial asset, it shall recognize the relevant asset and liability according to the extent of its continuous involvement in the transferred financial asset.

27.3 Chapter III: Measurement of Transfer of Financial Assets

Article 12 If the transfer of an entire financial asset satisfies the conditions for stopping recognition, the difference between the amounts of the following two items shall be recorded in the profits and losses of the current period:

1. The book value of the transferred financial asset;
2. The sum of consideration received from the transfer and the accumulative amount of the changes of the fair value originally recorded in the owner's equities (in the event that the financial asset involved in the transfer is a financial asset available for sale).

Where an enterprise obtains a new financial asset or undertakes a new financial liability due to the transfer of a financial asset, it shall, on the date of transfer, recognize the financial asset or liability according to its fair value (including the call option, put option, guaranteed liability, future contract, and interchange) and shall treat the net amount as an integral part of the aforesaid consideration through deducting the financial liability from the financial asset. Where an enterprise concludes a service contract with the transferee of a financial asset on providing relevant services (including receiving cash flow of the financial asset and delivering the received cash flow to the fund preservation institution as designated), it shall recognize a service asset or liability based on the service contract. The service liability shall be subject to the initial measurement according to its fair value and shall be treated as an integrate part of the aforesaid consideration.

Article 13 If the transfer of partial financial asset satisfies the conditions to stop the recognition, the entire book value of the transferred financial asset shall, between the portion whose recognition has been stopped and the portion whose recognition has not been stopped (under such circumstance, the service asset retained shall be deemed as a portion of financial asset whose recognition has not been stopped), be apportioned according to their respective relative fair value, and the difference between the amounts of the following two items shall be included into the profits and losses of the current period:

1. The book value of the portion whose recognition has been stopped;
2. The sum of consideration of the portion whose recognition has been stopped and the portion of the accumulative amount of the changes in the fair value originally recorded in the owner's equities which corresponds to the portion whose recognition has been stopped (in the event that the financial asset involved in the transfer is a financial asset available for sale). The portion of the accumulative amount of changes in the fair value originally recorded in the owner's equities which corresponds to the portion whose recognition has been stopped shall be recognized after the apportionment of the accumulative amount according to the relative fair values of the portion of financial asset whose recognition has been stopped and the portion of financial asset whose recognition has not been stopped.

Article 14 If the entire book value of the transferred financial asset is apportioned according to the relative fair values between the portion whose recognition has been stopped and the portion whose recognition has not been stopped in accordance with the provision of *Article 13* of these Standards, the fair value of the portion whose recognition has not been stopped shall be determined according to the following provisions:

1. It shall be determined based on the latest actual transaction price if the enterprise has ever sold any financial asset similar to the portion whose recognition has not been stopped, or has ever conducted any other market transaction related to the portion whose recognition has not been stopped;
2. If no quotation for the portion whose recognition has not been stopped is available in the active market and if there is no actual transaction price relating to it, it shall be determined based on the residual amount by deducting the consideration of the portion whose recognition has been stopped from the entire fair value of the transferred financial asset. If the entire fair value of the financial asset is really difficult to determine reasonably, it shall be determined based on the residual amount deducting the consideration of the portion whose recognition has been stopped from the entire book value of the financial asset.

Article 15 If an enterprise still retains nearly all of the risks and rewards related to the ownership of the transferred financial asset, it shall continue to recognize the entire financial asset to be transferred and shall recognize the consideration it receives as a financial liability. The financial asset shall not be used to offset the relevant financial liabilities it has recognized. In the subsequent accounting periods, the enterprise shall continue to recognize the income generated by the financial asset and the expenses generated by the financial liability. If the transferred financial asset is measured at the amortized cost, the relevant liability it has recognized shall not be designated as a financial liability which is measured at its fair value and the changes are recorded in the profits and losses of the current period.

Article 16 If an enterprise does not transfer or retain nearly all of the risks and rewards related to the ownership of the financial asset, and does not waive its control over the financial asset, the relevant asset and liability it recognizes according to these Standards shall fully reflect the rights it retains and the obligations it undertakes.

Article 17 If the enterprise is continuously involved in the transferred financial asset by way of providing a financial guarantee, it shall, on the date of transfer, recognize the assets formed by its continuous involvement based on the book value of the financial asset and the amount of financial guarantee, whichever is lower. In the meanwhile, it shall, based on the sum of amount of financial guarantee and the fair value of the financial guaranty contract (the charge for providing the guarantee), recognize the liability formed by its continuous involvement. The amount of financial guarantee shall refer to the highest amount of repayment to be demanded among the considerations the enterprise receives. In the subsequent accounting periods, the initially recognized amount of the financial guarantee contract shall be amortized in accordance with the time proportion within the period of the financial guarantee contract and shall be recognized as income for each period. The book value of the asset formed by the guarantee shall be conducted a devalue test on the balance sheet date.

Article 18 If an enterprise fails to satisfy the conditions to stop the recognition because it sells a put option or holds a call option, and if it measures the financial asset at the amortized cost, it shall recognize the liability formed by its continuous involvement in light of the consideration it receives on the date of transfer. The difference between the amount of the amortized cost of the transferred financial asset on the maturity date of the option and the amount of the initially recognized liability formed by its continuous involvement shall be amortized through the actual interest rate method and recorded into the profits and losses of the current period. In the meanwhile, an adjustment shall be made to the book value of the liability formed by its continuous involvement. For the relevant option exercise, the difference between the book value of the liability formed by its continuous involvement and the exercise price of option shall, when exercising the option, be recorded in the profits and losses of the current period.

Article 19 If an enterprise fails to satisfy the conditions to stop the recognition because it holds a call option, and if it measures the financial asset according to its fair value, it shall, on the date of transfer, recognize the transferred financial asset according to its fair value and shall, in light of the following provisions, simultaneously measure the liability formed by its continuous involvement: (1) If the option is an in-the-money option or at-the-money option, the liability formed by its continuous involvement shall be measured in accordance with the residual amount of the option exercise price minus the time value of the option; and (2) if the option is an out-of-the-money option, the liability formed by its continuous involvement shall be measured in accordance with the residual value of the fair value of the transferred financial asset minus the time value of the option.

Article 20 If an enterprise fails to satisfy the conditions to stop the recognition because it sells a put option and if it measures the financial asset according to its fair value, it shall, on the date of transfer, recognize the asset formed by its continuous involvement in accordance with the fair value of the financial asset and the option exercise price, whichever is lower. At the same time, it shall recognize the liability formed by its continuous involvement in accordance with the sum of option exercise price and the time value.

Article 21 If an enterprise fails to satisfy the conditions to stop the recognition for transferred financial asset because it sells a put option and purchases a call option (namely up-and-down options) and if it measures the financial asset according to its fair value, it shall, on the date of transfer, still recognize the transferred financial asset according to its fair value. At the same time, it shall measure the liability formed by its continuous involvement in accordance with the following provisions: (1) If the call option is an in-the-money option or at-the-money option, the liability formed by its continuous involvement shall be measured in accordance with the residual amount of the sum of option exercise price and the fair value of the put option minus the time value of the call option; and (2) if the call option is an out-of-the-money option, the liability formed by its continuous involvement shall be measured in accordance with the residual value of the sum of total fair value of the transferred financial asset and the fair value of the put option minus the time value of the call option.

Article 22 An enterprise shall recognize the relevant assets formed by its continuous involvement in the transferred financial assets as the relevant incomes and shall recognize the relevant liabilities formed by its continuous involvement therein as the relevant expenses. The relevant assets and liabilities so formed by its continuous involvement shall not be offset each other, and their subsequent measurement shall be governed by the Accounting Standards for Enterprises No. 22—Recognition and Measurement of Financial Instruments.

Article 23 An enterprise's continuous involvement in merely a portion of its transferred financial asset shall be treated according to the *Article 13* of these Standards.

Article 24 Where an enterprise provides the transferee of a financial asset with a non-cash guaranty (such as a liability instrument or equity instrument investment), this enterprise and the transferee shall make treatments in accordance with the provisions as follows:

1. If the transferee has the right to sell the guaranty or reuse it as a guaranty in accordance with the contract or practices, the enterprise shall put this non-cash guaranty into a new category in the balance sheet and present it separately;
2. If the transferee has sold this guaranty, the transferee shall recognize the liability according to fair value for the obligation to return the guaranty;
3. If the enterprise defaults and loses the right to redeem the guaranty, it shall stop recognizing the guaranty, and the transferee shall recognize the guaranty as an asset according to its fair value. If the transferee has sold the guaranty, it shall stop recognizing the obligation to return it; and
4. In a circumstance other than that as described in Item (3), the enterprise shall continue recognizing the guaranty as an asset.

27.4 Comments

ASBE No. 23 formalizes the requirements of "securitization of credit assets" issued by Ministry of Finance. Additionally, along with risks and rewards' tests, it is disposed also for those circumstances in which the enterprise has neither retained nor transferred substantially all of the risks and rewards of the assets. In such circumstances, derecognition is appropriate only if the enterprise does not control the asset. If the enterprise has retained control of the asset, then it continues to recognize the asset to the extent to which it has a continuing involvement in it.

ASBE No. 23 does not substantially differ from referred IAS 39 in that the regular way purchase or sale of financial assets is recognized and derecognized using either trade date or settlement date accounting. The method used is to be applied consistently for all purchases and sales of financial assets that belong to the same category of financial assets as defined in IAS 39 (note that for this purpose, assets held for trading form a different category from assets designated at fair value through profit or loss). The choice of method is an accounting policy.

Once an entity has determined that the asset has been transferred, it then determines whether or not it has transferred substantially all of the risks and rewards of ownership of the asset. If substantially all the risks and rewards have been transferred, the asset is derecognized. If substantially all the risks and rewards have been retained, derecognition of the asset is precluded.

If the entity has neither retained nor transferred substantially all of the risks and rewards of the asset, then the entity must assess whether it has relinquished control of the asset or not. If the entity does not control the asset, then derecognition is appropriate; however, if the entity has retained control of the asset, then the entity continues to recognize the asset to the extent to which it has a continuing involvement in the asset.

ASBE 23 requires that all financial assets and all financial liabilities be recognized on the balance sheet. That includes all derivatives. Historically, in many parts of the world, derivatives have not been recognized on company balance sheets. The argument has been that at the time the derivative contract was entered into, there was no amount of cash or other assets paid. Zero cost justified non-recognition, notwithstanding that as time passes and the value of the underlying variable (rate, price, or index) changes, the derivative has a positive (asset) or negative (liability) value.

27.5 Examples

On the 15 November in the current financial year, Company X sells its investment in Company Y's securities recorded at a carrying amount of 4,500,000 CNY, to Company Z for a total amount of 5,150,000 CNY.

Accordingly, Company X shall recognize the operation described above with total proceeds of 5,150,000 CNY in cash or cash equivalents, the derecognition of investment in securities for 4,500,000 CNY, and a capital gain of 650,000 CNY.

Now, let us assume Company X acquired the above shares intended for a long-term investment in Company Y two years ago for a total amount of 3,400,000 CNY. The fair values on respective balance sheet dates were 3,800,000 CNY and 4,500,000 CNY. Since long-term investment, Company X has recognized in previous years an overall capital surplus of 1,100,000 CNY (4,500,000–3,400,000) on occurred capital gains. On date of disposal, Company X shall record a capital gain of 650,000 CNY, while the capital surplus of 110,000 CNY is converted into a gain on disposal of long-term investment.

Chapter 28
Accounting Standards for Business Enterprises No. 24—Hedging

28.1 Chapter I: General Principles

Article 1 These Standards are formulated in accordance with the Accounting Standards for Enterprises—Basic Standards for the purpose of regulating the recognition and measurement of the hedging.

Article 2 The term "hedging" refers to one or more hedging instruments which are designated by an enterprise for avoiding the risks of foreign exchange, interest rate, commodity price, stock price, credit, etc., and which is expected to make the changes in fair value or cash flow of hedging instrument(s) to offset all or part of the changes in the fair value or cash flow of the hedged item.

Article 3 Hedging is classified into fair value hedging, cash flow hedging, and net investment hedging in an overseas operation.

1. A fair value hedging refers to a hedging of the risk to changes in the fair value of a recognized asset or liability or a previously unrecognized firm commitment, or to changes in the identifiable portion of the fair value of a recognized asset or liability or a previously unrecognized firm commitment. Such changes in value are attributable to a particular risk and could affect enterprise' profit or loss.
2. A cash flow hedging refers to a hedging of the risk to changes in cash flow. Such changes in cash flow are attributable to a particular risk related to a recognized asset or liability or a highly probable forecast transaction and could affect enterprise' profit or loss.
3. A net investment hedging in an overseas operation refers to hedging of the foreign exchange risk arising from net investment in an overseas operation. The "net investment in an overseas operation" refers to an enterprise' equity of rights and interests in the net assets in an overseas operation.

Article 4 For a hedging which satisfies the conditions as prescribed in Chapter III of these Standards, the enterprise may deal with it through the hedging accounting method. The "hedging accounting method" shall refer to a method to record the

L. Riccardi, *China Accounting Standards*,
DOI 10.1007/978-981-10-0006-5_28

result of offsetting the hedging instrument and the changes of the fair value of the hedged item.

28.2 Chapter II: Hedging Instruments and Hedged Items

Article 5 The term "hedging instrument" shall refer to a derivative instrument which is designated by an enterprise for hedging and by which it is expected that changes in its fair value or cash flow can offset the changes in fair value or cash flow of the hedged item. For a hedging of foreign exchange risk, a non-derivative financial asset or non-derivative financial liability may be used as a hedging instrument.

Article 6 To establish the hedging relationship, an enterprise shall designate all or certain proportion of the hedging instruments (excluding a certain time period within the residual time limit of the hedging instrument), but with the exception of the following circumstances:

1. For an option, the enterprise may separate the intrinsic value from the time value of the option and merely designate the option as a hedging instrument based on the changes of its intrinsic value; and
2. For a forward contract, the enterprise may separate the interest from the spot price of a forward contract and merely designate the forward contract as a hedging instrument based on the changes of spot price.

Article 7 Generally an enterprise may designate a single derivative instrument as a hedging for one kind of risk, but if the following conditions are met at the same time, it may designate a single derivative instrument as a hedging for one or more kinds of risks:

1. All risks to be hedged are clear and identifiable;
2. The effectiveness of hedging may be proved; and
3. It can insure that there is a specific specifying relationship between the derivative instrument and the different risk positions.

The "effectiveness of hedging" shall refer to the extent that the changes in the fair value or cash flow of a hedging instrument may offset the changes resulted from the hedging risks in the fair value or cash flow of a hedged item.

Article 8 An enterprise may designate a combination of two or more derivative instruments or a certain proportion of such a combination as a hedging instrument. For a foreign exchange hedging, the enterprise may designate a combination of two or more non-derivative instruments or a certain proportion of such a combination, or a combination of derivative instrument(s) and non-derivative instrument(s) or a certain proportion of such a combination as a hedging instrument. For a collar option, or for an option composed of an issued option and a purchased option, if its essential is equivalent to an option issued by the enterprise (that is to say, the enterprise charges for the net option), the enterprise cannot designate it as a hedging instrument.

Article 9 The "hedged item" shall refer to the following items which make an enterprise faced to changes in fair value or cash flow and are designated as the hedged objectives:

1. A single recognized asset, liability, firm commitment, highly probable forecast transaction, or a net investment in an overseas operation;
2. A group of recognized assets, liabilities, firm commitments, highly probable forecast transactions, or net investments in overseas operations with similar risk characteristics;
3. A portion of the portfolio of financial assets or financial liabilities that share the risk of interest rate of the same hedged (only applicable to a portfolio of hedging in the fair value of interest rate risk). The "firm commitment" shall refer to an agreement with legal control force regarding the exchange of a particular number of resources at the stipulated price on a specific future date or in a specific future period. The "forecast transaction" shall refer to a transaction for which no commitment is made, but which is expected to occur.

Article 10 If the hedged risk is a credit risk or foreign exchange risk, the held-to-maturity investment may be designated a hedged item. If the hedged risk is an interest rate risk or risk of repayment ahead of the schedule, the held-to-maturity investment shall not be designated as a hedged item.

Article 11 If the exchange gain or loss of any monetary item formed by an intra-group transaction of an enterprise is unable to be fully offset in the consolidated statements, the foreign exchange risk of this monetary item may be designated as a hedged item in the consolidated financial statements. For a highly probable forecast intra-group transaction of an enterprise, if its price is denominated in a currency other than the functional currency of the subject entering into that transaction (that is to say, its price is denominated in an overseas currency) and if the relevant foreign exchange risk will affect consolidated financial statements, such foreign exchange risk may be designated as a hedged item in the consolidated financial statements.

Article 12 For a portion of the risk relating to the cash flow or fair value of a financial liabilities or financial asset, if the effectiveness of hedging may be measured, the enterprise may, based on the risk, designate financial asset or financial liability as a hedged item.

Article 13 In the matter of a hedging in fair value of the interest rate risk of a portfolio of financial assets or financial liabilities, an asset or liability denominated in a certain currency (such as RMB, US dollar, or Euro dollar) may be designated as a hedged item.

Article 14 An enterprise may designate all of the cash flows of a financial asset or financial liability as a hedged item. However, if only a portion of the cash flows of a financial asset or financial liability is designated as a hedged item, the designated portion shall be less than the total amount of the cash flows of the financial asset or financial liability.

Article 15 Where a non-financial asset or non-financial liability is designated as a hedged item, the hedged risk shall be all risks or foreign exchange risks pertinent to this non-financial asset or non-financial liability.

Article 16 With regard to a hedging by the portfolio of assets or liabilities with similar risk characteristics, each single asset or liability among the portfolio shall undertake the hedged risk simultaneously, and the changes in fair value of each single asset or liability in the portfolio resulted from the hedged risk shall, by and large, be expected in proportion to the holistic changes in the fair value of the portfolio resulted from the hedged risk.

28.3 Chapter III: Recognition and Measurement of Hedging

Article 17 Where a fair value hedging, cash flow hedging, or a hedging of net investment in an overseas operation satisfies the following conditions simultaneously, it may be dealt with through the hedging accounting method as prescribed in these Standards:

1. At the commencement of the hedging, the enterprise shall specify the hedging relationship formally (namely the relationship between the hedging instrument and the hedged item) and prepare a formal written document on the hedging relationship, risk management objectives, and the strategies of hedging. This document shall at least specify the contents of hedging instrument, the hedged item, the nature of the hedged risk and the method for the effectiveness assessment of the hedging, etc. The hedging shall be relevant to the designated specific identifiable risk and will ultimately affect the profits and losses of the enterprise.
2. The hedging expectation is highly efficient and meets the risk management strategy, which is confirmed for the hedging relationship by enterprise at the very beginning.
3. For a cash flow hedging of forecast transaction, the forecast transaction shall be likely to occur and shall make the enterprise faced to the risk of changes in cash flow, which will ultimately affect the profits and losses.
4. The effectiveness of hedging can be reliably measured.
5. An enterprise shall continuously evaluate the effectiveness of hedging and ensure that this hedging is highly effective in accounting period in which the hedging relationship is specified.

Article 18 If a hedging satisfies the following conditions simultaneously, the enterprise shall recognize it as being highly efficient:

1. At the beginning and in subsequent periods of a hedging, this hedging expectation shall be highly effective in offsetting the changes in the fair value or cash flows caused by the hedged risk during the specified periods;

2. The hedging's actual offset results are within a range of 80–125 %.

Article 19 An enterprise shall at least evaluate the hedging effectiveness when formulating medium-term or annual financial statements.

Article 20 For a hedging of interest rate risk, the enterprise shall, by formulating the maturity timetable of financial assets and financial liabilities, mark out the net risk of interest rate for each period and evaluate the hedging effectiveness accordingly.

Article 21 If a fair value hedging satisfies the conditions for adopting the hedging accounting method, it shall be dealt with according to the following provisions:

1. If the hedging instrument is a derivative instrument, the gain or loss from the changes in the fair value of the hedging instrument shall be recorded in the profits and losses of the current period. If the hedging instrument is a non-derivative instrument, the gain or loss on the book value of the hedging instrument resulting from changes in exchange rate shall be recorded in the profits and losses of the current period.
2. The gain or loss of the hedged item resulting from the hedged risk shall be recorded in the profits and losses of the current period and the book value of the hedged item shall be adjusted at the same time. The said provision shall also be applicable if the hedged item is an inventory of which the subsequent measurement will be made at its cost and realizable net value, whichever is lower, or a financial asset of which the subsequent value will be made at the amortized cost, or a financial asset available for sale.

Article 22 With regard to a fair value hedging for the interest rate risk of a portfolio of financial assets or financial liabilities, for satisfying the requirements of *Article 21* (2) of these Standards, the enterprise may deal with the gain or loss formed by the hedged item according to the following methods:

1. If the hedged item is an asset within the repricing period, it shall be presented as a separate item under the assets item (presenting behind the financial assets) of the balance sheet and shall be written off after the termination of recognition.
2. If the hedged item is a liability within the repricing period, it shall be presented as a separate item under the liabilities item (presenting behind the financial liabilities) of the balance sheet and shall be written off after the termination of recognition.

Article 23 Where any of the following conditions is satisfied, the enterprise shall stop making the treatments according to the *Article 21* of these Standards:

1. The hedging instrument has been mature or has been sold, or the contract is terminated or has been exercised. Where the period of hedging instrument is extended, or where a hedging instrument is replaced by another one, if the extension or replacement is an composing part of the hedging strategy as specified in the formal written document of the enterprise, the enterprise shall not deal with it as being in the case of maturity or termination of contract.

2. The hedging does not satisfy the conditions for adopting the hedging accounting method as specified in these Standards any longer.
3. The enterprise has revoked the specifying of the hedging relationship.

Article 24 If a hedged item is a financial instrument measured at the amortized cost, an adjustment which is made to the book value of the hedged item according to the *Article 21* (2) of these Standards shall, during the period from the adjustment date to the maturity date, be amortized based on the effective interest rate recalculated on the adjustment date and shall be recorded in the profits and losses of the current period. With regard to a fair value hedging of interest rate risk portfolio, the relevant items separately presented in the balance sheet shall, during the period from the adjustment date to the relevant date on which the repricing period ends, be amortized based on the effective interest rate recalculated on the adjustment date. If it is not feasible to adopt the effective interest rate method for the amortization, the straight-line method may be adopted. The amortization of the above-mentioned adjustment amounts shall be finished on the maturity date of the financial instrument. For a fair value hedging of interest rate risk portfolio, the amortization shall be finished prior to the date of end of the relevant repricing period.

Article 25 If a hedged item is an unrecognized firm commitment, the accumulative amount of the changes in the fair value of the firm commitment resulting from the hedged risk shall be recognized as an asset or liability and the related gain or loss shall be included into the profits and losses of the current period.

Article 26 For a fair value hedging of firm commitment to purchase an asset or undertake a liability, an adjustment shall, based on the accumulative amount of the changes in the fair value resulting from the hedged risks (recognized to be an asset or liability), be made to the amount of initial recognition of the asset obtained or liability undertaken due to the firm commitment.

Article 27 Where a cash flow hedging meets the conditions for adopting the hedging accounting method, it shall be dealt with in accordance with the following provisions:

1. In the profit or loss of the hedging instrument, the portion, which is attributed to the effective hedging, shall be directly recognized as the owner's equity and shall be presented as a separate item. The amount of the portion of the effective hedging shall be confirmed in accordance with the absolute amounts of the following items whichever is lower:

   (a) The accumulative profit or loss of the hedging instrument as of the commencement of hedging; or
   (b) The accumulative amount of changes in the present value of the estimated future cash flow of the hedged item as of the commencement of the hedging.

2. In the profit or loss of the hedging instrument, the portion, which is attributed to the ineffective hedging (namely the other profit or loss after deducting the portion directly recognized as the owner's equity), shall be recorded in the profit and loss of the current period.

3. If the formal written document on the risk management strategy states that a certain portion of the profit or loss of a hedging instrument, or the relevant effects on the cash flow shall be excluded when evaluate the hedging effectiveness, the profit or loss of excluded portion shall be dealt with according to the Accounting Standards for Enterprises No. 22—Recognition and Measurement of Financial Instruments. An enterprise may deal with a hedging of foreign exchange risk of firm commitment as a cash flow hedging or fair value hedging.

Article 28 If a hedged item is a forecast transaction and if the forecast transaction makes the enterprise subsequently recognize a financial asset or financial liability, the relevant profit or loss directly recognized as the owner's equity originally shall be shifted out of the same period in which this financial asset or financial liability affects the profit or loss of the enterprise and shall be recorded in the profits and losses of the current period. However, when all or partial net loss expected by the enterprise to be directly recognized in the owner's equity originally cannot be made up in the future accounting period, the portion which cannot be made up shall be shifted out and shall be recorded in profits and losses of the current period.

Article 29 If a hedged item is a forecast transaction and if the forecast transaction makes the enterprise recognized a non-financial asset or non-financial liability subsequently, the enterprise may deal with it by choosing either of the following methods:

1. The relevant profit or loss directly recognized in the owner's equity originally shall be shifted out during the same period in which this non-financial asset or non-financial liability affects the profit or loss of the enterprise and shall be recorded in the current profits and losses of the current period. However, when all or partial net loss expected by the enterprise to be directly recognized in the owner's equity originally cannot be made up in the future accounting period, the portion which cannot be made up shall be shifted out and shall be recorded in profits and losses of the current period.
2. The relevant profit or loss directly recognized in the owner's equity originally shall be shifted out and shall be recorded in the amount of the initial recognition of the non-financial asset or non-financial liability.

When the forecast transaction of a non-financial asset or non-financial liability forms a firm commitment, if the firm commitment satisfies the conditions for adopting the hedging accounting method as prescribed in these Standards, either of the above-mentioned methods shall be chose to deal with it as well. When either of the above-mentioned methods is chosen by an enterprise as the accounting policy, it shall be applied to all relevant forecast transaction hedging and shall not be changed randomly.

Article 30 With regard to a cash flow hedging without involved in *Articles 28* and *29* of these Standards, the profit or loss of the hedging instrument directly recorded in the owner's equity originally shall be shifted out at the same period, during which the profits and losses of the hedged forecast transaction are affected, and shall be recorded in the profits and losses of the current period.

Article 31 Under the following circumstances, an enterprise may not make any treatment in accordance with the provisions from *Article 27* to *30* of these Standards:

1. The hedging instrument has been mature or sold, or the contract is terminated or has been exercised. The profit or loss of the hedging instrument, which is directly recorded in the owner's equity during effective period of the hedging, shall not be shifted out, until the forecast transaction actually occurs, it shall be dealt with according to *Article 28, 29,* or *30* of these Standards. If the period of a hedging instrument is extended, or if a hedging instrument is replaced by another, and if the extension or replacement is a composing part of the hedging strategy as specified in the formal written document of the enterprise, it shall not be dealt with as being in the case of maturity or termination of contract.
2. The hedging no longer satisfies the conditions for adopting the hedging accounting methods as prescribed in these Standards. The profit or loss of the hedging instrument, which is directly recorded in the owner's equity during the effective period of the hedging, shall not be shifted out, until the forecast transaction actually occurs it shall be dealt with according to the *Article 28, 29,* or *30* of these Standards.
3. It is expected that the forecast transaction will not occur. The profit or loss of the hedging instrument, which is directly recorded in the owner's equity during the effective period of the hedging, shall be shifted out and shall be recorded in the profits and losses of the current period.
4. An enterprise revokes the designation of the hedging relationship. For a hedging of forecast transaction, the profit or loss of the hedging instrument, which is directly recorded in the owner's equity during the effective period of the hedging, shall not be shifted out until the forecast transaction actually occurs, or until it is expected that it will not occur. If the forecast transaction actually occurs, it shall be dealt with according to the *Article 28, 29,* or *30* of these Standards. If it is expected that the forecast transaction will not occur, the relevant profit or loss directly recorded in the owner's equity originally shall be shifted out and shall be recorded in the profits and losses of the current period.

Article 32 A hedging of net investment in an overseas operation shall be dealt with according to the similar to the provisions of cash flow hedging accounting:

1. In the profit or loss formed by the hedging instrument, the portion that is attributed to the effective hedging shall be recognized as the owner's equity directly and shall be presented as a separate item. When disposing an overseas operation, the profit or loss of the hedging instrument reflected by the separately presented item in the owner's equity shall be shifted out and shall be recorded in the profits and losses of the current period.

2. In the profit or loss formed by the hedging instrument, the portion that is attributed to the ineffective hedging shall be recorded in the profits and losses of the current period.

28.4 Comments

New ASBE No. 24 introduces three types of hedges: fair value hedge; cash flow hedge; and hedge of a net investment in foreign operations. Activities of hedge accounting are optional. Furthermore, to qualify for hedge accounting, an enterprise shall prove the effectiveness of the hedge at inception. On conformity to the IAS counterpart, no relevant differences can be found against the equivalent IAS 39 on Financial Instruments.

A hedging instrument is an instrument whose fair value or cash flows are expected to offset changes in the fair value or cash flows of a designated hedged item. All derivative contracts with an external counterparty may be designated as hedging instruments except for some written options. A non-derivative financial asset or liability may not be designated as a hedging instrument except as a hedge of foreign currency risk.

ASBE 24 permits hedge accounting under certain circumstances. Formally designated and documented, including the entity's risk management objective and strategy for undertaking the hedge, identification of the hedging instrument, the hedged item, the nature of the risk being hedged, and how the entity will assess the hedging instrument's effectiveness and is expected to be highly effective in achieving offsetting changes in fair value or cash flows attributable to the hedged risk as designated and documented. Moreover, effectiveness can be reliably measured and assessed on an ongoing basis and determined to have been highly effective.

Under the fair value perspective, hedging is the exposure to changes in fair value of a recognized asset or liability or a previously unrecognized firm commitment or an identified portion of such an asset, liability, or firm commitment that is attributable to a particular risk and could affect profit or loss. The gain or loss from the change in fair value of the hedging instrument is recognized immediately in profit or loss. At the same time, the carrying amount of the hedged item is adjusted for the corresponding gain or loss with respect to the hedged risk, which is also recognized immediately in net profit or loss.

Under the cash flow point of view, hedging is the exposure to variability in cash flows that (i) is attributable to a particular risk associated with a recognized asset or liability (such as all or some future interest payments on variable rate debt) or a highly probable forecast transaction and (ii) could affect profit or loss. The portion of the gain or loss on the hedging instrument that is determined to be an effective hedge is recognized in other comprehensive income.

If a hedge of a forecast transaction subsequently results in the recognition of a financial asset or a financial liability, any gain or loss on the hedging instrument that was previously recognized directly in equity is "recycled" into profit or loss in the same period(s) in which the financial asset or liability affects profit or loss.

If a hedge of a forecast transaction subsequently results in the recognition of a non-financial asset or non-financial liability, then the entity has an accounting policy option that must be applied to all such hedges of forecast transactions. Same accounting is used for recognition of a financial asset or financial liability—any gain or loss on the hedging instrument that was previously recognized in other comprehensive income is "recycled" into profit or loss in the same period(s) in which the non-financial asset or liability affects profit or loss. "Basis adjustment" of the acquired non-financial asset or liability—the gain or loss on the hedging instrument that was previously recognized in other comprehensive income is removed from equity and is included in the initial cost or other carrying amount of the acquired non-financial asset or liability.

A hedge of a net investment in a foreign operation as defined in IAS 21 The Effects of Changes in Foreign Exchange Rates is accounted for similarly to a cash flow hedge.

A hedge of the foreign currency risk of a firm commitment may be accounted for as a fair value hedge or as a cash flow hedge.

ASBE 24 requires hedge effectiveness to be assessed both prospectively and retrospectively. To qualify for hedge accounting at the inception of a hedge and, at a minimum, at each reporting date, the changes in the fair value or cash flows of the hedged item attributable to the hedged risk must be expected to be highly effective in offsetting the changes in the fair value or cash flows of the hedging instrument on a prospective basis.

For hedge accounting purposes, only instruments that involve a party external to the reporting entity can be designated as a hedging instrument. This applies to intragroup transactions as well. However, they may qualify for hedge accounting in individual financial statements. A hedged item is an item that exposes the entity to risk of changes in fair value or future cash flows and is designated as being hedged. If hedge accounting ceases for a cash flow hedge because the forecast transaction is no longer expected to occur, gains and losses deferred in other comprehensive income must be taken to profit or loss immediately. If the transaction is still expected to occur and the hedge relationship ceases, the amounts accumulated in equity will be retained in equity until the hedged item affects profit or loss. If a hedged financial instrument that is measured at amortized cost has been adjusted for the gain or loss attributable to the hedged risk in a fair value hedge, this adjustment is amortized to profit or loss based on a recalculated effective interest rate on this date such that the adjustment is fully amortized by the maturity of the instrument. Amortization may begin as soon as an adjustment exists and must begin no later than when the hedged item ceases to be adjusted for changes in its fair value attributable to the risks being hedged.

28.5 Examples

On 1st December, Company X purchases a fixed-interest rate security for 600,000 CNY. The year-end fair value of the security is 630,000 CNY. Due to volatility in financial markets, Company X enters into a hedge by acquiring an interest rate swap.

At year-1-end, the security's value falls to 610,000 CNY.

Company X shall record in first financial year the acquisition of securities and the capital gain under capital surplus (the investment is not intended to be sold). During financial year 1, Company X is not required to record the interest rate swap. Rather at the date of balance sheet, it shall recognize a positive income item of 20,000 CNY due to the hedging instrument, and a negative income item for the same amount on securities held.

Chapter 29
Accounting Standards for Business Enterprises No. 25—Direct Insurance Contracts

29.1 Chapter I: General Provisions

Article 1 With a view to regulating the recognition, measurement of the original insurance contracts concluded by insurants, and the presentation of relevant information, the present Standards are formulated according to the Accounting Standards for Enterprises—Basic Standards.

Article 2 The term "insurance contract" refers to an agreement under which the insurer and the insured stipulate the insurance rights and obligations and the insurer undertakes the insurance risks sourced from the insured. Insurance contracts are classified into original insurance contracts and reinsurance contracts. The term "original insurance contract" refers to an insurance contract under which the insurer charges the insurance premium and undertakes the liability to pay the insurance money for the property losses resulted from the prescribed possible accident(s), or undertakes the liability to pay the insurance money when the insured dies, or is injured, disabled, or sick, or attains to the stipulated age or time period.

Article 3 The following items shall be subject to other relevant accounting standards:

1. The impairment of assets such as the post-loss goods produced by an original insurance contract issued by an insurer shall be subject to the Accounting Standards for Enterprises No. 1—Inventories.
2. A contract issued by an insurer to the insured on a risk other than the insurance risks shall be subject to the Accounting Standards for Enterprises No. 22—Recognition and Measurement of Financial Instruments and the Accounting Standards for Enterprises No. 37—Presentation of Financial Instruments.
3. A reinsurance contract issued or held by an insurer shall be subject to the Accounting Standard for Enterprises—Reinsurance Contracts.

L. Riccardi, *China Accounting Standards*,
DOI 10.1007/978-981-10-0006-5_29

29.2 Chapter II: Determination of Original Insurance Contracts

Article 4 No matter whether a contract concluded by an insurer and an insured is an original insurance contract or not, that whether or not the insurer has undertaken the insurance risks shall, on the basis of a single-item contract, be judged according to the contract terms. Where the occurrence of an insurance accident is likely to cause the insurer to undertake the liability to pay the insurance money, it shall be determined that the insurer has undertaken the insurance risks. The term "insurance accident" refers to accidents which are prescribed in an insurance contract and fall within the scope of insurance liabilities.

Article 5 Where a contract concluded by an insurer and an insured puts the insurer in a position of not only undertaking the insurance risks but also other risks, it shall be, respectively, treated according to the following circumstances:

1. Where the insurance risks can be distinguished from other risks and can be measured separately, the insurance risks may be separated from other risks. The part of insurance risks shall be determined as an original insurance contract. And the part of other risks may not be determined as an original insurance contract.
2. Where the insurance risks cannot be distinguished from other risks, or where the insurance risks can be distinguished from other risks but cannot be measured separately, the entire contract shall be determined as an original insurance contract.

Article 6 The insurer shall, in light of whether or not it undertakes the liability to pay the insurance money during the extension period of the original insurance contracts, classify the original insurance contracts into original life insurance contracts and original non-life insurance contracts. Where the insurer undertakes the liability to pay the insurance money during the extension period of an original insurance contract, it shall determine it as an original life insurance contract. Where it does not undertake the liability to pay insurance money during the extension period of an original insurance contract, it shall determine it as an original non-life insurance contract. The "extension period of an original insurance contract" refers to the period during which the insured does not pay premium from the maturity date of the previous period, but the insurer still undertake the liability to pay the insurance money.

29.3 Chapter III: The Income from Original Insurance Contracts

Article 7 The premium income, which can meet the following requirements simultaneously, may be recognized:

1. An original insurance contract has been established, and corresponding insurance liabilities have been undertaken;
2. The economic benefits related to the original insurance contract are highly probable to flow in; and
3. The income related to the original insurance contract can be measured reliably.

Article 8 An insurer shall, according to the following provisions, calculate and determine the amount of insurance income:

1. As for an original non-life insurance contract, the amount of insurance income shall be determined according to the total premium as stipulated in the original insurance contract.
2. As for an original life insurance contract, if the insurance premium as charged by installments, the amount of insurance income shall be the premium charged in the current period. If the premium is charged in a lump sum, the insurance income shall be determined according to the premium which shall be charged in a lump sum.

Article 9 Where an original insurance is canceled prior to the expiration date, the insurer shall, according to the stipulations of the original insurance contract, calculate and determine the refund to the insured as the refund premium, and record it in the profits and losses of the current period.

29.4 Chapter IV: Reserves for Original Insurance Contracts

Article 10 The reserves for original insurance contracts shall include unearned premium reserves, reserves for outstanding claims, reserves for life insurance liabilities, and reserves for long-term health insurance liabilities. The term "unearned premium reserves" refers to the reserves drawn by an insurer for unexpired non-life insurance liabilities. The term "reserve for outstanding claims" refers the reserves drawn by an insurer for the non-life insurance accidents which have already occurred but have not been settled. The term "reserves for life insurance liabilities" refers to the reserves drawn by an insurer for unexpired life insurance liabilities. The term "reserves for long-term health insurance liabilities" refers to the reserves calculated and drawn by an insurer for unexpired long-term health insurance liabilities.

Article 11 An insurer shall, in the current period of recognition of the income from non-life insurances, calculate and draw unearned premium reserve as an adjustment to the premium income of the current period in light of the actuarial amount, and recognize the unearned premium reserves as a liability. An insurer shall, on the balance sheet date, recalculate the balance between the recognized amount of the unearned premium reserves and the drawn amount of the unearned premium reserves in light of the actuarial amount, and shall make an adjustment to the unearned premium reserves.

Article 12 An insurer shall, in the current period when the non-life insurance accident happens, draw the reserve for outstanding claims in light of the actuarial amount and shall recognize the reserve for outstanding claims as a liability. The reserve for outstanding claims includes the reserve for outstanding claims that are incurred and reported, the reserve for outstanding claims that are incurred but not reported, as well as the reserve for the expenses of settlement of claims. The "reserve for outstanding claims that are incurred and reported" refers to the reserve made by an insurer for the compensation cases, in which non-life insurance accidents have occurred and claims are made to the insurer, but are not settled yet. The "reserve for outstanding claims that are incurred but not reported" refers to the reserve made by an insurer for the compensation cases, in which non-life insurance accidents have occurred, but no claim is made to the insurer yet. The "reserve for the expenses of settlement of claims" refers to the reserve made by an insurer for the attorney fees, litigation fees, loss inspection fees, wages, and salaries of the personnel for the settlement of claims and other expenses which are likely to incur in compensation cases, in which non-life insurance accidents have occurred but which have not been settled yet.

Article 13 An insurer shall, in the current period of recognition of life insurance premiums, draw reserves for life insurance liabilities and long-term health insurance liabilities in light of the actuarial amounts, and shall recognize the reserves for life insurance liabilities and those for long-term health insurance liabilities as liabilities.

Article 14 An insurer shall, at least by the end of each year, test the abundance of the reserves for outstanding claims, life insurance liabilities, and long-term health insurance liabilities. Where the amount of relevant reserves which are recalculated and determined by the insurer in light of the actuarial amount exceeds the drawn amount of the relevant reserves on the abundance test date, the relevant reserves shall be replenished on the basis of the difference. If the amount of relevant reserves which are recalculated and determined by the insurer in light of the actuarial amount is less than the residual amount of the relevant reserves on the abundance test date, no adjustment shall be made to the relevant reserves.

Article 15 Where an original insurance contract is canceled prior to its expiration date, the insurer shall write off the residue amounts of the relevant reserves for unearned premiums, life insurance liabilities, and long-term health insurance liabilities, and record them into the profits and losses of the current period.

29.5 Chapter V: Cost of Original Insurance Contracts

Article 16 The cost of an original insurance contract refers to the total outflow of economic benefits, which is incurred by the original insurance contract, will result in the decrease of the owner's equities and is irrelevant to the distribution of profits to the owners. The cost of an original insurance contract mainly includes the handling charges or commission, compensation cost, as well as the reserves for outstanding claims, life insurance liabilities, and long-term health insurance liabilities. The compensation cost includes the indemnity or payment made by the insurer, and the expenses for the attorney fees, litigation fees, loss inspection fees, wages and salaries of the personnel for the settlement of claims which are incurred during the settlement of the claims.

Article 17 The handling fees and commissions, which are incurred to the insurer during the course of obtaining the original insurance contracts, shall be recorded into the profits and losses of the current period.

Article 18 The reserves for outstanding claims, life insurance liabilities, and long-term health insurance liabilities, which are drawn by an insurer in light of the actuarial amounts, shall be recorded into the profits and losses of the current period. An insurer shall, in the current period of determination of the amount of compensation, record into the profits and losses of the current period the amount of compensation determined to make. Meanwhile, it shall offset the residual amount of the corresponding reserves for outstanding claims, life insurance liabilities, or long-term health insurance liabilities.

Article 19 The reserves for outstanding claims, life insurance liabilities, or long-term health insurance liabilities, which are replenished by an insurer according to the abundance test, shall be recorded into the profits and losses of the current period.

Article 20 Any post-loss goods obtained by an insurer due to undertaking the liability to pay the insurance money shall be recognized as an asset calculated at the market price of the same class of or similar asset and shall be used to offset the compensation cost of the current period. When disposing of any post-loss goods, the insurer shall adjust the compensation cost of the current period according to the balance between the amount received and the carrying amount of the post-loss goods.

Article 21 Where the subrogation recourse fee to be charged by an insurer for undertaking the liability to pay the insurance money meets the following requirements simultaneously, it shall be recognized as the receivable subrogation recourse fee and shall be used to offset the compensation cost of the current period:

1. The economic benefits related to this subrogation recourse fee is likely to flow in;
2. The amount of the subrogation recourse fee can be measured reliably.

When an insurer receives the receivable subrogation recourse fee, it shall, pursuant to the balance between the received amount and the carrying amount of the relevant receivable subrogation recourse fee, adjust the compensation cost of the current period.

29.6 Chapter VI: Presentation

Article 22 An insurer shall, in the balance sheet, separately present the following items related to the original insurance contract:

1. the unearned premium reserve;
2. the reserve for outstanding claims;
3. the reserve for life insurance liabilities; and
4. the reserve for long-term health insurance liabilities.

Article 23 An insurer shall, in the profit statement, present separately the following items related to the original insurance contract:

1. the income from premiums;
2. the refunded premiums;
3. the drawing of unearned premium reserve;
4. the premiums earned;
5. the disbursement of handling fee;
6. the compensation cost;
7. the reserve for outstanding claims;
8. the reserve for life insurance liabilities; and
9. the reserve for long-term health insurance liabilities.

Article 24 An insurer shall, in its annotations, disclose the following information related to the original insurance contract:

1. the relevant information on the subrogation recourse fee;
2. the relevant information on the post-loss goods;
3. the increase and decrease of each reserve; and
4. the main actuarial assumptions and methods for drawing these reserves and testing the abundance of the reserves.

29.7 Comments

Direct Insurance Contracts are introduced through ASBE No. 25. This *Article* prescribes the recognition, measurement, and presentation requirements of direct insurance costs issued by an insurer. Previously, just accounting and financial reporting were regulated.

Furthermore, it clarified the definition of an insurance contract and defined the concept of insurance risk.

With respect to contracts which expose the insurer to both insurance risk and financial risk, the insurer is allowed to unbundle the contract into different components if the insurance risk component and the other risk component can be separately identified and are separately measured. If the insurance risk component and the other risk component cannot be separately identified or measurable, the insurer shall account for the entire contract as a direct insurance contract. ASBE No. 25 requires an insurer to conduct an adequacy test for the claims outstanding reserve, the life insurance reserve, and the long-term medical insurance reserve, at least at each year-end.

Provisions under ASBE No. 25 refer to IFRS 4—Insurance Contracts. IFRS 4 does not specify the recognition and measurement requirements with respect to assets, liabilities, income, and expenses arising from insurance contracts. In practice, an insurer can continue to use its existing accounting practice. To a different extent, ASBE No. 25 requires the insurer to apply income, reserves, and cost.

Referred to the unbundling, IFRS 4 provides additional guidance on the treatment of contracts with insurance risks and/or financial risks. First, it clarifies that an insurer need not account for an embedded derivative separately at fair value if the embedded derivative meets the definition of an insurance contract. Second requires an insurer to separately account for deposit components of the insurance contracts if not all obligations and rights arising from the deposit component are recognized under the issuer's original accounting policy. Third, unbundling is permitted, but not required, if all obligations and rights arising from the deposit component are recognized under the issuer's original accounting policy. Finally, unbundling is not permitted if the deposit component is not measurable.

29.8 Examples

Following the provisioned end-year balance sheet for an insurer

Assets	Current period (RMB)	Prior period (RMB)
Cash and banks		
Other receivables		
Dividend receivables		
Interest receivables		
Premium receivables		
Available-for-sale financial assets		
Held-to-maturity investments		
Fixed assets		
Investment properties		
Total assets		

Liabilities	Current period (RMB)	Prior period (RMB)
Taxes payable		
Other payables		

(continued)

(continued)

Liabilities	Current period (RMB)	Prior period (RMB)
Dividends payables		
Claims payables		
Deferred tax liabilities		
Unearned premiums		
Provisions for		
– Undue obligations		
– Incurred but unsettled claims		
– Obligations arising on life insurance contracts		
– Obligations arising on LT health insurance contracts		
Total liabilities		

Shareholders' equity	Current period (RMB)	Prior period (RMB)
Stock		
Reserves		
Retained earnings		
Total liabilities and stockholders' equity		

Following the provisioned end-year income statement for an insurer

	Current period (RMB)	Prior period (RMB)
Revenue from operations		
Gross premium revenue		
Life direct insurance contracts		
General direct insurance contracts		
Less: premium refunds		
Net premium revenue		
Less: unearned premium revenue		
Premium earned		
Gains on changes in fair value		
Investment income		
Total revenue from operations		
Cost and expenses of operations		
Tax and surchargers		
Handling charges incurred		
Commission expenses		
Cost of paying claims		
Amounts of provisions accrued for		

(continued)

(continued)

	Current period (RMB)	Prior period (RMB)
– Undue obligations		
– Incurred but unsettled claims		
– Obligations arising on life insurance contracts		
– Obligations arising on LT health insurance contracts		
General and administrative expenses		
Total costs and expenses of operations		
Operating profit		
Add: Non-operating revenue		
Less: Non-operating expenses		
Profit before tax		
Less: Income tax expense		
Net profit		
Other comprehensive income		
Total comprehensive income		

Chapter 30
Accounting Standards for Business Enterprises No. 26—Reinsurance Contracts

30.1 Chapter I: General Principles

Article 1 With a view to regulating the recognition and measurement of reinsurance contracts, and the presentation of relevant information, the present Standards are formulated according to the Accounting Standards for Enterprises—Basic Standards.

Article 2 The term "reinsurance contract" refers to an insurance contract under which the insurer (reinsurance cedant) cedes a certain portion of a premium to another insurer (reinsurance acceptor) and the reinsurance acceptor makes compensation to the cedant for the compensation cost and other relevant expenses arising from the original insurance contract.

Article 3 The present Standards shall apply to the reinsurance contracts issued and held by insurers. A sub-reinsurance contract under which an insurer cedes a reinsurance business which is ceded to it to another insurer shall be subject to the present Standards.

Article 4 The original insurance contracts issued by insurers shall be subject to the Accounting Standards for Enterprises No. 25—Original Insurance Contracts.

30.2 Chapter II: Accounting Treatment of Ceded-Out Business

Article 5 No cedant may countervail the liabilities formed by relevant original insurance contracts with the assets formed by reinsurance contracts against. No cedant may countervail the expenses or incomes formed by the relevant original insurance contracts with the incomes or expenses formed by the reinsurance contracts.

L. Riccardi, *China Accounting Standards*,
DOI 10.1007/978-981-10-0006-5_30

Article 6 A cedant shall, in the current period of recognition of the premium income of an original insurance contract, calculate and determine the ceded premium in light of the reinsurance contract and record it into the profits and losses of the current period. Meanwhile, if the original insurance contract is a non-life original insurance contract, the cedant shall, according to relevant provisions of the reinsurance contract, calculate and recognize the receivable reinsurance unearned premium reserve as an asset and countervail with it the undue premium reserve. When the cedant adjusts the balance of the unearned premium reserve of the original insurance contract on the balance sheet date, it shall adjust the amount of the receivable reinsurance unearned premium reserve accordingly.

Article 7 A cedant shall, in the current period of recognition of the premium income of the original insurance contract, calculate and determine the reinsurance expenses which shall be recovered from the reinsurance acceptor and record them into the profits and losses of the current period.

Article 8 A cedant shall, in the current period of drawing the reserve for unearned premium, reserve for life insurance liabilities or reserve for long-term health insurance liabilities of an original insurance contract, calculate, and determine the corresponding reserves that shall be recovered from the reinsurance acceptor according to the provisions of the relevant reinsurance contract, and shall recognize the corresponding reinsurance reserve receivable as an asset.

Article 9 A cedant shall, in the current period of determining and offsetting the amount of an indemnity payment or the expenses actually incurred for the settlement of a claim against the balance of the corresponding reserve on the original insurance contract, offset it against the balance of the corresponding receivable reinsurance reserve. Meanwhile, it shall, according to the provisions of the reinsurance contracts, calculate and determine the compensation cost that shall be recovered from the reinsurance acceptor, and record it into the profits and losses of the current period.

Article 10 A cedant shall, in the current period of the canceling of an original insurance contract ahead of schedule, calculate and determine the amount of adjustment to the ceded premium or the recovered reinsurance expenses according to the provisions of the relevant reinsurance contract, and record it into the profits and losses of the current period. Meanwhile, it shall write off the amount of the relevant reinsurance reserves receivable.

Article 11 A cedant shall, in the current period of making an adjustment to the compensation cost of an original insurance contract because of the obtainment or disposal of any post-loss goods, or recognition and receipt of any subrogation recourse fee, calculate and determine the amount of adjustment to the to-be-recovered compensation cost according to the provisions of the relevant reinsurance contract, and record it into the profits and losses of the current period.

Article 12 When a cedant issues a reinsurance bill, it shall recognize the reinsurance guarantee deposited in the current period as described in the bill as the deposited-in reinsurance guarantee. Meanwhile, it shall write off the relevant deposited-in reinsurance guarantee in light of the refund of the deposited-in reinsurance guarantee of the previous period as described in the bill. The cedant shall, according to the relevant reinsurance contract, calculate the interest on the deposited-in reinsurance guarantee of each period and record it into the profits and losses of the current period.

Article 13 A cedant shall, when being able to calculate and determine the net profit commissions which it shall charge from the reinsurance acceptor, treat the profit commission as a recovered reinsurance expense according to the provisions of the relevant reinsurance contracts, and record it into the profits and losses of the current period.

Article 14 As for an excess of loss reinsurance or any other non-proportional reinsurance contract, the cedant shall, according to the provisions of the reinsurance contract, calculate and determine the premium to be ceded out, and record it into the profits and losses of the current period. A cedant shall, when making an adjustment to the premium, record the amount of adjustment into the profits and losses of the current period. A cedant shall, when being able to calculate and determine the compensation cost that shall be recovered from the reinsurance acceptor, record the to-be-recovered compensation cost into the profits and losses of the current period.

30.3 Chapter III: Accounting Treatment of Ceded-In Business

Article 15 No reinsurance premium income may be recognized unless it can simultaneously satisfy the following conditions:

1. The reinsurance contract is established and assumes relevant insurance liabilities;
2. The economic benefits related to the reinsurance contract are likely to flow in;
3. The economic benefits related to the reinsurance contract can be measured reliably.

The reinsurance acceptor shall, according to the provisions of the relevant reinsurance contracts, calculate and determine the amount of reinsurance premium income.

Article 16 The reinsurance acceptor shall, in the current period of recognizing a reinsurance premium income, calculate and determine the reinsurance expenses according to the provisions of the relevant reinsurance contracts, and record them into the profits and losses of the current period.

Article 17 The reinsurance acceptor shall, when being able to calculate and determine the net profit commissions that it shall pay to the cedant, treat the profit commissions as a reinsurance expense according to the provisions of the relevant reinsurance contracts, and record it into the profits and losses of the current period.

Article 18 The reinsurance acceptor shall, when receiving a reinsurance bill, make an adjustment to the relevant premium income and premium expenses in light of the amount as specified in the bill, and record the amount of adjustment into the profits and losses of the current period.

Article 19 The reinsurance acceptor shall accord with the relevant provisions of the Accounting Standards for Enterprises No. 25—Original Insurance Contracts when it draws reserves for unearned reinsurance premiums, outstanding reinsurance claims, reinsurance life insurance liabilities and the reinsurance of long-term health care insurance liabilities, and tests the adequacy of the relevant reserves.

Article 20 The reinsurance acceptor shall, in the current period of receipt of a reinsurance bill, treat the amount of the reinsurance indemnity payment as described in the said bill as the reinsurance compensation cost and record it into the profits and losses of the current period. Meanwhile, it shall offset it against the balance of the reinsurance reserve.

Article 21 The reinsurance acceptor shall, when receiving a reinsurance bill, shall recognize the reinsurance guarantee to be deposited in the current period as stated in the bill as the deposited-out reinsurance guarantee. Meanwhile, it shall write off the relevant deposited reinsurance guarantee in light of the refund of the deposit-out reinsurance guarantee of the previous period as stated in the bill. The reinsurance acceptor shall, according to the provisions of the reinsurance contract, calculate the interest on the deposit-out reinsurance guarantee of each period and record it into the profits and losses of the current period.

30.4 Chapter IV: Presentation

Article 22 An insurer shall, in its balance sheets, separately present the following items related to the reinsurance contract:

1. the receivable reinsurance;
2. the receivable unearned reinsurance premium reserve;
3. the receivable reserve for outstanding reinsurance claims;
4. the receivable reserve for reinsurance life insurance liabilities;
5. the receivable reserve for the reinsurance of long-term health insurance liabilities; and
6. the payable reinsurance.

Article 23 An insurer shall, in its profit statements, separately present the following items related to the reinsurance contract:

1. the reinsurance premium income;
2. the ceded-out premium;
3. the recovered reinsurance expense;
4. the reinsurance expense;
5. the recovered compensation cost;
6. the reinsurance compensation cost;
7. the recovered reinsurance compensation cost;

8. the recovered reserve for life insurance liabilities; and
9. the recovered reserve for long-term health insurance liabilities.

Article 24 An insurer shall, in its notes, discover the following information related to the reinsurance contract:

1. The information on the increase and decrease of reinsurance reserves for the ceded-in business.
2. The main actuarial assumptions and methods for making reinsurance reserves and testing the adequacy of the reinsurance reserves for the ceded-in business.

30.5 Comments

ASBE No. 26 has been introduced to prescribe the recognition, measurement, and presentation requirements of the reinsurance contract issued by an insurance company and assumed by an insurer. In such circumstances, the cedant shall not offset the following items on the balance sheet: the income or expense from reinsurance contracts against the expense or income from related direct insurance contracts; and the reinsurance assets arising from the reinsurance contracts against the related liabilities of the direct insurance contracts.

The cedant shall recognize the outward reinsurance premiums and commissions recoverable from the reinsurer in the period in which the cedant recognizes the premium income from the direct insurance contract. The cedant shall account for the reserves recoverable and claims recoverable under outward reinsurance contracts in the period in which the cedant accounts for the reserves in the insurance contracts. Under PRC GAAP, the cedant was required to recognize the outward reinsurance premiums and the various recoverable amounts from the reinsurer when the cedant issued a statement of the reinsurance transaction to the reinsurer.

The reinsurer shall recognize the inward premium income when the criteria for income recognition are met. The reinsured shall, at the same time, determine the commission payable for the inward reinsurance contracts according to the terms of the reinsurance contracts and recognize the amount in the profit or loss for the transactions, the reinsurer shall adjust the relevant inward premium income and commission expenses arising from inward reinsurance contracts according to the amounts indicated in the statement.

Like ASBE No. 25, also ASBE No. 26 refers to dispositions of IFRS 4. This, regarding the reinsurance point of view, disposes that there is no separate standard dealing with reinsurance under IFRSs. Nevertheless, the recognition and measurement requirements of ASBE No. 26 are generally consistent with the current market practice. IFRS 4 requires an impairment test for reinsurance assets. ASBE No. 8 requires an impairment test for reinsurance assets to be performed only when there is an impairment indication. Similarly to ASBE No. 26, income/expenses and assets/liabilities of reinsurance contracts are presented on a gross basis.

30.6 Examples

Following the provisioned End-Year Balance Sheet for a Reinsurer (or cedant insurer).

Assets	Current period (RMB)	Prior period (RMB)
Cash and banks		
Other receivables		
Dividend receivables		
Interest receivables		
Reinsurance receivables		
Premium receivables		
Recoveries on provisions for		
– Undue obligations from reinsurers		
– Incurred but unsettled claims from reinsures		
– Obligations arising on life insurance contracts from reinsurers		
– Obligations arising on LT health insurance contracts from reinsurers		
Available-for-sale financial assets		
Held-to-maturity investments		
Fixed assets		
Investment properties		
Total assets		

Liabilities	Current period (RMB)	Prior period (RMB)
Taxes payable		
Other payables		
Dividends payables		
Premium received in advance		
Commission payable		
Claims payable		
Reinsurance payables		
Deferred tax liabilities		
Unearned premium		
Provisions for		
– Undue obligations		
– Incurred but unsettled claims		
– Obligations arising on life insurance contracts		
– Obligations arising on LT health insurance contracts		
Total liabilities		

Shareholders' equity	Current period (RMB)	Prior period (RMB)
Stock		
Reserves		
Retained earnings		
Total liabilities and stockholders' equity		

Following the provisioned End-Year Income Statement for an insurer

	Current period (RMB)	Prior period (RMB)
Revenue from operations		
Gross premium revenue		
Direct insurance contracts		
Reinsurance contracts		
Less: premium refunds		
Net premium revenue		
Less: ceding premium		
Less: unearned premium revenue		
Premium earned		
Gains on changes in fair value		
Investment income		
Total revenue from operations		
Cost and expenses of operations		
Tax and surchargers		
Handling charges incurred		
Commission expenses		
Cost of paying claims for		
– Direct insurance contracts		
– Reinsurance contracts		
Less: recoveries of costs of paying claims		
Reinsurance expenses		
Less: recoveries of insurance expenses		
Amounts of provisions accrued for		
– Undue obligations		
– Incurred but unsettled claims		
– Obligations arising on life insurance contracts		
– Obligations arising on LT health insurance contracts		
Amounts of provisions recovered for		
– Incurred but unsettled claims		
– Obligations arising on life insurance contracts		

(continued)

(continued)

	Current period (RMB)	Prior period (RMB)
– Obligations arising on LT health insurance contracts		
General and administrative expenses		
Total costs and expenses of operations		
Operating profit		
Add: non-operating revenue		
Less: non-operating expenses		
Profit before tax		
Less: income tax expense		
Net profit		
Other comprehensive income		
Total comprehensive income		

Chapter 31
Accounting Standards for Business Enterprises No. 27—Exploitation of Petroleum and Natural Gas

31.1 Chapter I: General Provisions

Article 1 In order to regulate the accounting treatments for the exploitation activity of petroleum and natural gas (hereinafter referred to as oil and gas) and the disclosure of relevant information, these Standards are formulated in accordance with Accounting Standards for Enterprises—Basic Standards.

Article 2 The exploitation activity of oil and gas includes the stages of obtainment of rights and interests of mining areas, as well as exploration, development, and production of oil and gas.

Article 3 Except for the exploitation activity of oil and gas, the accounting treatments for the storage, centralized transport, processing, distribution of oil and gas shall be governed by other relevant accounting standards.

31.2 Chapter II: Accounting Treatments of Rights and Interests of Mining Areas

Article 4 The rights and interests of mining areas refers to the rights obtained by enterprises to explore, develop, and produce oil and gas in mining areas. The rights and interests of mining areas shall be classified into the rights and interests of proved and unproved mining areas. A proved mining area refers to a mining area in which an economically exploitable reserve has been discovered and proved after exploration. An unproved mining area refers to a mining area in which no economically exploitable reserve has been discovered and proved yet. The term "economically exploitable reserve is proved" refers to the amount of oil and gas that can be reasonably determined and be exploited from a known oil and gas reserve under the current technological and economic conditions in light of the geological and engineering analyses.

L. Riccardi, *China Accounting Standards*,
DOI 10.1007/978-981-10-0006-5_31

Article 5 The costs for obtaining the rights and interests of a mining area shall be capitalized when they are incurred. The rights and interests of a mining area obtained by an enterprise shall be measured initially according to the costs of obtainment:

1. The costs for the obtainment of the rights and interests of a mining area shall include the use fee of the exploration right, the use fee of the mining right, the disbursements for the use right of land or sea area, commissions, and other disbursements directly attributable to applying for obtainment of the rights and interests of the mining area.
2. The costs for the obtainment of the rights and interests of a mining area by way of purchase shall include the purchase price, commissions, and other purchasing disbursements directly attributable to the obtainment of the rights and interests of the mining area.

After the obtainment of the rights and interests of a mining area, the use fee of the exploration right, the use fee of mining right, rent, and other disbursements for maintaining the rights and interests of the mining area shall be recorded into the profits and losses of the current period.

Article 6 An enterprise shall adopt the output method or the average method of year limit to calculate the depletion of the rights and interest of the proved mining areas. If it adopts the output method to calculate the depletion, the depletion amount shall be calculated in light of each single mining area, or in light of a group of adjacent mining areas with identical or similar geological structure features or deposit layer conditions. The calculation formula shall be as follows:

The depletion amount of the rights and interests of the proved mining areas = the book value of the proved mining areas × the depletion rate of the rights and interests of the proved mining areas.

The depletion rate of the rights and interests of the proved mining areas = the output of the proved mining areas in the current period/(the proved economically exploitable reserve at the end of the period of the proved mining areas + the output of the proved mining areas of the current period).

Article 7 For the impairment of the rights and interests of a mining area, an enterprise shall recognize the impairment losses in accordance with the following different circumstances, respectively:

1. It shall treat the impairment of rights and interests of the proved mining areas in light of the Accounting Standard for Enterprises No. 8—Asset Impairment.
2. The rights and interests of the unproved mining areas shall be tested on impairment at least once a year. If the amount of costs incurred by the obtainment of a single mining area is relatively huge, the tests on impairment shall be performed on the basis of a single mining area and the amount of impairment of the rights and interests of the unproved mining area shall be confirmed. If the amount of costs incurred by the obtainment of a single mining area is relatively small and if its geological structure features or deposit layer conditions are the same as or similar to those of other adjacent mining areas, a

test on impairment may be performed on the basis of a group of mining areas consisting of several adjacent mining areas with identical or similar geological structure features or deposit layer conditions. If the fair value of the rights and interests of the unproved mining areas is lower than the book value thereof, the difference between them shall be considered as an impairment loss and shall be recorded in the profits and losses of the current period. Once an impairment loss on the rights and interests of the unproved mining areas has been recognized, it shall not be reversed.

Article 8 Where an enterprise transfers the rights and interests of a mining area, it shall be subject to the provisions as follows:

1. If it transfers all the rights and interests of a mining area, the difference between the transfer income and the book value of the rights and interests of the mining area shall be recorded in the profits and losses of the current period. If it transfers parts of the rights and interests of the mining area, in light of the proportion between the fair value of the transferred rights and interests and the fair value of the retained rights and interests, it shall calculate and determine the book value of the transferred portion of rights and interests of the mining area, and the difference between the transfer income and the book value of the transferred rights and interests of the mining area shall be recorded in the profits and losses of the current period.
2. If it transfers all the rights and interests of an unproved mining area, for which it calculates the impairment separately, the difference between the transfer income and the book value of the rights and interests of the unproved mining area shall be recorded in the profits and losses of the current period. If it transfers parts of the rights and interests of an unproved mining area, for which it calculates the impairment separately and if the transfer income is more than the book value of the rights and interests of the mining area, the difference between them shall be recorded in the profits and losses of the current period. If the transfer income is less than the book value of the rights and interests of the mining area, the transfer income shall offset against the book value of the rights and interests of the mining area and any profits and losses shall not be recognized.
3. If it transfers the rights and interests of any unproved mining areas, for which it calculates the impairment on the basis of a group of mining areas, and if the transfer income is more than the original book value of the rights and interests of the mining areas, the difference between them shall be recorded in the profits and losses of the current period; if the transfer income is less than the original book value of the rights and interests of the mining areas, the transfer income shall offset against the original book value of the rights and interests of the mining areas, any profits and losses shall not be recognized. When it transfers the residual rights and interests of the final unproved mining area among the group of the mining areas, the difference between the transfer income and the book value of the unproved mining area shall be recorded in the profits and incomes of the current period.

Article 9 Where an unproved mining area (portfolio) is changed into a proved mining area (or groups of mining areas) because an economically exploitable reserve is discovered and proved in such an unproved mining area (portfolio), it shall be shifted into the rights and interests of proved mining areas according to its book value.

Article 10 Where an enterprise eventually abandons an unproved mining area due to its failure to discover and prove any economically exploitable reserve therein, its book value at the time of abandonment shall be written off the rights and interests of the unproved mining area, and be recorded in the profits and losses of the current period. The abandonment costs, which are incurred due to the unfinished obligatory workload or other factors shall be recorded in the profits and losses of the current period.

31.3 Chapter III: Accounting Treatments of Oil and Gas Exploration

Article 11 The expression "oil and gas exploration" refers to the geological investigations, geophysical prospecting, drilling activities, and other relevant activities carried out for the purpose of identifying the exploration region or exploring the oil and gas reserve.

Article 12 The disbursements for oil and gas exploration shall include the drilling exploration disbursements and the non-drilling exploration disbursements. The drilling exploration disbursements shall mainly include the disbursements incurred by the exploratory drilling in the exploration region, the drilling for detailed prospecting, the appraisal well, the data well as well as other activities. The non-drilling exploration disbursements shall mainly include the disbursements for geological investigation, geophysical exploration, as well as other activities.

Article 13 With a view to the drilling exploration disbursements, after a well is completed, if it is sure that an economically exploitable reserve is discovered and proved in the well, the disbursements for drilling this well shall be carried forward as cost of the well and relevant facilities. If it is sure that no economically exploitable reserve is discovered and proved in the well, the result of the disbursements for drilling this well less the net salvage value shall be recorded in the profits and losses of the current period. If it is sure that an economically exploitable reserve is discovered and proved in a section of the well, among the portion of drilling exploration disbursements for the effective section of the well where an economically exploitable reserve is discovered and proved shall be carried forward as the cost of the well and relevant facilities. The accumulative drilling exploration disbursements for the ineffective section of the well shall be changed into the profits and currents of the current period. If it is not sure that whether or not an economically exploitable reserve is discovered and proved in the well, the disbursements for drilling the well shall be temporarily capitalized within 1 year after it is completed.

Article 14 If one year has lapsed since the completion of the well, it is still impossible to make sure whether or not an economically exploitable reserve is discovered and proved in a well, if the following conditions are satisfied simultaneously, the capitalized disbursements for drilling the well shall continue to be temporarily capitalized; otherwise, they shall be recorded in the profits and losses of the current period:

1. A sufficient reserve has been discovered in the well, but in order to make sure whether or not it is an economically exploitable reserve, it is necessary to carry out further exploration activities in order to make sure whether or not it is an proved economically exploitable reserve;
2. Further exploration activities are being implemented or are about to be implemented under a specific plan.

Where a new economically exploitable reserve is discovered and proved in a well for which the drilling exploration disbursements have been expensed, no adjustment may be made to the expensed drilling exploration disbursements and the disbursements for redrilling exploration and for the completion of the well shall be capitalized.

Article 15 The non-drilling exploration disbursements shall be recorded in the profits and losses of the current period at the time of incurrence.

31.4 Chapter IV: Accounting Treatments of Oil and Gas Development

Article 16 The term "oil development" refers to the activities such as the construction or renovation of wells and other relevant facilities in order to acquire the oil and gas of a proved mining area.

Article 17 The disbursements incurred during the oil and gas development activities shall be capitalized, respectively, in light of their purposes and be recognized as the cost of well and relevant facilities formed by the oil and gas development.

The cost of well and relevant facilities formed by the oil and gas development mainly includes:

1. The predrilling preparation disbursements, including the prephase research, project geological investigation, project design, determination of location of the well, cleaning up the well site, building roads, as well as other activities;
2. The disbursements for the purpose of purchasing equipment of the well and for the construction of the well. The equipment of the well shall include the casing pipes, oil pipes, oil pump equipment, and well mouth devices. The construction of the well shall include the drilling and completion of the well;
3. The disbursements for the purpose of purchasing and constructing the systems for promoting the exploitation rate; and

4. The disbursements for the purpose of purchasing and constructing the centralized transport facilities, separation processing facilities, measurement equipment, storage facilities, various offshore platforms, seabed and land cables, etc. within the mining area.

Article 18 In a proved mining area, the disbursements incurred during the process from the drilling to the current layer that has been proved shall be considered as the disbursements for oil and gas development. The disbursements incurred due to the continuous drilling till the unproved layer in order to obtain the new proved economically exploitable reserve shall be considered as the drilling exploration disbursements, and be treated in light of *Articles 13* and *14* of these Standards.

31.5 Chapter V: Accounting Treatments for the Oil and Gas Production

Article 19 The expression "oil and gas production" refers to the activities such as extracting any oil and gas from the oil and gas deposit to the surface of the earth, gathering, transporting, processing, storing on the spot within the scope of the mining area, as well as the management of the mining area.

Article 20 The cost of oil and gas production shall include the depletion of the rights and interests of the relevant mining area, the depletion of the wells and relevant facilities, the depreciation of the auxiliary equipment and facilities, as well as the operating expenses. The term "operating expenses" include the direct and indirect expenses incurred during the period of the oil and gas production and the management of the mining area.

Article 21 An enterprise shall compute the depletion of its wells and other relevant facilities by adopting the output method or the straight-line method. The wells and relevant facilities shall include the exploration wells where the economically exploitable reserve is discovered and proved, wells formed in the exploitation activities, and other various facilities directly related to the exploitation activities. If the output method is adopted for calculation of the depletion, the depletion amount shall be computed in light of a single mining area or in light of a group of adjacent mining areas with identical or similar geological structure features or deposit layer conditions. The calculation formula shall be given as follows: The depletion amount of the wells and other relevant facilities of the mining areas = the book value of the wells and relevant facilities of the mining areas at the end of the period × the depletion rate of the wells and relevant facilities of the mining areas.

The depletion rate of the wells and relevant facilities of the mining areas = the output of the proved mining areas in the current period/(the economically exploitable reserves at the end of the period which has been proved and have been exploited + the output of the mining areas in the current period). The economically exploitable reserves at the end of the period which have been proved and have been exploited include the economically exploitable reserves which have been proved and have been put into full exploitation after the completion of the drilling of the net of development wells and the construction of the supporting facilities, and the increased exploitable reserves correspondingly after the facilities necessary for the technologies to promote the exploitation rate have been finished and these facilities have been put into operation.

Article 22 The earthquake equipment, construction equipment, vehicles, maintenance workshops, warehouses, supply stations, communication equipment, office facilities, and other auxiliary equipment and facilities shall be treated in accordance with the Accounting Standard for Enterprises No. 4—Fixed Assets.

Article 23 For an enterprise's obligation to do the discarded dispose for any mining area, if this obligation satisfies the conditions for the recognition of the expected liabilities as prescribed in the Accounting Standards for Enterprises No. 13—Contingencies, it shall recognize this obligation as an expected liability and shall increase the corresponding book value of the wells and relevant facilities. If the conditions for the recognition of the expected liabilities are not satisfied, the disbursements for the disassembly, removal, and site cleaning at the time of discard shall be recorded in the profits and losses of the current period. The discard of a mining area refers to the termination of production of the last well of a mining area.

Article 24 The impairment of the wells and relevant facilities, auxiliary equipment and facilities shall be treated in light of the Accounting Standard for Enterprises No. 8—Impairment of Assets.

31.6 Chapter VI: Disclosure

Article 25 An enterprise shall disclose the information related to the oil and gas exploitation activities as follows in its notes:

1. The data of the beginning and the end of the year of the domestic and overseas oil and gas reserves that they possessed.
2. The total amount of all disbursements incurred in the current period in order to obtain the rights and interests of domestic and overseas mining areas, the oil and gas exploration as well as the oil and gas development.
3. The original book value of the rights and interests of the proved mining areas, wells and relevant facilities, the accumulative depletion amounts and the accumulative amounts of the impairment provisions as well as their calculation methods. The original book value of the auxiliary equipment and facilities for the oil and gas exploitation activities, the accumulative depreciation amounts, and the accumulative amounts of the impairment provisions as well as their calculation methods.

31.7 Comments

ASBE No. 27 introduces and formalizes the current market practice for the petroleum and natural gas extraction industry. Mineral interest in properties shall be classified as either mineral interests in proved properties (i.e., properties found to contain proved reserves that can be extracted economically) or mineral interests in unproved properties. Expenditures incurred in obtaining mineral interests in properties shall be capitalized as a cost when incurred. Expenditures incurred after acquisition of the mineral interests in properties such as fees for use of the exploration right and development right, and any rental payments, shall be recognized in the profit or loss for the current period.

Exploratory drilling costs incurred shall temporarily be capitalized. If, after completing the drilling of a well, it is discovered that the well contains proved reserves, the exploratory drilling costs shall be capitalized as costs of wells and related equipment. Otherwise, they shall be expensed in the current period unless they continue to meet the temporary capitalization criteria. Costs other than exploratory drilling costs, such as geological stud and geophysical prospecting, shall be expensed as incurred.

For mineral interests in proved properties, an enterprise shall assess whether there is an impairment indication on each balance sheet date in accordance with ASBE No. 8 for mineral interests in unproved properties, an enterprise shall perform impairment testing at least annually. If the fair value of an unproved property is less than its carrying amount, the difference shall be recognized as an impairment loss. Impairment losses are not reversed in the future.

If a portion of an asset of an interest in unproved properties (where an impairment loss has been recognized) is transferred, and the consideration obtained is higher than the carrying amount, the excess shall be recognized as a gain. If the consideration obtained is less than the carrying amount, it shall be offset against the cost of the mineral interest in the property and no gain or loss shall be recognized.

Furthermore, ASBE No. 27 allows the depletion of mineral interest in proved properties using either the straight-line method or the unit-of-production method (introduced after reform occurred in 2007). An enterprise shall recognize an obligation for decommissioning incurred during a particular period if it satisfies the recognition criteria of a provision under ASBE No. 13.

Several major differences can be recognized when comparing ASBE No. 27 with the equivalent IFRS 6. IFRS 6 applies to expenditure incurred for the exploration and evaluation of mineral resources (including petroleum and natural gas). ASBE No. 27 covers the accounting treatment of the exploration for exploitation and production of petroleum and natural gas.

Concerning the measurement, IFRS 6 allows enterprises to continue to use their existing accounting policies for exploration and evaluation assets (either the cost or the revaluation model), provided that, such polices, result in information that is relevant and reliable. At initial recognition, the costs of exploration and evaluation assets include expenditure on topographical, geological, geochemical, and geophysical studies. ASBE No. 27 only permits the cost model and capitalization of exploratory drilling costs. Costs other than exploratory drilling costs shall be expenses as incurred.

Finally, impairment testing is required only when facts and circumstances suggest the carrying amount of an exploration and evaluation asset may exceed its recoverable amount. IAS 36 does not prevent the reversal of impairment losses. ASBE No. 27 requires an impairment test to be performed for mineral interests at least annually. For mineral interests in proved properties, impairment testing shall be performed when there is an impairment indication. Impairment losses are not reversed in future.

31.8 Examples

Company X expends 250,000,000 CNY in development and production of unproved petroleum wells. Further drilling and non-drilling costs borne for exploration activities rise to 12,500,000 CNY. On 31 December, no proved reserves have still been found, and a recoverable value for the properties of 75 % is estimated.

According to these circumstances, Company X shall initially record the properties referred to petroleum wells for 250,000,000 CNY. Cost incurred for both drilling and non-drilling activities are recognized in profit or loss (12,500,000 CNY). Finally, the estimation of recoverable value up to 75 % leads to an impairment loss of 62,500,000 CNY, still referred to profit and loss.

Chapter 32
Accounting Standards for Business Enterprises No. 28—Changes of Accounting Policies and Accounting Estimates and Error Correction

32.1 Chapter I: General Provisions

Article 1 These Standards are formulated in accordance with the Accounting Standards for Enterprises—Basis Standards for the purpose of regulating the application of enterprise accounting policies, the changes of accounting policies and accounting estimates, the recognition, and measurement of the error correction in the prior periods, as well as the disclosure of relevant information.

Article 2 The effects on income tax by the changes of accounting policies and the error correction in the prior periods shall be governed by the Accounting Standards for Enterprises No. 18—Income Tax.

32.2 Chapter II: Accounting Policies

Article 3 With regard to identical or similar transactions or events, an enterprise shall adopt the same accounting policies, unless it is otherwise prescribed by other accounting standards. The term "accounting policies" refers to the specific principles, basis, and accounting treatment methods adopted by an enterprise for accounting recognition, measurement, and reporting.

Article 4 The accounting policies adopted by an enterprise shall be consistent for each accounting period and the prior and subsequent accounting periods and shall not be changed randomly. However, if one of the following conditions is satisfied, accounting policy may be changed:

1. The requirement by any law, administrative regulation, or national uniform accounting system changes; or
2. More reliable and more relevant accounting information shall be provided through changing the accounting policy.

L. Riccardi, *China Accounting Standards*,
DOI 10.1007/978-981-10-0006-5_32

Article 5 The following items shall not belong to the changes of accounting policies:

1. A new accounting policy is adopted for transactions or events occurred in the current period which are different essentially from those occurred in the prior periods; and
2. A new accounting policy is adopted for transactions or events which occur for the first time or are unimportant.

Article 6 Where an enterprise changes an accounting policy according to the requirement of any law, administrative regulation, or the national uniform accounting system, it shall implement it pursuant to the relevant accounting provisions of the state. If a change in accounting policy can provide more reliable and more relevant accounting information, the retrospective adjustment method shall be adopted for handling. The amount of cumulative effect by the change in accounting policy shall be adjusted and presented as the retained earnings at the beginning of the earliest prior period, and the beginning balance of other relevant items as well as other comparative data disclosed in the prior period presented shall be adjusted along with, unless the cumulative effect of a change in accounting policy is not feasible essentially. The retrospective adjustment method refers to a method whereby, for a change in accounting policy in respect of particular transactions or events, the changed accounting policy is adopted as if it had been in use from the day when such transactions or events first occurred, and the relevant items in the financial statements are adjusted accordingly. The cumulative effect of a change in accounting policy refers to the difference between the adjusted beginning balance of retained gain of the earliest prior period presented if the adjusted accounting policy had been applied retrospectively for all prior periods and the present amount of the retained earnings.

Article 7 If it is impracticable to determine the effect of a change in accounting policy for the prior period presented, the new accounting policy shall be applied from the beginning of the earliest period for which retrospective application is practicable. If, at the beginning of the current period, it is impracticable to determine the cumulative effect of the change in accounting policy for all prior periods, the prospective application method shall be adopted. The term "prospective application method" refers to a method whereby for a change in accounting policy, the new accounting policy is applied to the transactions or events occurring on the date of change and in subsequent periods, or refers to a method whereby for a change in accounting estimate, the effects of the change of the accounting estimate are recognized during the current period of the change of accounting estimate and in future periods.

32.3 Chapter III: Changes in Accounting Estimates

Article 8 An enterprise may need to revise its accounting estimates due to a change in the basis for estimates, or due to the obtainment of new information, accumulation of more experiences as well as the subsequent development and changes. The basis for the changes in accounting estimates shall be genuine and reliable. A change in accounting estimate refers to an adjustment to the book value of an asset or liability or to the amount of expense of an asset during a certain period, resulting from the changes in the current situation of the asset or liability and the expected economic benefits and obligations.

Article 9 The prospective application method shall be adopted by an enterprise for treating the changes in accounting estimates. If a change in accounting estimate affects only the current period of the change, the effect of the change shall be recognized in the period of the change. If any change in an accounting estimate affects both the period of the current change and future periods, the effects of the change shall be recognized in the period of the change and in future periods.

Article 10 Where it is difficult for an enterprise to determine a change as one in accounting policy or as one in an accounting estimate, it shall treat it as a change in an accounting estimate.

32.4 Chapter IV: Corrections of Prior Period Errors

Article 11 Prior period errors refer to the failure to use or misuse of the following two kinds of information and result in the omissions from or mispresentation in financial statements for the prior periods:

1. The reliable information that was available and could reasonably be expected to be obtained and taken into account when preparing the financial statements for the prior periods;
2. The reliable information that was available when the financial reports of prior periods are authorized for issue;

Generally, prior period errors include calculation mistakes, mistakes in applying accounting policies, oversights or misinterpretations of facts, consequences of fraud, inventory overage, and fixed asset overage.

Article 12 An enterprise shall adopt the retrospective restatement method to correct any important errors of prior period, however, unless it is impractical to recognize the amount of cumulative effects of the prior period error. The term "retrospective restatement method" refers to a method whereby, when a prior period error is discovered, the relevant items of the financial statements are corrected as if the prior period error had never occurred.

Article 13 If it is impracticable to recognize the effect of a prior period error, the enterprise may begin to adjust the beginning balance of the retained earnings of the earliest prior period for which the retrospective restatement is practical, and in the meanwhile, it may adjust the beginning balances of other relevant items in the financial statements, or may adopt the prospective application method.

Article 14 An enterprise shall, in the financial statements of the current period where it discovers any important prior period error, adjust the comparative data of the prior period.

32.5 Chapter V: Disclosure

Article 15 An enterprise shall, in its notes, disclose the following information related to the changes in accounting polices:

1. The character, contents, and reasons for the changes of accounting policies;
2. The names of the affected items and the adjusted amounts in the financial statements for the current period and all the prior periods presented; and
3. If it is unable to make retrospective adjustments, it shall state the facts, reasons, date of beginning of the application of the new accounting policies as well as the information about the concrete application thereof.

Article 16 An enterprise shall, in its notes, disclose the following information related to the changes in accounting estimates:

1. The contents of and reasons for the changes in accounting estimates;
2. The effect amount in the current period and future periods by changes in accounting estimates; and
3. If it is unable to recognize the effect amount of a change in the accounting estimate, it shall disclose the facts and reasons.

Article 17 An enterprise shall, in its notes, disclose the following information related to the corrections in prior period errors:

1. The nature of the prior period errors;
2. The names of the affected items and the corrected amounts in the financial statements for all prior periods presented;
3. If it is unable to make a retrospective restatement, it shall state the facts, reasons, time point of beginning the correction of the prior period error as well as the information about the concrete correction.

Article 18 In the financial statements of subsequent periods, it is not required to repeatedly disclose any information about the changes of accounting policies and corrections of prior period errors which have been disclosed in the notes of prior periods.

32.6 Comments

ASBE No. 28 introduces the term "prior period errors" and removes the concept of "significant accounting errors in prior periods." An enterprise shall correct materials' prior period errors by retrospective restatements. Changes in accounting policies shall be accounted for using retrospective application. No substantial differences can be recognized against comparable IAS 8.

When a Standard or an Interpretation specifically applies to a transaction, other event, or condition, the accounting policy or policies applied to that item must be determined by applying the Standard or Interpretation and considering any relevant Implementation Guidance issued by the Standard or Interpretation. In the absence of a Standard or an Interpretation that specifically applies to a transaction, other event, or condition, management must use its judgement in developing and applying an accounting policy that results in information that is relevant and reliable. In making that judgement, management must refer to and consider the applicability of: the requirements and guidance in IASB standards and interpretations dealing with similar and related issues, and the definitions, recognition criteria and measurement concepts for assets, liabilities, income and expenses in the framework.

An entity shall select and apply its accounting policies consistently for similar transactions, other events, and conditions, unless a Standard or an Interpretation specifically requires or permits categorization of items for which different policies may be appropriate. If a Standard or an Interpretation requires or permits such categorization, an appropriate accounting policy shall be selected and applied consistently to each category.

An entity is permitted to change an accounting policy only if the change is required by a standard or interpretation, or results in the financial statements providing reliable and more relevant information about the effects of transactions, other events, or conditions on the entity's financial position, financial performance, or cash flows.

Note that changes in accounting policies do not include applying an accounting policy to a kind of transaction or event that did not occur previously or was immaterial. If a change in accounting policy is required by a new IASB standard or interpretation, the change is accounted for as required by that new pronouncement, or if the new pronouncement does not include specific transition provisions, then the change in accounting policy is applied.

If an entity has not applied a new standard or interpretation that has been issued but is not yet effective, the entity must disclose that fact and any known or reasonably estimable information relevant to assessing the possible impact that the new pronouncement will have in the year it is applied. The effect of a change in an accounting estimate shall be recognized prospectively by including it in profit or loss in the period of the change—if the change affects that period only, or the period of the change and future periods; if the change affects both.

However, to the extent that a change in an accounting estimate gives rise to changes in assets and liabilities, or relates to an item of equity, it is recognized by adjusting the carrying amount of the related asset, liability, or equity item in the period of the change.

The disclosure of changes in accounting policies and estimates copes with the nature and amount of a change in an accounting estimate that has an effect in the current period or is expected to have an effect in future periods, and if the amount of the effect in future periods is not disclosed because estimating it is impracticable, an entity shall disclose that fact.

32.7 Examples

Company X buys at the beginning of Year N a new item in PPE for RMB 1,000,000 with an estimated useful life of 8 years and no residual value. After the end of Year 3, due to a new technology, it is estimated that the reviewed remaining life of the Asset is expected to be 2 years. According to data, let us compute changes in estimate for the asset.

For the first 4 years, the annual depreciation is computed as RMB 125,000 ($125,000 \times 4 = 500,000$ the overall value of depreciation, whereas 500,000 the carrying amount of the asset). Since the new expected useful life is now 2 years, the depreciation to be computed is now RMB 250,000.

Now, let us assume that Company X borne out borrowing expenses for financing the acquisition of the asset. Company X previously capitalized interest estimated in RMB 60,000, but after that decides to write it off immediately as an expense when occurred. This is a change in accounting policy because there is a change in the accounting recognition and the interest is now to be recognized as an expense rather than the cost of Asset.

Chapter 33
Accounting Standards for Business Enterprises No. 29—Events After the Balance Sheet Date

33.1 Chapter I: General Provisions

Article 1 These Standards are formulated in accordance with the Accounting Standards for Enterprises—Basic Standards for the purpose of regulating the recognition and measurement of the matters after the balance sheet date, as well as the disclosure of relevant information.

Article 2 The term "event after the balance sheet date" refers to an event, either favorable or unfavorable, that occurs between the balance sheet date and the date when the financial statements are authorized for issuance. The date that the financial statements are authorized for issuance refers to the date when the financial statements are authorized by the board of directors or equivalent governing body for issuance. The events after the balance sheet date include the adjusting events and non-adjusting events occurring after the balance sheet date. The term "adjusting event after the balance sheet date" refers to an event after the balance sheet date that provides any new or further evidence for the conditions that has existed on the balance sheet date. The term "non-adjusting event after the balance sheet date" refers to an event that a condition occurs after the balance sheet date.

Article 3 Where any event after the balance sheet date indicates the going concern assumption is no longer appropriate, the enterprise should not make the financial statements on the basis of going concern.

33.2 Chapter II: Adjusting Events After the Balance Sheet Date

Article 4 An enterprise shall adjust its financial statements on the date of the balance sheet date for any adjusting event occurring in an enterprise after the balance sheet date.

L. Riccardi, *China Accounting Standards*,
DOI 10.1007/978-981-10-0006-5_33

Article 5 The adjusting events occurring in an enterprise after the balance sheet date generally include the following:

1. Any litigations completed after the balance sheet date, wherein the court judgment confirms that the enterprise has any present obligation which has existed on the balance sheet date, thus it is necessary to adjust the expected liability related to such litigation originally recognized, or to recognize a new liability;
2. Any exact evidence obtained after the balance sheet date indicating that an asset is devalued on the balance sheet date, or that the amount of a recognized devalue for that asset needs to be adjusted;
3. The cost of an asset purchased prior to the balance sheet date or the income generated from an asset sold prior to the balance sheet date is further confirmed after the balance sheet date; and
4. Any fraud or error that is found in the financial statements after the balance sheet date.

33.3 Chapter III: Non-adjusting Events After the Balance Sheet Date

Article 6 No enterprise may adjust the financial statements on the date of the balance sheet date for any non-adjusting event occurring in an enterprise after the balance sheet date.

Article 7 The non-adjusting events occurring in an enterprise after the balance sheet date generally include the following:

1. Significant lawsuits, arbitrations, or commitments occurring after the balance sheet date;
2. Any significant change in the asset price, tax policy, or foreign exchange rate occurring after the balance sheet date;
3. Any severe loss on an asset resulted from a natural disaster after the balance sheet date;
4. The issuance of stocks or bonds, or any other huge amount borrowing from an outside party after the balance sheet date;
5. The capitalization of capital reserves after the balance sheet date;
6. Any significant loss occurring after the balance sheet date;
7. The important change in account policy after the balance sheet date; and
8. Any enterprise combination or disposal of subsidiary after the balance sheet date;

Article 8 After the balance sheet date, the profits or dividends to be distributed and declared to be distributed upon deliberation and approval under the profit distribution plan of an enterprise shall not be recognized as a liability on the balance sheet date, but shall be separately disclosed in the notes.

33.4 Chapter IV: Disclosure

Article 9 An enterprise shall, in its notes, disclose the following information related to the events after the balance sheet date:

1. The organ which authorizes the issuance of the financial statements, and the date on which the financial statements are authorized to be issued. According to the provisions of the relevant laws and administrative regulations, if the owner of an enterprise or any other party has the power to revise the issued financial statements, it shall disclose the relevant information.
2. The nature and content of each important non-adjusting event after the balance sheet date, as well as its effect on the financial status and operating outcomes. If it is unable to make an estimate, an explanation shall be made.

Article 10 Where an enterprise, after the balance sheet date, obtains any new or further evidence that affects the conditions existed on the balance sheet date, it shall adjust the relevant information of disclosures.

33.5 Comments

ASBE No. 29 is related to several basic concepts, defined as follows.

Adjusting event: An event after the reporting period that provides further evidence of conditions that existed at the end of the reporting period, including an event that indicates that the going concern assumption in relation to the whole or part of the enterprise is not appropriate.

Event after the reporting period: An event, which could be favorable or unfavorable, that occurs between the end of the reporting period and the date that the financial statements are authorized for issue.

Adjust financial statements for adjusting events—events after the balance sheet date that provide further evidence of conditions that existed at the end of the reporting period, including events that indicate that the going concern assumption in relation to the whole or part of the enterprise is not appropriate. Do not adjust for non-adjusting events—events or conditions that arose after the end of the reporting period. If an entity declares dividends after the reporting period, the entity shall not recognize those dividends as a liability at the end of the reporting period. That is a non-adjusting event.

An entity shall not prepare its financial statements on a going concern basis if management determines after the end of the reporting period either that it intends to liquidate the entity or to cease trading, or that it has no other realistic alternative.

Companies must disclose the date when the financial statements were authorized for issue and who gave that authorization. If the enterprise owners or others have the power to amend the financial statements after issuance, the enterprise must disclose that fact.

Non-adjusting events should be disclosed if they are of such importance that non-disclosure would affect the ability of users to make proper evaluations and decisions. The required disclosure is (a) the nature of the event and (b) an estimate of its financial effect or a statement that a reasonable estimate of the effect cannot be made. A company should update disclosures that relate to conditions that existed at the end of the reporting period to reflect any new information that it receives after the reporting period about those conditions. Dispositions provisioned in ASBE No. 29 are in full conformity with the equivalent IAS 10.

33.6 Examples

Company X at the end of Year N enters in its balance sheet all records concerning outstanding accounting receivables. Among these a receivable of RMB 200,000 from Company Y has been recognized. Few days after the closing of the financial year, Company Y is placed under receivership, and it is already in financial difficulties.

At this point, the repayment capacity for Company X is assessed in 30 % of the face value of the debt (RMB 200,000 × 30 % = RMB 60,000). Accordingly, Company X should proceed with an adjustment entry of RMB 140,000 in the financial statement for year N recognizing provision for this bad debt.

Chapter 34
Accounting Standards for Business Enterprises No. 30—Presentation of Financial Statements

34.1 Chapter I: General Provisions

Article 1 With a view to regulating the presentation of financial statements and guaranteeing the commensurability between the financial statements of a same enterprise in different periods and between the financial statements of different enterprises in a same period, the present Standards is formulated according to the Accounting Standards for Enterprises—Basic Standards.

Article 2 The "financial statements" are structural reports on the financial status, business performance, and cash flow of an enterprise, which shall at least include the following parts:

1. the balance sheet;
2. the profit statement;
3. the cash flow statement;
4. the statement of changes in the owner's equities (or shareholder's equities, the same below); and
5. the notes.

Article 3 The preparation and presentation of a cash flow statement and the special presentation requirements of other accounting standards shall be subject to the Accounting Standards for Enterprises No. 31—Cash Flow Statement and other relevant accounting standards.

34.2 Chapter II: Basic Requirements

Article 4 An enterprise shall, on the basis of continuous operation, recognize and measure the actually occurred transactions and events according to the Accounting Standards for Enterprises—Basic Standards and the provisions of other accounting

L. Riccardi, *China Accounting Standards*,
DOI 10.1007/978-981-10-0006-5_34

standards, and then prepare financial statements. No enterprise may substitute the note disclosure for the recognition and measurement. Where it is not reasonable any more to prepare financial statements on the basis of continuous operation, the enterprise shall prepare financial statements with other basis and shall disclose this fact in its notes.

Article 5 The presentations of items in financial statements in different accounting periods shall be kept consistent, which shall not be changed randomly with the exception of those under the following circumstances:

1. It is required to change the presentation of the items of financial statements according to some accounting standards; and
2. After great change of the nature of business operation of an enterprise, the presentation of items of post-change financial statements can be able to provide more reliable and more relevant accounting information.

Article 6 Items with different nature or function shall be separately presented in financial statements, with the exception of those of no importance. As for items with similar nature or function, if the category in which they fall is of importance, they must be presented separately in the financial statements. The term "importance" refers to that an item is of significance when the omission or false reporting thereof may affect the economic decision making of the user on the basis of it. Then, the item shall be considered of importance. The importance shall, in light of the environment in which the enterprise is situated, be judged on the basis of the nature and amount of the item.

Article 7 The amounts of the items of assets and liabilities, incomes, and expenses in financial statements shall not countervail each other, unless it is otherwise provided for in other accounting standards. The presentation of the net amount of an asset item minus the impairment provision is not an offset. The presentation of the net amount of any gain or loss produced by any non-routine activity minus the expenses is not an offset.

Article 8 The presentation of financial statements of the current period shall at least provide the comparative data of all items of the previous comparative period, as well as the explanations on the understanding of the financial statements of the current period, unless it is otherwise provided for in other accounting standards. According to the provisions of *Article 5* of the present Standards, where there is any change to the items presented in the financial statements, an adjustment shall be made to the comparative date of the previous period in light of the presentation requirements of the current period, and the reasons and nature of the adjustment and the adjustment amount to each item shall be disclosed in the notes. In case it is not feasible to adjust the comparative data of the previous period, the reasons for the failure of adjustment shall be disclosed in the notes. The term "infeasibility" refers to that an enterprise is still unable to adopt a certain provision after it makes all reasonable efforts.

Article 9 An enterprise shall, at the eye-catching place of the financial statements, disclose the following items:

1. the name of the presenting enterprise;
2. the balance sheet date or the accounting period covered by the financial statements;
3. the unit of RMB amount;
4. If the financial statements are consolidated financial statements, an indication shall be given.

Article 10 An enterprise shall at least prepare financial statements on a yearly basis. If the period covered by the annual financial statements is less than one year, the period covered by the annual financial statements and the reasons for being less than one year shall be disclosed. If an enterprise offers interim financial reports to outsiders, it shall accord with the Accounting Standards for Enterprises No. 32—Interim Financial Reports as well.

Article 11 The items that are required to be presented separately according to the present Standards shall be separately presented. Items that are required to be separately presented according to other accounting standards shall be added.

34.3 Chapter III: Balance Sheets

Article 12 The assets and liabilities shall be presented as current and non-current assets and liabilities, respectively. As for the assets and liabilities of a financial enterprise, if the presentation based on fluidity provides reliable and more relevant information, the assets and liabilities may be presented on the basis of the fluidity order.

Article 13 Where an asset meets any of the following conditions, it shall be classified as current assets:

1. It is expected to be realized, sold, or consumed within a normal business cycle;
2. It is held mainly for trading;
3. It is expected to be realized within one year as of the balance sheet date (including one year, the same below); and
4. It is cash or cash equivalent, which is subject to no limit when it is used to exchange other assets or to pay off the liabilities as of the balance sheet date.

Article 14 The assets other than current assets shall be classified as non-current assets and shall be presented on the basis of their respective nature.

Article 15 The liability that can meet the following conditions shall be classified as current liabilities:

1. It is expected to be repaid within a normal business cycle;
2. It is held mainly for trading;
3. It shall be repaid at maturity within one year as of the balance sheet date; and
4. It is an asset for which the enterprise does not have an unconditional right to delay payment more than one year after the balance sheet date.

Article 16 The liabilities other than current liabilities shall be classified as non-current liabilities and shall be presented on the basis of their nature.

Article 17 As for a liability which will be at maturity within one year as of the balance sheet date, if the enterprise predicts that it can independently extend the repayment obligation by one year or more after the balance sheet date, it shall be classified as non-current liabilities. If it predicts that it is unable to independently extend the repayment obligation, even if an agreement on the rearrangement of the repayment plan is signed during the period after the balance sheet date but prior to the approval date of the financial reports, it shall be still classified as current liabilities.

Article 18 If a liability has become payable on demand because an enterprise has breached an undertaking under a long-term loan agreement, it shall be classified as current liabilities. The liability is classified as non-current liabilities if the lender has agreed, on or before the balance sheet date, to provide a grace period ending one year or more after the balance sheet date, during which the entity can rectify the breach and the lender cannot demand immediate repayment. Where any other long-term liability is under a similar circumstance, it shall be treated according to the provisions of the preceding 2 paragraphs.

Article 19 The category of assets in the balance sheets shall at least separately present items reflecting the following information:

1. money;
2. receivable and advance payments;
3. transaction investments;
4. inventories;
5. held-to-maturity investments;
6. long-term equity investments;
7. investment real estates;
8. fixed assets;
9. biological assets;
10. deferred income tax assets; and
11. Intangible assets.

Article 20 The category of assets in the balance sheets shall at least include the aggregate item of current assets and non-current assets.

Article 21 The category of liabilities in the balance sheets shall at least separately present items reflecting the following information:

1. the short-term borrowings;
2. the payable and advance receipts;
3. the payable taxes;
4. the payable wages and salaries of employees;
5. the expected liabilities;
6. the long-term borrowings;
7. the long-term accounts payable;
8. the payable bonds; and

9. the deferred income tax liabilities.

Article 22 The category of liabilities in the balance sheets shall at least include the aggregate item of current liabilities, non-current liabilities, and liabilities.

Article 23 The category of the owner's equities in the balance sheets shall at least separately present items reflecting the following information:

1. the paid-in capital (capital stock);
2. the additional paid-in capital;
3. the surplus reserves; and
4. the undistributed profits.

In the consolidated balance sheets, the equities of minority shareholders shall be separately presented in the category of equities.

Article 24 The category of equities in the balance sheets shall include the aggregate item of the owner's equities.

Article 25 The balance sheets shall present the total amount of the asset items, total amount of liability items, and total amount of items of the owner's equities.

34.4 Chapter IV: Profit Statements

Article 26 The expenses shall, on the basis of functions, be classified into costs, administrative expenses, sale expenses, and financial expenses occurred in business operation.

Article 27 The profit statements shall at least separately present items reflecting the following information:

1. the business incomes;
2. the business costs;
3. the business taxes;
4. the sale expenses;
5. the administrative expenses;
6. the financial expenses;
7. the investment gains;
8. the profits and losses on the changes in fair value;
9. the losses on the asset impairment;
10. the profits and losses on the disposal of non-current assets;
11. the income tax expenses; and
12. the net profits.

The financial enterprise may, according to its particularities, present the items in the profits.

Article 28 In the consolidated profit statements, an enterprise shall, under the item of net profits, separately present the profits and losses attributable to the parent company and the profits and losses attributable to the minority shareholders.

34.5 Chapter V: Statements of Changes in the Owner's Equities

Article 29 The statements of changes in the owner's equities shall reflect the increases and decreases in the current period as integrate parts of the owner's equities. The changes in the owner's equities, which result from the profits and losses in the current period, the gains and losses directly recorded into the owner's equities as well as the capital transaction with the owner (or shareholder, the same below), shall be presented, respectively.

Article 30 The statements of changes in the owner's equities shall at least separately present items reflecting the following information:

1. the net profits;
2. the items of gains and losses directly recorded into the owner's equities, and the total amount of the said items;
3. the accumulative amount affected by changes in accounting policies and estimates? And correction of errors;
4. the capital invested by the owners and the profits distributed to them;
5. the surplus reserves made according to the relevant provisions; and
6. the information on the balance of the paid-in capital (stock capital), additional paid-in capital, surplus reserves, the undistributed profits at the beginning and at the end of the period, and the adjustments made to them.

34.6 Chapter VI: Notes

Article 31 The notes are word descriptions or detailed information on the items presented in the balance sheets, profits statements, cash flow statements and statements of changes in the owner's equities, and the explanations on the items that are not presented in these statements.

Article 32 The notes shall disclose the basis for the preparation of financial statements. The relevant information in the notes shall be cross-referenced with the items presented in the balance sheets, profits statements, and cash flow statements and statements of changes in the owner's equities.

Article 33 Generally, the notes shall disclose the following items according to the following order:

1. the basis for the formulation of financial statements;
2. the declaration on compliance with the accounting standards for enterprises;
3. the explanations on the important accounting policies, including the basis for the measurement of items of the financial statements and the basis for the determination of accounting policies;

4. the explanations on the accounting estimates, including the basis for the determination of the accounting estimates that may result in a significant adjustment to the carrying amount of the assets or liabilities in the next accounting period;
5. the explanations on the changes in accounting policies and estimates? And explanations on the correction of errors;
6. the more detailed explanations on the important items presented in the balance sheets, profit statements, and cash flow statements and statements of changes in the owner's equities, including the amount of the profit after the termination of business operation and its composition; and
7. the contingencies and commitments, non-adjustment events occurring after the balance sheet date, the relationship of connected parties and their transactions, and other items that need to be explanted.

Article 34 An enterprise shall, during the period after the balance sheet date but before the financial statements are authorized for issue, disclose the total amount of dividends and the related amount per share it proposes or declares to distribute (or the total amount of profits to be distributed to investors).

Article 35 In case an enterprise fails to disclose the following items along with other information publicized in the financial statements, it shall disclose them in its notes:

1. the registered place and organizational form, and the address of its headquarters;
2. the nature of its business operation and its principal business activities; and
3. the name of its parent company and the ultimate parent company of the group.

34.7 Comments

New ASBE No. 30 introduces the definition of "materiality." Moreover, it also sets the requirement to classify assets and liabilities as current and non-current assets, and current and non-current liabilities.

An entity may use titles for the statements other than those stated above. All financial statements are required to be presented with equal prominence. When an entity applies an accounting policy retrospectively, or makes a retrospective restatement of items in its financial statements, or when it reclassifies items in its financial statements, it must also present a statement of financial position (balance sheet) at the beginning of the earliest comparative period. Reports that are presented outside the financial statements—including financial reviews by management, environmental reports, and value-added statements—are outside the scope of standards.

The financial statements must "present fairly" the financial position, financial performance, and cash flows of an entity. Fair presentation requires the faithful representation of the effects of transactions, other events, and conditions in accordance with the definitions and recognition criteria for assets, liabilities, income, and expenses. The application of ASBEs, with additional disclosure when necessary, is presumed to result in financial statements that achieve a fair presentation.

ASBE No. 30 requires an entity's financial statements (aligned with IFRSs) to make an explicit and unreserved statement of such compliance in the notes. Inappropriate accounting policies are highlighted either by disclosure of the accounting policies used or by notes or explanatory material.

It is acknowledged that, in extremely rare circumstances, compliance with an IFRS requirement may result in misleading information and such information may conflict with the objective of financial statements set out in the framework. In such a case, the entity is required to depart from the international requirement, with detailed disclosure of the nature, reasons, and impact of the departure.

The conceptual framework notes that financial statements are normally prepared under the going concern assumption and assumes that the entity will continue in operation for the foreseeable future. ASBE No. 30 requires management to make an assessment of an entity's ability to continue as a going concern. If management has significant concerns about the entity's ability to continue as a going concern, the uncertainties must be disclosed. If management concludes that the entity is not a going concern, the financial statements should not be prepared on a going concern basis.

It is required that an entity prepares its financial statements, except for cash flow information, using the accrual basis of accounting. The presentation and classification of items in the financial statements shall be retained from one period to the next unless a change is justified either by a change in circumstances or a requirement of a new standard.

Each material class of similar items must be presented separately in the financial statements. Dissimilar items may be aggregated only if they are individually immaterial.

However, information should not be obscured by aggregating or by providing immaterial information, materiality considerations apply to all the parts of the financial statements, and even when a standard requires a specific disclosure, materiality considerations do apply.

Assets and liabilities, and income and expenses, may not be offset unless required or permitted.

When a presentation based on liquidity provides information that is reliable and more relevant for a financial institution, assets and liabilities may be presented in order of liquidity. After the reform of 2007, comparative information shall be disclosed in respect of the previous period for all amounts reported in the financial statements. Previously, PRC GAAP only required disclosure of comparative information on the primary statements and selected notes.

ASBE No. 30 does not prescribe the format of the financial position's statement. Assets can be presented as current then non-current, or vice versa. Liabilities and equity can be presented as current, non-current, and then equity, or vice versa. The net asset presentation (assets minus liabilities) is allowed. The long-term financing approach used internationally and elsewhere (fixed assets + current assets—short-term payables = long-term debt + equity) is also acceptable.

In the consolidated income statement, profit attributable to minority interests and profit attributable to owners of the parent company should be presented separately after the profit of the year. Profit attributable to minority interests is not presented as a deduction item (as income or expense) before profit of the year in the income statement required under past PRC GAAP. Lastly, instead of preparing a statement of profit appropriation, an enterprise shall prepare a statement of changes in equity and present minority interests separately.

Accounting for differences with IAS/IFRS, under ASBE No. 30, expenses are analyzed by function, but the correspondent IAS 1 allows an enterprise to present an analysis of expenses using a classification based on either the nature of expenses or their function, whichever provides information that is more reliable and more relevant.

34.8 Examples

Following a format of balance sheet in accordance with ASBE No. 30's dispositions.

Assets	Ending balance (RMB)	Beginning balance (RMB)
Current assets		
Monetary funds		
Trading financial assets		
Notes receivable		
Accounts receivable		
Payments in advance		
Interest receivables		
Dividends receivable		
Other receivables		
Inventories		
Non-current assets due within one year		
Other current assets		
Total current assets		
Non-current assets		
Available-for-sale financial assets		
Held-to-maturity investments		
Long-term receivables		
Long-term equity investments		
Investment properties		

(continued)

(continued)

Assets	Ending balance (RMB)	Beginning balance (RMB)
Fixed assets		
Construction in progress		
Construction materials		
Fixed assets for disposal		
Biological assets		
Oil and gas assets		
Intangible assets		
Development expenditures		
Goodwill		
Long-term prepaid expenses		
Deferred tax assets		
Other non-current assets		
Total non-current assets		
Total assets		

Liabilities and owners' (stockholders') equity	Ending balance (RMB)	Beginning balance (RMB)
Current liabilities		
Short-term borrowings		
Trading financial liabilities		
Notes payable		
Accounts payable		
Receipts in advance		
Employee compensation payable		
Tax payable		
Interest payable		
Dividend payable		
Other payable		
Non-current liabilities due within one year		
Total current liabilities		
Non-current liabilities		
Long-term borrowings		
Bonds payable		
Long-term payables		
Special fund payables		
Estimated liabilities		
Deferred tax liabilities		
Other non-current liabilities		
Total non-current liabilities		

(continued)

(continued)

Liabilities and owners' (stockholders') equity	Ending balance (RMB)	Beginning balance (RMB)
Total liabilities		
Owners' (stockholders') equity		
Paid-in capital (stock)		
Capital surplus		
Less: Treasury stock		
Surplus reserve		
Undistributed profit		
Total owners' (stockholders') equity		
Total liabilities and owners' (stockholders') equity		

Following a format of income statement in accordance with ASBE No. 30's dispositions.

Item	Current period (RMB)	Prior period (RMB)
1. ***Revenue from operations***		
Less: cost of operations		
Tax and surcharge for operations		
Selling expenses		
Administrative expenses		
Financial expenses		
Impairment losses of assets		
Add: Gains on changes in fair value (or losses)		
Investment income including investment income from associated entities and joint venture enterprises		
2. ***Operating profit (or loss)***		
Add: non-operating revenue		
Less: non-operating expenses including losses on disposal of non-financial assets		
3. ***Profit before tax (or loss)***		
Less: Income tax expense		
4. ***Net profit (or loss)***		
5. ***Earnings per share***		
(a) **Basic earnings per share**		
(b) **Diluted earnings per share**		

Following a format of statement of changes in owners' equity in accordance with ASBE No. 30's dispositions.

Item	Current period (RMB)	Prior period (RMB)
1. ***Ending balance of prior year***		
Add: Changes in accounting policies		
Corrections of prior period errors		
2. ***Beginning balance of current year***		
3. ***Changes in amount for the current year***		
A. Net profit		
B. Other comprehensive income		
(b1) Net changes in fair value on available-for-sale financial assets		
(b2) Effect of other changes in owners' equity of investee enterprise accounted for under equity method		
(b3) Tax on items recognized directly in owners' equity		
(b4) Other subtotal of points a. and b. above		
Subtotal of a. and b. above		
C. Owners' contributed or reduction of capital		
(c1) Owners' contributed capital		
(c2) Amount recognized in owners' equity in respect of share-based payment		
D. Profit distribution		
(d1) Appropriation of surplus reserve		
(d2) Distribution to owners (Stockholders)		
(d3) Other		
E. Transfers within owners' equity		
(e1) Transfer from capital surplus to capital (for stock)		
(e2) Transfer from surplus reserve to capital (for stock)		
(e3) Surplus reserve for recovery of losses		
(e4) Other		
4. ***Ending balance of current year***		

Chapter 35
Accounting Standards for Business Enterprises No. 31—Cash Flow Statements

35.1 Chapter I: General Provisions

Article 1 These Standards are formulated in accordance with the Accounting Standards for Enterprises—Basic Standards for the purpose of regulating the preparation and presentation of cash flow statements.

Article 2 The term "cash flow statement" refers to a statement which reflects the inflows and outflows of cash and cash equivalents of an enterprise in a certain accounting period. The term "cash" refers to cash on hand and deposits that are available for payment at any time. The term "cash equivalents" refers to short-term and highly liquid investments that are readily convertible to known amounts of cash and which are subject to an insignificant risk of change in value. The cash as mentioned in these Standards shall include cash and cash equivalents unless the cash equivalents are mentioned simultaneously.

Article 3 The Accounting Standards for Enterprises No. 33—Consolidated Financial Statements shall be applicable to the preparation and presentation of consolidated cash flow statements.

35.2 Chapter II: Basic Requirements

Article 4 Cash flow statements shall be reported for operating activities, investing activities, and financing activities, respectively.

Article 5 Cash flows shall be presented, respectively, according to the total amounts of inflows and outflows of cash. However, the following items shall be presented according to the net amounts:

1. Cash received or paid on behalf of customers;
2. Cash inflows and outflows on items which are quick in circulation, large in amounts, and short in maturity; and

L. Riccardi, *China Accounting Standards*,
DOI 10.1007/978-981-10-0006-5_35

3. Items relating to financial enterprises, including short-term loans granted and repayment of principal of such loans, the acceptance of current deposits and the repayment of the principal of such deposits, financial institution deposits and deposits from or to other financial institutions, funds borrowed from or lent to other financial institutions, and purchase and sale of securities.

Article 6 Some extraordinary items, such as a loss from a natural disaster or an insurance claim, shall be classified into the cash flow of operating activities, investing activities, or financing activities, respectively, according to their features and shall be presented separately.

Article 7 The exchange rate used for the translation of cash flows in a foreign currency and the cash flows of an overseas subsidiary shall be the spot exchange rate on the date of the cash flows or shall be the rate which is determined through a systematic and reasonable method and which is approximate to the spot exchange rate. The effect of a change in exchange rate on cash shall, as an adjustment item, be separately presented in the cash flow statement.

35.3 Chapter III: Cash Flows Arising from Operating Activities

Article 8 An enterprise shall adopt the direct method to present the cash flows arising from operating activities. The term "operating activities" refers to all transactions and events except the investing and financing activities of an enterprise. The term "direct method" refers to a method whereby major classes of cash receipts and cash payments are presented for the cash flows arising from operating activities.

Article 9 The relevant information about the cash flows arising from the operating activities may be acquired through either of the following ways:

1. The accounting records of the enterprise.
2. Making adjustment on the business revenue, business costs, and other items in the income statement according to the following items:
   (a) The changes of inventory of current period and the changes of items of operating receivables and payables;
   (b) The depreciation of fixed assets, amortization of intangible assets, provision for asset impairment, and other non-cash projects; and
   (c) Other non-cash items falling into the scope of cash flows arising from investing activities or financing activities.

Article 10 The items to reflect the following information for cash flows arising from operating activities shall be presented separately at least:

1. Cash received from the sale of goods and the rendering of services;
2. Tax refunds received;

3. Cash received relating to other operating activities;
4. Cash paid for goods purchased and labor services received;
5. Cash paid to employee and for employee.
6. Payments of all types of taxes; and
7. Cash payments relating to other operating activities.

Article 11 The financial enterprises may, according to the industrial features and the actual situation of cash flows, reasonably determine the categories of cash flows arising from operating activities.

35.4 Chapter IV: Cash Flows Arising from Investing Activities

Article 12 The term "investing activities" refers to those activities of an enterprise, such as the purchase and construction of long-term assets and the investments and disposal activity that are not considered to be cash equivalents.

Article 13 At least, the items reflecting the following information for the cash flows arising from investing activities shall be presented separately:

1. Cash received from returns of investments;
2. Cash received from returns on investments;
3. Net cash received from the disposal of fixed assets, intangible assets, and other long-term assets;
4. Net cash received from the disposal of subsidiaries and other business entities;
5. Other cash received relating to investing activities;
6. Cash paid for the purchase and construction of fixed assets, intangible assets, and other long-term assets;
7. Cash paid for investments;
8. Net cash paid for the acquisition of subsidiaries and other business entities; and
9. Other cash payments relating to investing activities.

35.5 Chapter V: Cash Flows Arising from Financing Activities

Article 14 The term "financing activities" refers to those activities that result in changes in the scale and composition of the capital and debts of an enterprise.

Article 15 At least, the items reflecting the following information for the cash flows arising from financing activities shall be presented separately:

1. Cash received by absorbing investments;
2. Cash received from debts;

3. Cash received relating to other financing activities.
4. Cash paid for repayments of debts;
5. Cash paid for distribution of dividends or profits, or cash payments for interests; and
6. Cash payments relating to other financing activities.

35.6 Chapter VI: Disclosure

Article 16 An enterprise shall, in its notes, disclose the information about the reconciliation of net profits to cash flows arising from operating activities. It shall at least disclose the following items separately for the reconciliation of net profits to cash flows arising from operating activities:

1. The provision for impairment losses of assets;
2. The depreciation of fixed assets;
3. The amortization of intangible assets;
4. The amortization of long-term deferred expenses;
5. The deferred expenses;
6. The accrued expenses;
7. The profit or losses on the disposal of fixed assets, intangible assets, and other long-term assets;
8. The losses on the discard of fixed assets;
9. The profit and losses on the changes in fair value;
10. The financial expenses;
11. The profit or losses arising from investments;
12. The deferred income tax assets and the deferred income tax liabilities;
13. The inventories;
14. The item of operating receivables; and
15. The item of operating payables;

Article 17 An enterprise shall, in its notes, disclose the following information about the total amounts of acquisition or disposal of subsidiaries and other business entities in the current period:

1. The price for acquisition or disposal;
2. The portion of cash paid for the acquisition or disposal;
3. The portion of cash received for the acquisition or disposal of subsidiaries and other business entities; and
4. The non-cash assets and liabilities classified according to the major categories arising from the acquisition or disposal of subsidiaries and other business entities.

Article 18 An enterprise shall, in its notes, disclose the significant activities on investment and financing, which do not concern the cash receipts and payments of the current period but affect its financial status or will possibly affect its future cash flows.

Article 19 An enterprise shall, in its notes, disclose the following information related to cash and cash equivalents:

1. The composition of cash and cash equivalents and the corresponding amounts thereof in the balance sheets; and
2. The large sums of cash and cash equivalents held by an enterprise that are not available for use by the parent company or by any other subsidiary within the group.

35.7 Comments

ASBE No. 31 basically leaves unchanged provisions stated in previous PRC GAAP. Rather, some key divergences arise comparing ASBE No. 31 with the equivalent IAS 7. An entity is required to present a statement of cash flows as an integral part of its primary financial statements. Cash flows are classified and presented into operating activities, investing activities, or financing activities, with the latter two categories generally presented on a gross basis.

The statement of cash flows analyses changes in cash and cash equivalents during a period. Cash and cash equivalents comprise cash on hand and demand deposits, together with short-term, highly liquid investments that are readily convertible to a known amount of cash, and that are subject to an insignificant risk of changes in value. Guidance notes indicate that an investment normally meets the definition of a cash equivalent when it has a maturity of three months or less from the date of acquisition. Equity investments are normally excluded, unless they are in substance a cash equivalent (e.g., preferred shares acquired within three months of their specified redemption date). Bank overdrafts which are repayable on demand and which form an integral part of an entity's cash management are also included as a component of cash and cash equivalents.

First of all, ASBE No. 31 requires the use of the direct method, accompanied by a note showing the reconciliation of profit and net cash flow from operating activities using the indirect method. IAS 7 encourages the use of the direct method but allows the use of the indirect method as well. The direct method shows each major class of gross cash receipts and gross cash payments.

Another major issue regards dividends and interests. ASBE No. 31 specifies the appropriate classification for interest received (cash inflow from investing activities) and paid (cash outflow from financing activities) and dividends received (cash inflow from investing activities). Under IAS 7, these items are required to be classified as operating, investing, or financing activities in a consistent manner.

35.8 Examples

Below is the framework to be followed by enterprises under ASBEs when presenting the year-end statement of cash flow:

Item	Amount (RMB)
1. ***Cash flows from operating activities***	
Cash receipts from sale of goods and rendering of services	
Refund of taxes	
Other cash receipts relating to operating activities	
Subtotal of cash inflows from operating activities	
Cash payments for goods and services	
Cash paid to and on behalf of employees	
Payments of all types of taxes	
Other cash payments relating to operating activities	
Subtotal of cash outflows from operating activities	
Net cash flow from operating activities	
2. ***Cash flow from investing activities***	
Net cash receipts from sales of fixed assets, intangibles, and other long-term assets	
Cash receipts from return of investments, other than receipts for those instruments considered to be cash equivalents	
Net cash receipts form the disposal of subsidiaries or other business units	
Other cash receipts relating to investing activities	
Subtotal of cash inflows from investing activities	
Cash payments to acquire fixed assets, intangibles, and other LT assets	
Cash payments to acquire investments, other than payments for those instruments considered to be cash equivalents	
Net cash payments to acquire subsidiaries or other business units	
Other cash payments relating to investing activities	
Subtotal of cash outflows from investing activities	
Net cash flow from investing activities	
3. ***Cash flows from financing activities***	
Cash proceeds from investment by others	
Cash proceeds from borrowings	
Other cash receipts relating to financing activities	
Subtotal of cash inflows from financing activities	
Cash payments of amounts borrowed	
Cash payments for distribution of dividends or interest expenses	
Other cash payments relating to financing activities	
Subtotal of cash outflows from financing activities	
Net cash flows from financing activities	

(continued)

(continued)

Item	Amount (RMB)
4. ***Effect of foreign exchange rate changes on cash and cash equivalents***	
5. ***Net increase in cash and cash equivalents***	
Cash and cash equivalents balance at the beginning of the period	
6. ***Cash and cash equivalents balance at the end of the period***	

Chapter 36
Accounting Standards for Business Enterprises No. 32—Interim Financial Reporting

36.1 Chapter I: General Provisions

Article 1 These Standards are formulated in accordance with the Accounting Standards for Enterprises—Basic Standards for the purpose of regulating the contents of interim financial reports, and the principles of recognition and measurement to be followed when working out the interim financial reports.

Article 2 An interim financial report refers to a financial report worked out on the basis of an interim period. An interim period refers to a reporting term which is shorter than a full fiscal year.

36.2 Chapter II: Contents of Interim Financial Reports

Article 3 An interim financial report shall at least include a balance sheet, an profit statement, a cash flow statement, and explanatory notes.

The balance sheet, profit statement, and cash flow statement included in an interim financial report shall be presented in their complete forms. Their format and contents shall be consistent with the annual accounting statements of the prior fiscal year. If the format and content of the financial statements have been changed due to the adoption of new accounting standards for the current year, the interim financial statements shall be worked out according to the amended format and content. In addition, the format and content of comparative financial statements for the prior fiscal year shall also be adjusted accordingly. The basic earnings per share and the diluted earnings per share shall be separately presented in the interim profit statement.

Article 4 Where consolidated financial statements were worked out for the prior year, consolidated financial statements shall be worked out by the end of the interim period. If a financial report for the prior year includes financial statements of the

L. Riccardi, *China Accounting Standards*,
DOI 10.1007/978-981-10-0006-5_36

parent company besides the consolidated financial statements, the interim financial report shall include the financial statements of the parent company as well. If a financial report for the prior year includes consolidated financial statements, but if all subsidiaries that were included in the consolidation scope were disposed during the period of interim reporting, the interim financial report shall be only required to provide the financial statements of the parent company, but the comparative financial statements for the prior year shall still include the consolidated financial statements unless there is no subsidiary in the comparative interim period of the prior year.

Article 5 An interim financial report shall, according to the following provision, provide the comparative financial statements:

1. The balance sheet statement at the end of the current interim period and the balance sheet statement at the end of the prior year;
2. The profit statement for the current interim period, the profit statement for the period from the beginning of the year to the end of the current interim period, as well as the profit statement of the comparative period of the prior year; and
3. The cash flow statement for the period from the beginning of the year to the end of the current interim period, and the cash flow statement for the period from the beginning of the prior year to the end of the comparative current interim period.

Article 6 Where any adjustment or revision is made to the items of the financial statements in an interim report, the relevant amounts of the items in the comparative financial statements for the prior year shall be reclassified according to the requirements of the interim financial statements for the current year, and the reasons and contents of the reclassification shall be explained in the notes. If the reclassification is impracticable, the reasons shall be given in the notes.

Article 7 The notes in an interim financial report shall be worked out based on the period from the beginning of the year to the end of the current interim, and shall disclose any significant events or transactions, which occurred after the balance sheet date of the prior year and which may be helpful to the understanding of financial status, operating performance, and cash flow changes of the enterprise. The enterprise shall, in its notes, disclose any significant events or transactions, which may be helpful to the understanding of its financial status, operating performances, and cash flows during the current interim period.

Article 8 The notes in an interim financial report shall at least include the following information:

1. A declaration that the accounting policies adopted for the interim financial statements are consistent with those for the financial statements of the prior year. If the accounting policy altered, the nature, details, reasons, and effect of the change of the accounting policy shall be explained. If it is unable to make a retrospective adjustment, the reasons shall be explained.
2. The details, reasons, and effect of alteration of accounting estimates, or if the effect cannot be determined, the reason shall be explained;

3. The nature of any prior period error and the amount of correction; if the retrospective restatement is impractical, the reasons shall be explained;
4. The seasonal or periodicity features of the enterprise's operations;
5. The details of changes in affiliated enterprises where a control relationship exists. Where there are related party transactions, the nature of the affiliated party relationship, the types of transactions, and the essential elements of the transactions shall be disclosed;
6. The details of changes in the consolidation scope for the consolidated financial statements;
7. The explanatory comments about the financial statement items that are abnormal in terms of their nature or amounts;
8. The details of issuance, repurchase, and repayment of securities;
9. The details of any distribution of profits to the enterprise's owners, including profits distributed and distribution proposed or approved but not yet made in the interim period;
10. If any segment reporting information is required to be disclosed under the Accounting Standards for Enterprises, the segment revenue and segment profit (loss) under primary segment reporting shall be disclosed;
11. The non-adjusting events occurring during the period from interim balance sheet date to the date on which the interim financial report is authorized for issuance;
12. The details of any changes in contingent liabilities and contingent assets after the prior year's balance sheet date;
13. A description of any changes in the composition of the enterprise such as business combination, acquisition, or disposal of long-term investments for which the enterprise can exercise significant influence and has joint control or control over the investees, or termination of business operations;
14. Other significant transactions or events such as transfer and sale of significant long-term assets, significant acquisitions of fixed assets and intangible assets, significant research and development disbursements, and significant assets impairment losses.

When an enterprise provides information about the affiliated party transactions, and segment revenue and segment profit (loss) as mentioned in the preceding Items (5) and (10), it shall simultaneously provide the figures of the current interim period (or the end of the current interim period), the figures during the period from the beginning of the current year to the end of the current interim period, the comparative figures of the comparative current period of the prior year (or the end of the comparative period), and comparative figures during the period from the beginning of the comparative year to the end of the current interim period.

Article 9 In the recognition, measurement, and report of the each line item on the interim financial statements, the enterprise shall base its judgment about the importance of each line item on the interim financial figure other than on the annual financial figure. As compared with annual financial figures, the interim accounting measurement may rely on the estimates to a greater extent; however, the enterprise shall ensure that the interim financial report it provides includes the relevant important information.

Article 10 During the same fiscal year, if an estimate amount reported in an prior interim financial report is changed significantly during the final interim period, but a separate financial report is not published for that final interim period by enterprise, the details, reasons, and effect amount of that alteration of estimate should be disclosed in the notes of the annual financial statements.

36.3 Chapter III: Recognition and Measurement

Article 11 The accounting policies adopted by an enterprise for its interim financial statements shall be consistent with those as adopted for its annual financial statements. If any accounting policy alters after the balance sheet date of prior year and if the accounting policy after alteration will be adopted for the annual financial statements, the accounting policy after alteration shall be adopted for the interim financial statements and shall be treated according to the provision of Article 14 of these Standards.

Article 12 The interim accounting measurement shall be based on the period from the beginning of the year to the end of the current interim period. The frequency of the financial reports shall not affect the measurement of the annual results. Within a same accounting year, if the accounting estimate for an accounting statement item reported in a prior interim period alters in the subsequent interim period, such amount after accounting estimate alteration should be reflected in the subsequent interim accounting statements, but the amount of the item as reported in the prior interim period should not be adjusted. In the meanwhile, the alteration of the accounting estimate shall also be disclosed in the notes according to provisions of Article (2) or Article 10 of these Standards.

Article 13 An enterprise should recognize and measure revenues that are received seasonally, cyclically, or occasionally when they are occurred and shall not anticipate or defer such revenues in interim accounting statements unless anticipation or deferral was permitted at the end of the accounting year. An enterprise shall recognize and measure costs that are incurred unevenly during an accounting year when they are incurred and shall not anticipate or defer such costs in the interim accounting statements unless the anticipation or deferral would be acceptable at the end of the fiscal year.

Article 14 If there is any alteration in an accounting policy during the interim period for an enterprise, it shall be treated according to the Accounting Standards for Enterprises No. 28—Changes in Accounting Policies and Accounting Estimates, and Corrections of Errors shall be disclosed accordingly in the notes pursuant to the provision of *Article* 8 (1) of these Standards. If the cumulative effect of a change in accounting policy can be reasonably determined and if the change in accounting policy affects the figures of any line items on the interim financial statements for the prior interim period in the current fiscal year, these items shall be adjusted retrospectively as if the same accounting policy has been adopted throughout the whole fiscal year. In the meanwhile, the comparative financial statements of the prior year shall also be adjusted accordingly.

36.4 Comments

New ASBE No. 32 does not introduce any important provision upon prior PRC GAAP.

Interim Financial Reporting standard applies when an entity prepares an interim financial report, without mandating when an entity should prepare such a report. Permitting less information to be reported than in annual financial statements (on the basis of providing an update to those financial statements), the standard outlines the recognition, measurement, and disclosure requirements for interim reports. The objective under ASBE No. 32 is to prescribe the minimum content of an interim financial report and to prescribe the principles for recognition and measurement in financial statements presented for an interim period.

The explanatory notes required are designed to provide an explanation of events and transactions that are significant to an understanding of the changes in financial position and performance of the entity since the last annual reporting date. It is stated a presumption that anyone who reads an entity's interim report will also have access to its most recent annual report. Consequently, ASBE No. 32 avoids repeating annual disclosures in interim condensed reports.

The same accounting policies should be applied for interim reporting as are applied in the entity's annual financial statements, except for accounting policy changes made after the date of the most recent annual financial statements that are to be reflected in the next annual financial statements. A key provision of ASBE No. 32 is that an entity should use the same accounting policy throughout a single financial year. If a decision is made to change a policy mid-year, the change is implemented retrospectively, and previously reported interim data are restated.

In deciding how to recognize, measure, classify, or disclose an item for interim financial reporting purposes, materiality is to be assessed in relation to the interim period financial data, not forecast annual data. If an estimate of an amount reported in an interim period is changed significantly during the financial interim period in the financial year, but a separate financial report is not published for that period, the nature and amount of that change must be disclosed in the notes to the annual financial statements.

However, unlike IAS 34 on Interim Financial Report, ASBE No. 32 does not require a statement of changes in equity to be presented. IAS 34 allows the presentation of condensed statement of changes in equity and condensed cash flow statement. At the same time, ASBE No. 32 requires the interim balance sheet, interim income statement, and interim cash flow statements to be complete statements (i.e., it is disposed that form and content shall conform to the annual financial statements).

36.5 Examples

Company X presents semiannual interim financial statements. Let us suppose that at the end of June of the financial year N the enterprise estimates that some items recorded in inventories have a net realizable value lower than their cost. In accordance with the provisions disposed in ASBE N0. 32, the company should proceed with the writing down of the loss (e.g., RMB 15,000) in the first semiannual interim financial statement.

Assuming now that the same items are still handled in inventories at December 31 of financial year N and that at the same time, the net realizable value turns higher than the cost. In this situation, the inventory should still be recorded at the cost. However, in the end-year financial statement, the loss initially written-off (RMB 15,000) should be reversed.

Chapter 37
Accounting Standards for Business Enterprises No. 33—Consolidated Financial Statements

37.1 Chapter I: General Provisions

Article 1 This standard, formulated in accordance with ASBE—Basic Standard, should be applied in the preparation and presentation of consolidated financial statements for a group of entities under the control of a parent.

37.2 Chapter II: Introduction

Article 2 Individual financial statements are those presented by a parent or by its subsidiary before the consolidation.

Article 3 Consolidated financial statements are the financial statements of a group presented as those of a single economic entity.

Article 4 A parent is an enterprise that has one or more subsidiaries.

Article 5 A subsidiary is an enterprise that is controlled by another entity (known as the parent).

Article 6 A parent should present consolidated financial statements in which it consolidates its investments in subsidiaries.

Article 7 Consolidated financial statements should, at a minimum, include the following components:

1. Consolidated balance sheet;
2. Consolidated income statement;
3. Consolidated cash flow statement;
4. Consolidated statements of changes in owner's equity; and
5. Notes.

Article 8 Scope of consolidation for consolidated financial statements should be determined on the basis of the concept of control. Consolidated financial statements

L. Riccardi, *China Accounting Standards*,
DOI 10.1007/978-981-10-0006-5_37

should include all subsidiaries of the parent. A subsidiary is not excluded from consolidation because its business activities are dissimilar from those of the other enterprises within the group.

Article 9 Control is the power to govern the financial and operating policies of an enterprise so as to obtain benefits from its activities.

Article 10 Control is presumed to exist when the parent owns, directly or indirectly through subsidiaries, more than half of the voting power of an enterprise unless, in exceptional circumstances, it can be clearly demonstrated that such ownership does not constitute control. Control also exists when the parent owns half or less of the voting power of an enterprise when there is:

1. Ownership of more than half of the voting rights by virtue of an agreement with other investors;
2. Power to govern the financial and operating policies of the enterprise under a statute or an agreement;
3. Power to appoint or remove the majority of the members of the board of directors or equivalent governing body and the control of the enterprise is by that board or body; or
4. Power to cast the majority of votes at meetings of the board of directors or equivalent governing body and the control of the enterprise is by that board or body.

Article 11 An enterprise may own instruments that are convertible into ordinary shares, or other similar instruments that have the potential, if exercised or converted, to give the enterprise voting power or to reduce another party's voting power over the financial and operating policies of another enterprise (potential voting rights). The existence and effect of potential voting rights that are currently exercisable or convertible, including potential voting rights held by another enterprise, are considered when assessing whether an enterprise has the power to govern the financial and operating policies of another enterprise. Potential voting rights are not currently exercisable or convertible when, for example, they cannot be exercised or converted until a future date or until the occurrence of a future event.

37.3 Chapter III: Consolidation Procedures

Article 12 In preparing consolidated financial statements, an enterprise combines the financial statements of the parent and its subsidiaries line by line by adding together items of assets, liabilities, equity, income, and expenses.

Article 13 Consolidated financial statements should be prepared using uniform accounting policies for transactions and other events in similar circumstances.

If a member of the group uses accounting policies other than those adopted in the consolidated financial statements for transactions and events in similar circumstances, appropriate adjustments are made to its financial statements in preparing the consolidated financial statements.

Article 14 The financial statements of the parent and its subsidiaries used in the preparation of the consolidated financial statements should be prepared as of the same date. When the end of the reporting period of the parent is different from that of a subsidiary, the subsidiary prepares, for consolidation purposes, additional financial statements as of the same date as the financial statements of the parent unless it is impracticable to do so, or makes adjustments to its individual financial statements according to the parent's reporting period.

Article 15 When preparing consolidated financial statements, a subsidiary is required to provide its individual financial statements to its parent and the following information:

1. The application of accounting policies other than those adopted by the parent and the effected amounts;
2. The reporting period if different from that of the parent;
3. Relevant information about intragroup transactions incurred with the parent or other subsidiaries;
4. Relevant information about changes in owner's equity; and
5. Any other information that is necessary for the preparation of consolidated financial statements.

37.3.1 Consolidated Balance Sheet

Article 16 When preparing consolidated financial statements, the parent should rely on its individual balance sheets and on those of its subsidiaries and must eliminate intragroup balances and transactions on the consolidated balance sheet. In particular, in order that the consolidated financial statements present financial information about the group as that of a single economic entity, the parent must:

1. Eliminate the carrying amount of the parent's investment in each subsidiary and the parent's portion of equity of each subsidiary. The difference between these two amounts should be accounted for as goodwill, whose amount should be presented as after the impairment test, if any. Concurrently, the provision for impairment of long-term equity investments is eliminated.
2. Eliminate intragroup items of payables and receivables. Concurrently, the provision for bad debts and the provision for impairment of the debt investments should be eliminated. The difference between the investments in the subsidiary's bonds should be eliminated against the subsidiary's bonds payable and accounted for in "investment income."
3. Eliminate unrealized profit or loss arising from intragroup sales of goods or rendering of services. Unrealized profits and losses resulting from intragroup transactions that are recognized in assets, such as inventory, fixed assets, construction contracts, and intangible assets, are eliminated in full.
4. Eliminate the effects of other intragroup transactions on the consolidated balance sheet.

Article 17 The subsidiary's stockholders equity that is not attributable to the parent's portion of equity should be accounted for as non-controlling interest. Non-controlling interests are identified separately from the parent's ownership interests in the consolidated balance sheet and should be presented below "minority stockholder's interest" item.

Article 18 For business combinations of enterprises not under common control, when preparing the consolidated balance sheet, the beginning amount of the consolidated balance sheet should not be adjusted for a subsidiary acquired during the accounting period.

Article 19 For business combinations of enterprises under common control, when preparing the consolidated balance sheet, the beginning amount of the consolidated balance sheet should be adjusted for a subsidiary acquired during the accounting period.

Article 20 Upon disposal of a subsidiary during the accounting period, when preparing the consolidated balance sheet, the parent should not adjust the beginning amount of the consolidated balance sheet.

Article 21 Consolidation issue occurs if the identifiable assets, liabilities, and contingent liabilities of the subsidiary that are acquired are not presented at their respective fair values.

This could happen if:

1. Some of the subsidiary's assets, liabilities, and contingent liabilities are undervalued, overvalued, or not recognized;
2. The carrying amount of the parent's investment in each subsidiary is not equal to the fair value of the net identifiable assets of the subsidiary that is acquired; and
3. The parent does not acquire the 100 % of the subsidiary's issued paid-in capital.

37.3.2 Consolidated Income Statement

Article 22 Consolidated income statement is obtained by combining line items of income and expenses of the parent and the subsidiaries.

Article 23 If the parents acquire less than 100 % of a subsidiary's paid-in capital, profit or loss is attributed to the owners of the parent and to the non-controlling interests. In order to determine the total net profit, 100 % of the subsidiary's individual income statement items are added to those of the parent. The total net profit is then decomposed into the following amounts:

1. Net profit attributable to the stockholders of the parent; and
2. Net profit attributable to the non-controlling interests.

Article 24 The subsidiary's net profit or loss for the period that is attributable to non-controlling interests should be accounted for in the consolidated income statement below "minority stockholder's profit or loss" item.

Article 25 When preparing consolidated financial statements, the parent should rely on its individual income statements and those of its subsidiaries and must eliminate intragroup balances and transactions on the consolidated income statement. In order that the consolidated financial statements present financial information about the group as that of a single economic entity, the following steps are then taken:

1. Eliminate operating revenue and operating costs occurred in intragroup sales of goods. Furthermore, unrealized profits and losses resulting from intragroup transactions that are recognized in assets, such as inventory, fixed assets, construction contracts, and intangible assets, are eliminated in full. In such circumstances, the accumulated depreciation of fixed assets or amortized amount of intangible assets and the relevant portion of unrealized intragroup sales should also be eliminated.
2. Eliminate the intragroup investment income of bonds and the corresponding interest expense of the issuer.
3. Eliminate the intragroup investment income of long-term equity investments.
4. Eliminate the effect of other intragroup transactions on the consolidated income statement.

Article 26 The excess of the losses attributable to non-controlling interests in a consolidated subsidiary over the non-controlling interests in the subsidiary's equity at the beginning of the period should be accounted for as follows:

1. If the non-controlling interests have an obligation under a memorandum and article of association or an agreement to cover the loss, the excess is charged against the non-controlling interest's equity.
2. If the non-controlling interests have no obligation under a memorandum and Article of association or an agreement to cover the loss, the excess is charged against the parent's stockholders equity. Profits realized by the subsidiary in subsequent periods are allocated to the parent's stockholders equity until the non-controlling interest's share of losses absorbed previously by the parent has been recovered.

Article 27 For business combinations of enterprises not under common control, the subsidiary's income, expenses, and profit are included in the consolidated income statement from the acquisition date to the end of the accounting period.

Article 28 For business combinations of enterprises under common control, the subsidiary's income, expenses, and profit are included in the consolidated income statement from the beginning to the end of the accounting period for a combination during the period.

Article 29 Upon disposal of a subsidiary during the accounting period, the parent should only include the income, expenses, and profit or loss of the subsidiary in the consolidated income statement from the beginning of the period until the date of disposal of the subsidiary.

Article 30 If a subsidiary incurs a loss, the non-controlling interests will be allocated their share of loss.

37.3.3 Consolidated Cash Flow Statement

Article 31 When preparing consolidated financial statements, the parent should rely on its individual cash flow statements and those of its subsidiaries and must eliminate intragroup balances and transactions on the consolidated cash flow statement. In order that the consolidated financial statements present financial information about the group as that of a single economic entity, the following steps are then taken:

1. Eliminate cash flows arising from intragroup investments made by cash or acquiring shares during the period;
2. Eliminate cash receipts from returns on investments and cash payments for the distribution of dividends or profit, or for interest expenses among group enterprises;
3. Eliminate cash receipts from the settlement of debts and cash payments of amounts borrowed among group enterprises;
4. Eliminate cash flows arising from intragroup sales of goods during the period;
5. Eliminate net cash receipts from the disposal of fixed assets, intangible assets, and other long-term assets and cash payments to acquire fixed assets, intangible assets, and other long-term assets among group enterprises; and
6. Eliminate the effect of other intragroup transaction occurred during the period on the consolidated cash flow statement.

Article 32 Additional information for the cash flow statement can be provided based on the consolidated balance sheet and the consolidated income statement.

Article 33 For business combinations of enterprises not under common control, a subsidiary's cash flows are included in the consolidated cash flow statement from the acquisition date to the end of the accounting period.

Article 34 For business combinations of enterprises under common control, a subsidiary's cash flows are included in the consolidated cash flow statement from the beginning to the end of the accounting period for a combination during the period.

Article 35 Upon disposal of a subsidiary during the accounting period, the parent should only include the cash flows of the subsidiary in the consolidated cash flow statement from the beginning of the period until the date of disposal of the subsidiary.

37.3.4 Consolidated Statement of Changes in Owner's Equity

Article 36 When preparing consolidated financial statements, the parent should rely on its individual statement of changes in owner's equity and those of its subsidiaries and must eliminate intragroup balances and transactions on the consolidated statement of changes in owner's equity. In order that the consolidated financial statements present financial information about the group as that of a single economic entity, the following steps are then taken:

1. Eliminate the carrying amount of the parent's investment in each subsidiary against the parent's portion of equity of each subsidiary;
2. Eliminate intragroup investment income of long-term equity investments; and
3. Eliminate the effect of other intragroup transactions on the consolidated statement of changes in owner's equity.

Article 37 Additional information for the consolidated statement of changes in owner's equity can be provided based on the consolidated balance sheet and the consolidated income statement.

Article 38 When there are non-controlling interests, the consolidated statement of changes in owner's equity should present the "minority stockholder's interests in equity" line item in order to reflect the changes in non-controlling interests in equity.

37.4 Chapter IV: Disclosure

Article 39 An enterprise should, in the notes, disclose the following information:

1. A list of subsidiaries, including the name, country of incorporation, nature of business, the parent's portion of ownership interest, and portion of voting power held;
2. The nature of the relationship between the parent and a subsidiary when the parent does not own, directly or indirectly through subsidiaries, more than half of the voting power, but such ownership constitutes control;
3. The reasons why the ownership, directly or indirectly through subsidiaries, of more than half of the voting or potential voting power of an investee does not constitute control;
4. The method to account for different accounting policies used by a subsidiary in the preparation of consolidated individual financial statements and its effect;
5. The end of the reporting period of the financial statements of a subsidiary when such financial statements are used to prepare consolidated financial statements and are as of a date or for a period that is different from that of the parent's financial statements, and the reason for using a different date or period;
6. The inclusion of additional subsidiaries during the period;
7. If control of a subsidiary is lost, a description of the name of the subsidiary; country of incorporation; nature of business; the parent's portion of ownership interest and portion of voting power held; the reason why it is no longer a subsidiary; the amount of assets, liabilities, or owner's equity on the date of disposal and the previous accounting period; the amount of income, expenses, and profit form the beginning of the period until the date of disposal;

8. The nature and extent of any significant restrictions on the ability of subsidiaries to transfer funds to the parent;
9. The nature of the business, business activities, etc., of the special purpose enterprises treated as subsidiaries that are consolidated; and
10. Other necessary items to be explained in the notes.

37.5 Comments

ASBE No. 33 requires a parent entity to prepare consolidated financial statements. This standard does not mention whether there are any circumstances where a parent is allowed not to prepare consolidated financial statements—this may be addressed in the guidance to ASBE No. 33. In the precedent dispositions under PRC GAAP, there were three types of enterprises required to prepare consolidated financial statements. Other enterprises might choose to prepare consolidated financial statements on a voluntary basis.

It is also specified that the scope of consolidation shall be determined on "control." All subsidiaries under the control of a parent shall be consolidated. PRC GAAP is exempt from the consolidation of certain subsidiaries. For example, when total assets, sales revenue, and profits of the subsidiary are less than 10 % of the corresponding amount of the group, subsidiaries declared bankrupt and subsidiaries engaged in specific industries.

A set of consolidated financial statements shall include a consolidated statement of changes in equity. For a business combination not under common control, the identifiable net assets of the subsidiary shall be adjusted to their fair values at the date of acquisition when preparing the consolidated financial statements.

For a business combination involving enterprises under common control during the reporting period, the consolidated balance sheet includes the net assets of the combining entities using the book values, and the consolidated income statements include the results of the combining entities for the full period.

If the losses applicable to the minority shareholders in a subsidiary exceed the minority interest in that subsidiary's owners' equity at the beginning of the period, the excess is used to reduce minority interest in equity to the extent that the minority shareholder has a binding obligation and is able to make an additional investment to cover the losses. Otherwise, the excess is allocated against the owners' equity of the parent instead of being allocated to "unrecognized investment loss" as provisioned under previous PRC GAAP.

In assessing an enterprise's ability to control another enterprise, the effect of "potential voting rights" shall be considered. The equity method instead of proportionate consolidation shall be used to account for equity interests in jointly controlled entities. The latter were required under PRC GAAP.

Intragroup balances, transactions, income, and expenses should be eliminated in full amount. Intragroup losses may indicate that an impairment loss on the related asset should be recognized. The financial statements of the parent and its subsidiaries used in preparing the consolidated financial statements should all be prepared as of the same reporting date, unless it is impracticable to do so. If it is impracticable, a particular subsidiary to prepare its financial statements as of the same date as its parent, adjustments must be made for the effects of significant transactions or events that occur between the dates of the subsidiary's and the parent's financial statements. And in no case may the difference be more than three months.

Consolidated financial statements must be prepared using uniform accounting policies for transactions and other events in similar circumstances. Minority interests should be presented in the consolidated balance sheet within equity, but separately from the parent's shareholders' equity. Minority interests in the profit or loss of the group should also be disclosed separately. Where losses applicable to the minority exceed the minority interest in the equity of the relevant subsidiary, the excess losses, and any further losses attributable to the minority, are charged to the group unless the minority has a binding obligation to, and is able to, make the losses good. Where excess losses have been taken up by the group, if the subsidiary in question subsequently reports profits, all such profits are attributed to the group until the minority's share of losses previously absorbed by the group has been recovered.

Accounting for the differences against IAS/IFRS systems, two main issues arise in comparison with IAS 27. When the reporting dates of the parent and a subsidiary are different, the subsidiary prepares, for consolidation purposes, additional financial statements as of the same date as the financial statements of the parent unless it is impracticable to do so. In any case, the difference between the reporting date of the subsidiary and that of the parent shall be no more than three months. The length of the reporting periods and any difference in the reporting dates shall be the same from period to period. ASBE No. 33 requires the reporting periods of the parent and the subsidiaries to be the same. In addition, a venturer may choose the equity method or proportionate consolidation method to account for its interest in a jointly controlled entity. Under ASBE No. 33, only the use of the equity method is allowed.

37.6 Examples

Company X and Company Y are initially two stand-alone companies. At the end of financial year N, Company X acquires 100 % of Company Y.

Assets	Company X (RMB)	Company Y (RMB)
Current assets		
Cash	70,000	180,000
Accounts receivable	130,000	–

(continued)

(continued)

Assets	Company X (RMB)	Company Y (RMB)
Non-current assets		
LT equity investment in Company Y (cost method)	300,000	–
Fixed assets	1,000,000	170,000
Total assets	**1,500,000**	**350,000**
Liabilities		
Current liabilities		
Accounts payable	200,000	–
Non-current liabilities		
Long-term borrowings	–	50,000
Owners' (stockholders') equity		
Paid-in capital	800,000	200,000
Capital surplus	100,000	30,000
Surplus reserve	80,000	20,000
Retained earnings	220,000	50,000
Total liabilities and equity	**1,500,000**	**350,000**

Items to be offset in consolidation:
Assets
LT equity investment in Company Y (cost method): RMB 300,000
Liabilities
Paid-in capital (Y): RMB 200,000
Capital surplus (Y): RMB 30,000
Surplus reserve (Y): RMB 20,000
Retained earnings (Y): RMB 50,000

Assets	Company X (RMB)
Current assets	
Cash	250,000
Accounts receivable	130,000
Non-current assets	
Fixed assets	1,170,000
Total assets	**1,550,000**
Liabilities	
Current liabilities	
Accounts payable	200,000
Non-current liabilities	
Long-term borrowings	50,000

(continued)

(continued)

Assets	Company X (RMB)
Owners' (stockholders') equity	
Paid-in capital	800,000
Capital surplus	100,000
Surplus reserve	80,000
Retained earnings	220,000
Total liabilities and equity	**1,550,000**

Chapter 38
Accounting Standards for Business Enterprises No. 34—Earings per Share

38.1 Chapter I: General Provisions

Article 1 In order to regulate the methods for the calculation of the earnings per share (EPS) and the presentation thereof, these Standards are formulated according to the Basic Standards of Accounting Standards for Enterprises.

Article 2 These Standards apply to enterprises whose ordinary shares or potential ordinary shares have been traded publicly, and those that are going on a public offering of ordinary stocks or potential ordinary shares. The term "potential ordinary stock" refers to a financial instrument or other contract that could endow its holder ordinary with ordinary share rights within reporting term or the following term, such as convertible corporate bonds, share warrants, and share options.

Article 3 In the consolidated financial statements, an enterprise shall calculate and present the EPS based on the consolidated financial statements.

38.2 Chapter II: Basic Earnings per Share

Article 4 For an enterprise, the basic EPS shall be calculated by dividing the current net profits belonging to the shareholders of ordinary shares by the weighted average number of ordinary shares issued to the public.

Article 5 The weighted average number of ordinary shares which are issued to the public shall be calculated in light of the formulas as follows:

The weighted average number of ordinary shares issued to the public = the number of ordinary shares issued to the public at the beginning of the period + the number of shares newly issued in the current period × the lapsed time after issuance ÷ the time during the reporting period − the number of ordinary shares repurchased in the current period × the lapsed time after repurchase ÷ the time during the reporting period.

L. Riccardi, *China Accounting Standards*,
DOI 10.1007/978-981-10-0006-5_38

The lapsed time after issuance, the time during the reporting period, and the time after the repurchase shall be calculated by days. On the precondition of not affecting the reasonableness of calculation result, a simplified calculation method may be employed.

Article 6 In accordance with the specific terms and clauses of the issuance contract, the number of newly issued ordinary shares shall be calculated and decided as of the date of receivable consideration (generally the date of issuance of stocks), consisting of the circumstances as follows:

1. The number of ordinary shares issued for cash collection shall be calculated as of the date of cash receivable;
2. The number of ordinary shares issued as a result of conversion of debt to capital shall be calculated as of the date of cessation of calculation of debt interest or the settlement date;
3. As to a business combination not under the same control, the number of ordinary shares issued as a consideration shall be calculated as of the purchase date. As to a business combination under the same control, the number of ordinary shares issued as a consideration shall be charged to the weighted average number of ordinary shares presented during each reporting period; and
4. The number of ordinary shares issued for buying non-cash assets shall be calculated as of the date of recognition of the purchase.

38.3 Chapter III: Diluted Earnings per Share

Article 7 If an enterprise has any diluted potential ordinary shares, it shall modulate the current net profits belonging to the shareholder of ordinary shares, and the weighted average number of ordinary shares issued to the public in a separately way, and then calculate the diluted EPS according to the adjusted results. The term "diluted potential ordinary shares" refers to the potential ordinary shares of which the EPS shall be reduced on supposing they would be converted to ordinary shares in the current period.

Article 8 When calculating the diluted EPS, an enterprise shall modulate the current net profits belonging to the shareholders of ordinary shares in accordance with the items as follows:

1. The interests of the diluted potential ordinary shares determined to be expenses in the current period; and
2. The gains or expenses to be resulted from the conversion of the diluted potential ordinary shares.

The effects of the income tax on the aforesaid modulation shall be taken into consideration.

Article 9 When calculating the diluted EPS, the weighted average number of the ordinary shares issued to the public in the current period shall be the sum of the weighted average number of ordinary shares in calculating the basic EPS and the weighted average number of increased ordinary shares on supposing that the diluted potential ordinary shares are converted into ordinary shares already issued. When calculating the weighted average number of increased ordinary shares resulted from that the diluted potential ordinary shares are converted into ordinary shares already issued, the diluted potential ordinary shares issued in prior periods shall be supposed to be converted at the beginning of the current period. The diluted potential ordinary shares issued in the current period shall be supposed to be converted on the date of issuance.

Article 10 In case the exercise prices of the share warrant and share options are lower than the average market price of the ordinary shares of the current period, the dilution shall be taken into consideration. When calculating the diluted EPS, an enterprise shall calculate the number of the ordinary shares increased in accordance with the formula as follows:

The number of ordinary shares increased = the number of ordinary shares to be converted in the exercise of warrants − the exercise price × the number of ordinary shares to be converted in the exercise of warrants ÷ the average market price of ordinary shares in the current period.

Article 11 The dilution shall be taken into consideration when an enterprise promises that the price for the repurchase of its shares provided in the contract is higher than the average market price of the current period. When calculating the diluted EPS, an enterprise shall calculate the number of the ordinary shares increased in accordance with the formula as follows:

The number of ordinary shares increased = the repurchase price × the number of ordinary shares promised to repurchase ÷ the average market price of the current period − the number of ordinary shares promised to repurchase.

Article 12 The diluted potential ordinary shares shall be charged to the diluted EPS based on the extent of dilution according to the sequential order from the big to the small, until the diluted EPS to be the minimum.

38.4 Chapter IV: Presentation

Article 13 If the number of ordinary shares issued to the public or of potential ordinary shares is increased because of the distribution of stocks or dividends, the increase of capital converted by accumulation fund or share split-up is reduced because of reverse split-up, but causing no effect on the amount of the owner's equities. An enterprise shall recalculate the EPS in each presentation period in accordance with the number of post-adjustment shares. In case the aforesaid changes occur during the period from the balance sheet date to the date on which the financial reports are authorized for issue, the EPS in each presentation period shall be recalculated in light of the number of post-modulation shares. In case any of the profits and losses of any previous year are retroactively modulated or restated in light of the Accounting Standards for Enterprises No. 28—Changes of

Accounting Policies, Estimates and Corrections of Errors, the EPS during the period of presentation shall be recalculated.

Article 14 The basic EPS and the diluted EPS shall be, respectively, shown in the profit statements of an enterprise.

Article 15 The information related to the EPS shall be brought into open by an enterprise in its notes:

1. The calculating process of the numerators and denominators on the basic EPS and diluted EPS;
2. The potential ordinary that not possessing dilution during the presentation period but likely to possess dilution in the subsequent periods; and
3. The information about the great changes on the number of the ordinary shares issued by the enterprise to the public or the potential ordinary shares during the period from the balance sheet date to the date on which the financial reports are authorized for issue.

38.5 Comments

New ASBE No. 34 requires listed companies or companies in process of issuing shares and applying for a listing status to disclose the basic and diluted EPS amounts. If the number of shares increases as a result of stock dividend, capitalization of surplus reserves or share split decreases as a result of share consolidation, but there is no effect to the amount of owners' equity. EPS for all periods presented shall be recalculated on the basis of the adjusted number of shares.

The previous regulation lacked specific provisions; however, enterprises listed on the PRC stock exchange were required by China Securities Regulatory Commission (CSRC) to present the EPS figures in the interim report and annual report in accordance with a simple formula provided by the CSRC rules.

This Standard sets out how to calculate both basic EPS and diluted EPS. The calculation of basic EPS is based on the weighted average number of ordinary shares outstanding during the period, whereas diluted EPS also includes dilutive potential ordinary shares (such as options and convertible instruments) if they meet certain criteria.

If an entity presents the components of profit or loss in a separate income statement, it presents EPS only in that separate statement. Basic and diluted EPS must be presented with equal prominence for all periods presented.

Basic EPS is calculated by dividing profit or loss attributable to ordinary equity holders of the parent entity (the numerator) by the weighted average number of ordinary shares outstanding (the denominator) during the period. The earnings numerators (profit or loss from continuing operations and net profit or loss) used for the calculation should be after deducting all expenses including taxes, minority interests, and preference dividends.

The denominator (number of shares) is calculated by adjusting the shares in issue at the beginning of the period by the number of shares bought back or issued during the period, multiplied by a time-weighting factor. ASBE No. 34 includes guidance on appropriate recognition dates for shares issued in various circumstances.

Contingently issuable shares are included in the basic EPS denominator when the contingency has been met. Diluted EPS is calculated by adjusting the earnings and number of shares for the effects of dilutive options and other dilutive potential ordinary shares. The effects of anti-dilutive potential ordinary shares are ignored in calculating diluted EPS.

Basic and diluted EPS must be presented even if the amounts are negative (i.e., a loss per share). If an entity reports a discontinued operation, basic and diluted amounts per share must be disclosed for the discontinued operation either on the face of the comprehensive income (or separate income statement if presented) or in the notes to the financial statements.

Finally, whereas ASBE No. 34 only requires the calculation of EPS based on net profit or loss for the current period, IAS 33 requires disclosure of the basic and diluted EPS amounts for profit or loss from continuing operations and those for discontinued operations.

38.6 Examples

Company X has fully paid-up capital of RMB 80,000,000 (10,000,000 shares at RMB 8.00 each). On year N, Company X issues RMB 40,000,000 convertible loan stocks. And at the end of financial year N + 1, RMB 20,000,000 of the loan is converted into 2 million shares. Let us assume that in the financial year N + 1, the net income is RMB 12,000,000. The converted shares are fully eligible for 100 % earnings.

Basic EPS

Net profit attributable to ordinary shareholders: RMB 12,000,000
Number of shares outstanding: 10,000,000
Ordinary shares issued for convertible loan stocks: 2,000,000
Basic EPS: RMB 12,000,000/12,000,000 = 1.00 RMB/stock

Diluted EPS

Net profit attributable to ordinary shareholders: RMB 12,000,000
Number of shares outstanding: 10,000,000
Ordinary shares issued for convertible loan stocks: 2,000,000
Other ordinary shares resulting from assumed conversion of CLS: 2,000,000
Basic EPS: RMB 12,000,000/14,000,000 = 0.86 RMB/stock

Chapter 39
Accounting Standards for Business Enterprises No. 35—Segment Reporting

39.1 Chapter I: General Provisions

Article 1 This standard, formulated in accordance with ASBE—Basic Standard, provides guidance on the disclosure of information relating to the segments of an enterprise, except for the provisions stipulated in other laws or regulations.

Article 2 An enterprise should present segment information on the basis of the financial statements provided for public use. If a financial report contains both the consolidated financial statements of a parent and the parent's separate financial statements, segment information is required only in the consolidated financial statements.

39.2 Chapter II: Identification of Segments

Article 3 An enterprise should disclose segment information to enable users of its financial statements to evaluate the nature and financial effects of the business activities in which it engages and the economic environments in which it operates.

Article 4 An enterprise should disclose segment information based on both business segments and geographical segments.

Article 5 A business segment is defined as a component of an enterprise that is involved in providing an individual product or service or a group of related products or services and that is subject to risks and returns that are different from those of other business segments.

Article 6 Two or more business segments may be aggregated into a single business segment if aggregation is consistent with the requirements of internal management, and the segments have similar financial performance and are similar in each of the following respects:

L. Riccardi, *China Accounting Standards*,
DOI 10.1007/978-981-10-0006-5_39

1. The nature of the products and services;
2. The nature of the production processes;
3. The type or class of customer for their products and services;
4. The methods used to distribute their products or provide their services; and
5. If applicable, the nature of the regulatory environment.

Article 7 A geographical segment is defined as a component of an enterprise that is involved in providing products or services within a particular economic and environment and that is subject to risks and returns that are different from those components operating in other economic environments.

Article 8 Two or more geographical segments may be aggregated into a single geographical segment if aggregation is consistent with the requirements of internal management, and the segments have similar financial performance and are similar in each of the following respects:

1. Economic and political conditions;
2. Relationship between operations in different geographical areas;
3. Proximity of operations;
4. Special risks associated with operations in a particular area;
5. Exchange control regulations; and
6. Exchange risks.

39.3 Chapter III: Identification of Reportable Segments

Article 9 An enterprise should report the information separately about a business segment or geographical segment that meets any of the following quantitative thresholds:

1. Its reported revenue, including both sales to external customers and interseg-ment sales or transfers, is 10 % or more of the combined revenue, internal and external, of all operating segments.
2. The absolute amount of its reported profit or loss is 10 % or more of the greater, in absolute amount, of (i) the combined reported profit of all operating segments that did not report a loss and (ii) the combined reported loss of all operating segments that reported a loss.
3. Its assets are 10 % or more of the combined assets of all operating segments.

Business segments or geographical segments that do not meet any of the quantitative thresholds may be considered reportable, and separately disclosed, if management believes that information about the segment would be useful to users of the financial statements.

Article 10 An enterprise may combine information about operating segments that do not meet the quantitative thresholds with information about other operating segments that do not meet the quantitative thresholds to produce a reportable segment.

Article 11 Information about other business activities and operating segments that are not reportable should be combined and disclosed separately in an "all other segments" category.

Article 12 If the total external revenue reported by operating segments constitutes less than 75 % of the enterprise's revenue, additional operating segments shall be identified as reportable segments (even if they do not meet the criteria in *Article 9*) until at least 75 % of the enterprise's revenue is included in reportable segments.

Article 13 When separate segments are identified according to different stages of vertically integrated operations, the enterprise can report vertically integrated activities as a separate reportable business segment, even if it does not generate significant external sales revenue.

Article 14 If management judges that an operating segment identified as a reportable segment in the immediately preceding period is of continuing significance, information about that segment should continue to be reported separately in the current period even if it no longer meets the criteria for reportability in *Article 9*.

39.4 Chapter IV: Identification of Primary and Secondary Reportable Segments

Article 15 Primary and secondary segments require different disclosures, primary reporting format and secondary reporting format, respectively.

Article 16 To determine which format is primary or secondary, the following criteria should be applied:

1. If the enterprise's risk and returns are affected predominantly by differences in the products and services it produces, the enterprise should use business segments as its primary format for reporting segment information, and geographical segments as its secondary format;
2. If the enterprise's risk and returns are affected predominantly by differences in the countries or geographical areas in which it operates, the enterprise should use geographical segments as its primary format for reporting segment information, and business segments as its secondary format; and
3. If the enterprise's risk and returns are strongly affected both by the differences in the products and services it produces and by the fact that it operates in different countries or other geographical areas, then the enterprise's primary segment reporting format is business segments and its secondary segment reporting format is geographical segments.

39.5 Chapter V: Segment Information Disclosure

Article 17 For each primary segment, the following information has to be disclosed in the notes:

1. Segment revenue (i.e., revenue from external customers and revenue from transactions with other segments of the same enterprise);
2. Segment expenses (i.e., expenses from external customers and expenses from transactions with other segments of the same enterprise);
3. Segment profit or loss (in the consolidated income statement, segment profit or loss should be determined before any adjustments for non-controlling interest are made);
4. Segment assets (i.e., assets that are employed by a segment in its operating activities and that are attributable to the segment, net of the accumulated depreciation or amortization, and accumulated impairment losses);
5. Segment liabilities (i.e., liabilities that result from the operating activities of the segment and that are attributable to the segment);

Article 18 An enterprise should report interest revenue and interest expense separately for each reportable segment unless the segment's daily operations are of financial nature. In that situation, an enterprise may report segment's interest income and interest expense, respectively, as segment revenue and segment expense.

Article 19 An enterprise should provide reconciliation between the information disclosed for reportable segments and the aggregated information in the enterprise's financial statements. In particular, an enterprise should provide reconciliations of all of the following:

1. The total of the reportable segments' revenues to the enterprise's revenue from external clients;
2. The total of the reportable segments' measures of profit or loss to the enterprise's profit or loss;
3. The total of the reportable segments' assets to the enterprise's assets; and
4. The total of the reportable segments' liabilities to the enterprise's liabilities.

Article 20 For secondary segments that are geographical segments, the following information has to be disclosed in the notes:

1. Segment revenue from external customers if it accounts for 10 % or more of the total enterprise revenue from external customers; and
2. Segment total assets if they account for 10 % or more of the total assets of all geographical segments.

Article 21 For secondary segment that are business segments, the following information has to be disclosed in the notes:

1. Segment revenue from external customers if it accounts for 10 % or more of the total enterprise revenue from external customers; and
2. Segment total assets if they account for 10 % or more of the total assets of all business segments.

Article 22 Segment accounting policies are defined as the accounting policies adopted both for preparing and for presenting the individual or consolidated financial statement of the enterprise and the segment reporting information.

Article 23 Intersegment transactions should be measured on the basis of the pricing policies that the enterprise actually used to price those transactions. The intersegment pricing policies and any change therein should also be disclosed.

Article 24 An enterprise is required to disclose the segment accounting policies only if they are not in conformity with the accounting policies used by the enterprise to prepare and present its individual or consolidated financial statements.

Article 25 Changes in accounting policies adopted for segment reporting should be disclosed in accordance with ASBE 28, and related comparative data should be provided, unless the enterprise is impracticable to do so, and in this case, the reason of impracticability should be stated.

Article 26 If an enterprise has changed the structure of its internal organization in a manner that causes the composition of its reportable segments to change and if segment information for earlier periods is not restated to reflect the change, the enterprise should disclose in the year in which the change occurs segment information for the current period on both the old basis and the new basis of segmentation.

Article 27 In disclosing segment information, an enterprise is required to provide the prior period's comparative data unless it is impracticable to do so.

39.6 Comments

The major introduction of new ASBE No. 35 involves the requirement as the basis of presentation, of primary and secondary, with considerably less information to be disclosed for the secondary segment. This different treatment did not figure under past PRC GAAP where the same amount of information was required for both business segments and geographical segments. Segment Reporting requires reporting of financial information by business or geographical area. It requires disclosures for "primary" and "secondary" segment reporting formats, with the primary format based on whether the entity's risks and returns are affected predominantly by the products and services it produces or by the fact that it operates in different geographical areas.

Segments deemed too small for separate reporting may be combined with each other, if related, but they may not be combined with other significant segments for which information is reported internally. Alternatively, they may be separately reported. If neither combined nor separately reported, they must be included as an unallocated reconciling item.

When comparing dispositions of ASBE No. 35 with the equivalent IAS 14, some divergences stem out from scope perspective. Unless stipulated in other laws or regulations, ASBE No. 35 requires an enterprise which has different operations or operates in different geographical areas to provide segment information. IAS 14 only applies to the published financial statements of enterprises whose equity or debt securities are publicly traded and enterprises that are in the process of issuing equity or debt securities in public securities market.

39.7 Examples

Following the segment information disclosure for two business segments under ASBEs.

Item	Segment A (RMB)	Segment B (RMB)	Elimination (RMB)	Total (RMB)
1. Revenue from operations				
2. Cost of operations				
3. Operating profit				
4. Total identifiable assets				
5. Total liabilities				
6. Supplementary information				
Depreciation and amortization				
Capital expenditure				
Non-cash expenses				

Geographical segments

Item	Country A (RMB)	Country B (RMB)	Total (RMB)
1. Revenue from operations			
2. Total assets			

Chapter 40
Accounting Standards for Business Enterprises No. 36—Related Party Disclosures

40.1 Chapter I: General Provisions

Article 1 With a view to regulating the disclosure of information about affiliated parties and transactions among them, these Standards are formulated in accordance with Accounting Standards for Enterprises—Basic Standards.

Article 2 An enterprise shall, in its financial statements, disclose the related information about all affiliated party relationships and the transactions among them. If it offers consolidated financial statements to outsiders, it is not required to disclose the transactions among the enterprises that have been included in the scope consolidation, but it shall disclose the affiliated party relationships and transactions beyond the scope of consolidation.

40.2 Chapter II: Affiliated Parties

Article 3 When a party controls, jointly controls, or exercises significant influence over another party, or when two or more parties are under the control, joint control, or significant influence of the same party, the affiliated party relationships are constituted. The term "control" means having the power to decide an enterprise's financial and operating policy and obtains benefits from its business activities. The term "joint control" means control over an economic activity as specified by contract, which exists only when the investing parties that need to share the power of control in important financial and operating decision making agree unanimously. The term "significant influence" means having the power to participate in the formulation of financial and operating policies of an enterprise, but not the power to control or jointly control the formulation of these policies together with other parties.

L. Riccardi, *China Accounting Standards*,
DOI 10.1007/978-981-10-0006-5_40

Article 4 The following parties constitute the affiliated parties of an enterprise:

1. The parent company thereof;
2. The subsidiaries thereof;
3. Other enterprises under the control of the same parent company thereof;
4. The investors having joint control over the enterprise;
5. The investors having significant influence thereon;
6. The joint ventures thereof;
7. The associated enterprises thereof;
8. The main individual investors and the close family members thereof. A main individual investor refers to an individual investor who can control or jointly control an enterprise, or has significant influence thereon; and
9. Key managerial personnel of the enterprise or of its parent company and the close family members thereof. Key managerial personnel refer to those who have the power of and responsibility for planning, directing, and controlling the activities of the enterprise. The close family members of a main individual investor or of a key managerial person refer to the family members who may influence or be influenced by that individual in handling transactions with the enterprise.
10. Other enterprises the main individual investors, key managerial personnel, or close family members of such individuals control, jointly control, or have significant influence over.

Article 5 Where one party has the following relationship with one enterprise, it is not an affiliated party thereof.

1. The capital providers, public utility units, government departments, and organs which have normal dealings therewith;
2. A single customer, supplier, franchiser, distributor, or agent with whom an enterprise transacts a significant volume of business by virtue only of the resulting economic dependence; and
3. The joint venture operators which jointly control a joint venture therewith.

Article 6 Enterprises shall not be regarded as affiliated parties simply because they are all under the control of the state.

40.3 Chapter III: Affiliated Party Transaction

Article 7 The term "affiliated party transaction" refers to an event whereby a transfer of resources, labor services, or obligations takes place between affiliated parties, irrespective of whether money is charged.

Article 8 The types of affiliated party transaction usually include as follows:

1. Purchases or sales of goods;
2. Purchasing or selling assets other than goods;
3. Rendering or receiving labor services;
4. Guarantying;
5. Providing capital (including loans or equity contributions);
6. Leasing;
7. Agency;
8. Transfer of research and development projects;
9. License agreements;
10. Settling debts on behalf of an enterprise or by this enterprise that represents another party; and
11. The emoluments for key managerial personnel.

40.4 Chapter IV: Disclosure

Article 9 An enterprise shall, in the annotations to the financial statements, disclose the following information about the parent company and subsidiaries thereof, irrespective of whether there have been transactions between them:

1. The names of the parent company and subsidiaries thereof where the parent company is not the ultimate controlling party of the enterprise, it shall disclose the name of the ultimate controlling party. Where neither the parent company nor the ultimate controlling party provides the financial statements to outsiders, it shall disclose the name of the parent company which is its closest superior parent company providing financial statements to outsiders.
2. The nature of business, name, place of registration, and registered capital (or actually paid-in capital, stock capital) and changes therein of the parent company and its subsidiaries; and
3. The proportion of shares or voting rights held by the parent company in this enterprise or by this enterprise in its subsidiaries.

Article 10 Where there have been transactions between an enterprise and its affiliated parties, it shall disclose the nature of the affiliated party relationships, the types of transactions, and the elements of transaction in the annotations. The elements of transaction shall at least include the following:

1. The amount of transactions;
2. The amounts, terms, and conditions of outstanding items, and the information about the guaranties granted to others or obtained;
3. The amounts of provisions for nonperforming debts under outstanding items; and
4. Price policies.

Article 11 Affiliated party transactions shall be disclosed on the basis of the affiliated parties and the types of the transactions involved. The affiliated party transactions of similar types may be disclosed in aggregate in case that it does not affect readers' correct understanding of the financial statements.

Article 12 No enterprise may disclose an affiliated party transaction as a fair transaction unless it provides exact proofs.

40.5 Comments

ASBE No. 36 expands the scope of related party. If two parties are subject to joint control or to significant influence from the same party, they are regarded as related parties, differently from the previous PRC GAAP. If the separate financial statements of the parent are presented together with its consolidated financial statement, information concerning related party relationship and related party transactions of the parent shall be disclosed as well. Disclosures that related party transactions were conducted at the fair value are allowed only if the enterprise is able to provide supporting evidence.

Related party disclosures require disclosures about transactions and outstanding balances with an entity's related parties. The standard defines various classes of entities and people as related parties and sets out the disclosures required in respect of those parties, including the compensation of key management personnel. The objective of ASBE No. 36 is to ensure that an entity's financial statements contain the disclosures necessary to draw attention to the possibility that its financial position and profit or loss may have been affected by the existence of related parties and by transactions and outstanding balances with such parties.

A related party transaction is a transfer of resources, services, or obligations between related parties, regardless of whether a price is charged. Regardless of whether there have been transactions between a parent and a subsidiary, an entity must disclose the name of its parent and, if different, the ultimate controlling party. If neither the entity's parent nor the ultimate controlling party produces financial statements available for public use, the name of the next most senior parent that does so must also be disclosed.

If there have been transactions between related parties, disclose the nature of the related party relationship as well as information about the transactions and outstanding balances necessary for an understanding of the potential effect of the relationship on the financial statements.

Related party disclosures treated under ASBE No. 36 acknowledge state-controlled entities are not regarded as related parties simply because they are state-controlled. However, state-controlled entities are not exempted under IAS 24. Moreover, two parties subject to joint or significant influence from the same party are clearly defined as related parties under ASBE No. 36, but this point is not specifically addressed in IAS 24.

40.6 Examples

In this case, let us show a diagram representing relationships lying among all entities under the same control. The group consists of the parent Company X and other three entities strictly interrelated. In particular, Company X exerts direct control over Company Y, whereas indirect control to Company W and Company Z. Company Y exerts direct control over both Company Y and Company Z. For any enterprise identified as the reporting enterprise, all the other three enterprises are related to that reporting enterprise.

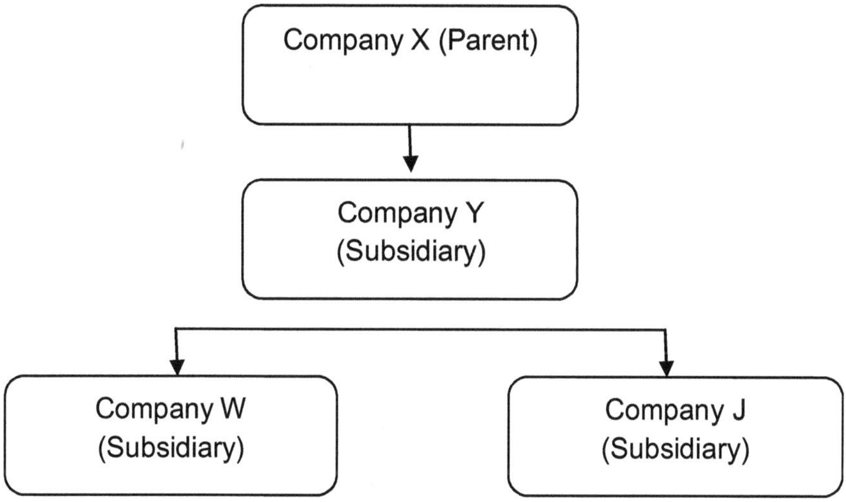

Chapter 41
Accounting Standards for Business Enterprises No. 37—Presentation of Financial Instruments

41.1 Chapter I: General Provisions

Article 1 This standard, formulated in accordance with ASBE—Basic Standard, prescribes the basis for the presentation of financial instruments.

Article 2 When this standard requires disclosures by the class of financial instrument, an enterprise should group financial instruments into classes that are appropriate to the nature of the information disclosed and that take into account the characteristics of those financial instruments. An enterprise should provide sufficient information to permit reconciliation to the line items presented in the balance sheet.

Article 3 This standard should be applied by all enterprises to all types of financial instruments except:

1. Long-term equity investments (ASBE No. 2—Long-term Equity Investments);
2. Share-based payments (ASBE No. 11—Share-based Payments);
3. Debt restructuring (ASBE No. 12—Debt Restructuring);
4. Contracts for contingent consideration of the acquirer in a business combination (ASBE No. 20—Business Combinations);
5. Rights and obligations under leases (ASBE No. 21—Leases);
6. Rights and obligations under direct insurance contracts (ASBE No. 25—Direct Insurance Contracts); and
7. Rights and obligations under reinsurance contracts (ASBE No. 25—Reinsurance Contracts).

Article 4 This standard should be applied to those contracts to buy or sell a non-financial item that can be settled net in cash or another financial instrument, with the exception of contracts that were entered into and continue to be held for the purpose of the receipt or delivery of a non-financial item in accordance with the enterprise's expected purchase, sale, or usage requirements.

L. Riccardi, *China Accounting Standards*,
DOI 10.1007/978-981-10-0006-5_41

41.2 Chapter II: Presentation of Financial Instruments

41.2.1 Liabilities and Equity

Article 5 The issuer of a financial instrument should classify the instrument, or its component parts, on initial recognition as a financial liability, a financial asset, or an equity instrument in accordance with the substance of the contractual arrangement and the definitions of a financial liability, a financial asset, and an equity instrument.

Article 6 When an issuer has to determine whether a financial instrument is an equity instrument rather than a financial liability, the instrument is an equity instrument if, and only if, both conditions (1) and (2) below are met.

1. The instrument includes no contractual obligation:
   a. to deliver cash or another financial asset to another entity; or
   b. to exchange financial assets or financial liabilities with another entity under conditions that are potentially unfavorable to the issuer.
2. If the instrument will or may be settled in the issuer's own equity instruments, it is:
   a. a non-derivative that includes no contractual obligation for the issuer to deliver a variable number of its own equity instruments; or
   b. a derivative that will be settled only by the issuer exchanging a fixed amount of cash or another financial asset for a fixed number of its own equity instruments. For this purpose, the issuer's own equity instruments do not include instruments that are contracts for the future receipt or delivery of the issuer's own equity instruments.

Article 7 A critical feature in differentiating a financial liability from an equity instrument is the existence of a contractual obligation of one party to the financial instrument (the issuer) either to deliver cash or another financial asset to the other party (the holder) or to exchange financial assets or financial liabilities with the holder under conditions that are potentially unfavorable to the issuer.

Article 8 The substance of a financial instrument, rather than its legal form, governs its classification in the enterprise's statement of financial position.

Article 9 If an enterprise does not have an unconditional right to avoid delivering cash or another financial asset to settle a contractual obligation, the obligation meets the definition of a financial liability.

Article 10 A financial instrument that gives the holder the right to put it back to the issuer for cash or another financial asset (a "puttable instrument") is a financial liability.

Article 11 An enterprise may have a contractual right or obligation to receive or deliver a number of its own shares or other equity instruments that vary so that the fair value of the entity's own equity instruments to be received or delivered equals the amount of the contractual right or obligation. Such a contractual right or obligation may be for a fixed amount or an amount that fluctuates in part or in full in response to changes in a variable other than the market price of the enterprise's own equity instruments. Such a contract is a financial liability of the enterprise even though the enterprise must or can settle it by delivering its own equity instruments. It is not an equity instrument because the entity uses a variable number of its own equity instruments as a means to settle the contract. Accordingly, the contract does not evidence a residual interest in the enterprise's assets after deducting all of its liabilities.

Article 12 A financial instrument may require the enterprise to deliver cash or another financial asset, or otherwise to settle it in such a way that it would be a financial liability, in the event of the occurrence or non-occurrence of uncertain future events that are beyond the control of both the issuer and the holder of the instrument. The issuer of such an instrument does not have the unconditional right to avoid delivering cash or another financial asset (or otherwise to settle it in such a way that it would be a financial liability). Therefore, it is a financial liability of the issuer unless:

1. The part of the contingent settlement provision that could require settlement in cash or another financial asset (or otherwise in such a way that it would be a financial liability) is not genuine and
2. The issuer can be required to settle the obligation in cash or another financial asset (or otherwise to settle it in such a way that it would be a financial liability) only in the event of liquidation of the issuer.

Article 13 When a derivative financial instrument gives one party a choice over how it is settled (e.g., the issuer or the holder can choose settlement net in cash or by exchanging shares for cash), it is a financial asset or a financial liability unless all of the settlement alternatives would result in it being an equity instrument.

An example of a derivative financial instrument with a settlement option that is a financial liability is a share option that the issuer can decide to settle net in cash or by exchanging its own shares for cash.

Article 14 Interest, dividends, losses, and gains relating to a financial instrument or a component that is a financial liability should be recognized as income or expense in profit or loss. Distributions to holders of an equity instrument should be debited by the enterprise directly to equity, net of any related income tax benefit.

Article 15 Changes in the fair value of an equity instrument are not recognized in the financial statements.

41.3 Compound Financial Instruments

Article 16 The issuer of a non-derivative financial instrument should evaluate the terms of the financial instrument to determine whether it contains both a liability and an equity component. Such components should be classified separately as financial liabilities, financial assets, or equity instruments.

Article 17 An enterprise recognizes separately the components of a financial instrument that (a) creates a financial liability of the enterprise and (b) grants an option to the holder of the instrument to convert it into an equity instrument of the enterprise. For example, a bond or similar instrument convertible by the holder into a fixed number of ordinary shares of the entity is a compound financial instrument. From the perspective of the enterprise, such an instrument comprises two components: a financial liability (a contractual arrangement to deliver cash or another financial asset) and an equity instrument (a call option granting the holder the right, for a specified period of time, to convert it into a fixed number of ordinary shares of the entity). Accordingly, the enterprise presents the liability and equity components separately in its statement of financial position.

Article 18 When the initial carrying amount of a compound financial instrument is allocated to its equity and liability components, the equity component is assigned the residual amount after deducting from the fair value of the instrument as a whole the amount separately determined for the liability component. The fair value of the liability component is the present value of the contractually determined stream of future cash flows discounted at the interest rate applied at the time by the market to instruments of comparable credit status and providing substantially the same cash flows on the same terms but without the conversion option.

41.3.1 Settlement in the Enterprise's Own Equity Instruments

Article 19 Any consideration received from issuing an equity instrument is added directly to equity after deducting transaction costs. Any consideration paid in relation to share issues is deducted directly from equity.

41.4 Treasury Shares

Article 20 If an enterprise reacquires its own equity instruments, those instruments ("treasury shares") should be deducted from equity. No gain or loss shall be recognized in profit or loss on the purchase, sale, issue, or cancelation of an enterprise's own equity instruments.

41.5 Offsetting a Financial Asset and a Financial Liability

Article 21 A financial asset and a financial liability should be offset and the net amount presented in the statement of financial position when, and only when, an enterprise:

1. Currently has a legally enforceable right to set off the recognized amounts; and
2. Intends either to settle on a net basis or to realize the asset and settle the liability simultaneously.

In accounting for a transfer of a financial asset that does not qualify for derecognition, the enterprise should not offset the transferred asset and the associated liability.

Article 22 This standard requires the presentation of financial assets and financial liabilities on a net basis when doing so reflects an enterprise's expected future cash flows from settling two or more separate financial instruments. When an enterprise has the right to receive or pay a single net amount and intends to do so, it has, in effect, only a single financial asset or financial liability. In other circumstances, financial assets and financial liabilities are presented separately from each other consistently with their characteristics as resources or obligations of the enterprise.

Article 23 Offsetting a recognized financial asset and a recognized financial liability and presenting the net amount differ from the derecognition of a financial asset or a financial liability. Although offsetting does not give rise to recognition of a gain or loss, the derecognition of a financial instrument not only results in the removal of the previously recognized item from the statement of financial position but also may result in the recognition of a gain or loss.

41.6 Chapter III: Disclosure of Financial Instruments

Article 24 Disclosures of financial instruments refer to related information of recognized and unrecognized financial instruments that are disclosed by an enterprise in the notes. An enterprise should disclose information that enables users of its financial statements to evaluate the significance of financial instruments for its financial position and performance.

Article 25 An enterprise discloses, in the summary of significant accounting policies, the measurement basis (or bases) used in preparing the financial statements and the other accounting policies used that are relevant to an understanding of the financial statements.

Specifically, an enterprise should disclose the following information:

1. For financial assets or financial liabilities at fair value through profit or loss:
    a. The basis for designating financial assets and financial liabilities as at fair value through profit or loss;
    b. The nature of the financial assets or financial liabilities so designated; and
    c. How, after designation, it eliminates or significantly reduces a recognition and measurement inconsistency that would otherwise arise from recognizing the gains or losses related to the financial asset or financial liability on different measurement bases, and a narrative description of how the designation satisfies the enterprise's documented risk management or investment strategy.

2. The criteria for designating financial assets as available for sale;
3. Objective evidence indicating that an impairment of a financial asset has been incurred and the method used to calculate the impairment loss on the financial asset;
4. The bases for measuring gains and losses on financial assets and financial liabilities;
5. The criteria applied in determining when to derecognize financial assets and financial liabilities; and
6. Other accounting policies related to financial instruments.

Article 26 An enterprise should group financial assets and financial liabilities into classes according to their nature and characteristics. Specifically, an enterprise should disclose information that enables users of its financial statements to evaluate the significance of financial instruments and the nature and extent of risks arising from financial instruments to which the enterprise is exposed at the reporting date.

41.7 Balance Sheet

Article 27 The carrying amounts of each of the following categories should be disclosed:

1. Financial assets at fair value through profit or loss;
2. Held-to-maturity investments;
3. Loans and receivables;
4. Available-for-sale financial assets;
5. Financial liabilities at fair value through profit or loss; and
6. Other financial liabilities.

Article 28 If the enterprise has designated a loan or receivable (or group of loans or receivables) as at fair value through profit or loss, it should disclose:

1. The maximum exposure to credit risk at the reporting date;
2. The amount by which any related credit derivatives or similar instruments mitigate that maximum exposure to credit risk.
3. The amount of change, during the period and cumulatively, in the fair value of the loan or receivable (or group of loans or receivables) that is attributable to changes in the credit risk of the financial asset determined.
4. The amount of the change in the fair value of any related credit derivatives or similar instruments that has occurred during the period and cumulatively since the loan or receivable was designated.

Article 29 If the enterprise has designated a financial liability as at fair value through profit or loss, it should disclose:

1. The amount of change, during the period and cumulatively, in the fair value of the financial liability that is attributable to changes in the credit risk of that liability; and

2. The difference between the financial liability's carrying amount and the amount the enterprise would be contractually required to pay at maturity to the holder of the obligation.

Article 30 If the enterprise has reclassified a financial asset as one measured:

1. At cost or amortized cost, rather than at fair value; or
2. At fair value, rather than at cost or amortized cost,

it should disclose the amount reclassified into and out of each category and the reason for that reclassification.

Article 31 An enterprise may have transferred financial assets in such a way that part or all of the financial assets do not qualify for derecognition. The enterprise should disclose for each class of such financial assets:

1. The nature of the assets;
2. The nature of the risks and rewards of ownership to which the enterprise remains exposed;
3. When the enterprise continues to recognize all of the assets, the carrying amounts of the assets and of the associated liabilities; and
4. When the enterprise continues to recognize the assets to the extent of its continuing involvement, the total carrying amount of the original assets, the amount of the assets that the enterprise continues to recognize, and the carrying amount of the associated liabilities.

Article 32 An enterprise should disclose:

1. The carrying amount of financial assets it has pledged as collateral for liabilities or contingent liabilities, including amounts that have been reclassified; and
2. The terms and conditions relating to its pledge.

Article 33 When an enterprise holds collateral (of financial or non-financial assets) and is permitted to sell or repledge the collateral in the absence of default by the owner of the collateral, it should disclose:

1. The fair value of the collateral held;
2. The fair value of any such collateral sold or repledged, and whether the enterprise has an obligation to return it; and
3. The terms and conditions associated with its use of the collateral.

Article 34 When financial assets are impaired by credit losses, the enterprise should disclose for each class of financial assets the beginning balances of the provision for the impairment of financial assets, the amount of the impairment loss recognized during the period, the amount of impairment loss reversed during the period, and a reconciliation of changes during the period.

Article 35 For loans payable recognized at the reporting date, an enterprise should disclose:

1. Details of any defaults during the period of principal, interest, sinking fund, or redemption terms of those loans payable;

2. The carrying amount of the loans payable in default at the reporting date; and
3. Whether the default was remedied, or the terms of the loans payable were renegotiated, before the financial statements were authorized for issue.

41.7.1 Income Statement and Statement of Changes in Owner's Equity

Article 36 An enterprise should disclose the following items of income, expense, gains, or losses either on the face of the financial statements or in the notes:

1. Net gains or net losses on:
   i. financial assets or financial liabilities at fair value through profit or loss;
   ii. available-for-sale financial assets;
   iii. held-to-maturity investments;
   iv. loans and receivables; and
   v. financial liabilities measured at amortized cost;
2. Total interest income and total interest expense (calculated using the effective interest method) for financial assets or financial liabilities;
3. Fee income and expense (other than amounts included in determining the effective interest rate) arising from:
   i. financial assets or financial liabilities that are not at fair value through profit or loss; and
   ii. trust and other fiduciary activities that result in the holding or investing of assets on behalf of individuals, trusts, retirement benefit plans, and other institutions;
4. Interest income on impaired financial assets accrued; and
5. The amount of any impairment loss for each class of financial asset.

41.8 Other Disclosures

Article 37 An enterprise should disclose the following separately for each type of hedge (i.e., fair value hedges, cash flow hedges, and hedges of net investments in foreign operations):

1. A description of each type of hedge;
2. A description of the financial instruments designated as hedging instruments and their fair values at the reporting date; and
3. The nature of the risks being hedged.

Article 38 For cash flow hedges, an enterprise should disclose:

1. The periods when the cash flows are expected to occur and when they are expected to affect profit or loss;
2. A description of any forecast transaction for which hedge accounting had previously been used, but which is no longer expected to occur;
3. The amount that was recognized in equity during the period;
4. The amount that was removed from equity and included in profit or loss for the period; and
5. The amount that was removed from equity during the period and included in the initial cost or other carrying amount of a non-financial asset or non-financial liability whose acquisition or incurrence was a hedged highly probable forecast transaction.

Article 39 An enterprise should disclose separately:

1. In fair value hedges, gains, or losses:

   a. on the hedging instrument; and
   b. on the hedged item attributable to the hedged risk.

2. The ineffectiveness recognized in profit or loss that arises from cash flow hedges; and
3. The ineffectiveness recognized in profit or loss that arises from hedges of net investments in foreign operations.

Article 40 Except as set out in *Article 43*, for each class of financial assets and financial liabilities, an enterprise should disclose the fair value of that class of assets and liabilities in a way that permits it to be compared with its carrying amount.

Article 41 An enterprise should disclose:

1. The methods applied in determining fair values of each class of financial assets or financial liabilities.
2. Whether fair values are determined, in whole or in part, directly by reference to published price quotations in an active market or are estimated using a valuation technique.
3. Whether the fair values recognized or disclosed in the financial statements are determined in whole or in part using a valuation technique based on assumptions that are not supported by prices from observable current market transactions in the same instrument and not based on available observable market data. For fair values that are recognized in the financial statements, if changing one or more of those assumptions to reasonably possible alternative assumptions would change fair value significantly, the enterprise should state this fact and disclose the effect of those changes. For this purpose, significance should be judged with respect to profit or loss, and total assets or total liabilities, or, when changes in fair value are recognized in equity, total equity.
4. If (3) applies, the total amount of the change in fair value estimated using such a valuation technique that was recognized in profit or loss during the period.

Article 42 If the market for a financial instrument is not active, an enterprise establishes its fair value using a valuation technique. Nevertheless, the best evidence of fair value at initial recognition is the transaction price (i.e., the fair value of the consideration given or received). It follows that there could be a difference between the fair value at initial recognition and the amount that would be determined at that date using the valuation technique. If such a difference exists, an enterprise should disclose, by class of financial instrument:

1. Its accounting policy for recognizing that difference in profit or loss; and
2. The aggregate difference yet to be recognized in profit or loss at the beginning and end of the period.

Article 43 Disclosures of fair value are not required:

1. When the carrying amount is a reasonable approximation of fair value, for example, for financial instruments such as short-term trade receivables and payables; or
2. For an investment in equity instruments that do not have a quoted market price in an active market, or derivatives linked to such equity instruments, and must be settled by delivery of such equity instruments.

Article 44 In the cases described in *Article 43* (2), an enterprise should disclose information to help users of the financial statements make their own judgements about the extent of possible differences between the carrying amount of those financial assets or financial liabilities and their fair value, including:

1. The fact that fair value information has not been disclosed for these instruments because their fair value cannot be measured reliably;
2. A description of the financial instruments, their carrying amount, and an explanation of why fair value cannot be measured reliably;
3. Information about the market for the instruments;
4. Information about whether and how the enterprise intends to dispose of the financial instruments; and
5. If financial instruments whose fair value previously could not be reliably measured are derecognized, that fact, their carrying amount at the time of derecognition, and the amount of gain or loss recognized.

41.9 Nature and Extent of Risks Arising from Financial Instruments

Article 45 For each type of risk arising from financial instruments, an enterprise should disclose:

1. The exposures to risk and how they arise;
2. Its objectives, policies, and processes for managing the risk and the methods used to measure the risk; and
3. Any changes in (1) or (2) from the previous period.

Article 46 For each type of risk arising from financial instruments, an enterprise should disclose:

1. Summary quantitative data about its exposure to that risk at the reporting date. This disclosure should be based on the information provided internally to key management personnel of the enterprise, for example, the enterprise's board of directors or chief executive officer.
2. The disclosures required by *Articles 47–57.*
3. Concentrations of risk at the reporting date.

If the quantitative data disclosed as at the reporting date are unrepresentative of an enterprise's exposure to risk during the period, an enterprise should provide further information that is representative.

Article 47 For credit risk, an enterprise should disclose by class of financial instrument:

1. The amount that best represents its maximum exposure to credit risk at the reporting date without taking account of any collateral held or other credit enhancements (e.g., netting agreements that do not qualify for offset);
2. In respect to the amount disclosed in (1), a description of collateral held as security and other credit enhancements;
3. Information about the credit quality of financial assets that are neither past due nor impaired; and
4. The carrying amount of financial assets that would otherwise be past due or impaired whose terms have been renegotiated.

Article 48 Enterprise should disclose the book value of financial assets that are warranties for liabilities, the related article, and condition. Thereinto, for the transferred financial assets, the party that transfers in has the right to sell and grant. The party that transfers out should disclose these financial assets separately.

Article 49 The warranties that gained by enterprises should disclose the fair value, articles, and conditions about the warranties.

Article 50 Enterprises should set up contra accounts to record the impairment and disclose the opening balance, accrue, restitution, write-off, and closing balance of the impairment provision

Article 51 enterprises should disclose the related nature of the compounded financial instruments which combined financial liabilities, equity, and the derivatives.

Article 52 The financial liabilities except short-term account payment should disclose the following information:

1. The detail information on the principal, interest, sinking fund, and payment articles;
2. The closing balance of the delayed financial liabilities; and

3. Before the issue of the financial reports, the remediation actions, and updated information on the liabilities articles.

If the enterprises have delay issues, they should disclose the above information. If the delay issue settled before the end of the period, enterprises no need to disclose related information

Article 53 In preparing the contractual maturity analysis, an enterprise should base disclosure on the earliest contractual maturity date in order to show the worst-case scenario. Specifically:

1. When counterparty has a choice of when an amount is paid, the liability is included on the basis of the earliest date on which the enterprise can be required to pay.
2. When an enterprise is committed to make amounts available in installments, each installment is allocated to the earliest period in which the enterprise can be required to pay.
3. When the amount payable is not fixed, the amount disclosed is determined by reference to the conditions existing at the reporting date.
4. Demand deposits and other deposits that are repayable on demand should be included in the earliest time band.

Article 54 Market risk is the risk that the fair value or future cash flows of a financial instrument will fluctuate because of the changes in market prices. Market risk comprises three types of risk: currency risk, interest rate risk, and other price risk.

Article 55 For market risk, an enterprise should disclose:

1. A sensitivity analysis for each type of market risk to which the enterprise is exposed at the reporting date, showing how profit or loss and equity would have been affected by changes in the relevant risk variable that were reasonably possible at that date;
2. The methods and assumptions used in preparing the sensitivity analysis; and
3. Changes from the previous period in the methods and assumptions used, and the reasons for such changes.

Article 56 If an enterprise prepares a sensitivity analysis, such as value-at-risk, that reflects interdependencies between risk variables (e.g., interest rates and exchange rates) and uses it to manage financial risks, it may use that sensitivity analysis in place of the analysis specified in *Article 55*. The enterprise should also disclose:

1. An explanation of the method used in preparing such a sensitivity analysis and of the main parameters and assumptions underlying the data provided; and
2. An explanation of the objective of the method used and of limitations that may result in the information not fully reflecting the fair value of the assets and liabilities involved.

Article 57 When the sensitivity analyses disclosed in accordance with *Article 55* or 56 are unrepresentative of a risk inherent in a financial instrument (e.g., because the year-end exposure does not reflect the exposure during the year), the enterprise should disclose that fact and the reason it believes the sensitivity analyses are unrepresentative.

41.10 Comments

New ASBE No. 37 requires the issuer of a financial instrument to classify the instrument, or its component parts, on initial recognition as a financial liability or an equity instrument. If an instrument has both liability and equity components, the instrument needs to be split into two components and the components accounted for separately. Financial Instruments: Presentation outlines the accounting requirements for the presentation of financial instruments, particularly as to the classification of such instruments into financial assets, financial liabilities, and equity instruments. The standard also provides guidance on the classification of related interests, dividends, and gains/losses and when financial assets and financial liabilities can be offset.

The fundamental principle of ASBE No. 37 is that a financial instrument should be classified as either a financial liability or an equity instrument according to the substance of the contract, not its legal form, and the definitions of financial liability and equity instrument. Two exceptions of this principle are certain potable instruments meeting specific criteria and certain obligations arising on liquidation (see below). The entity must make the decision at the time the instrument is initially recognized. The classification is not subsequently changed based on changed circumstances.

A financial instrument is an equity instrument only if (a) the instrument includes no contractual obligation to deliver cash or another financial asset to another entity and (b) if the instrument will or may be settled in the issuer's own equity instruments, it is either.

A non-derivative includes no contractual obligation for the issuer to deliver a variable number of its own equity instruments. A derivative will be settled only by the issuer exchanging a fixed amount of cash or another financial asset for a fixed number of its own equity instruments.

If an entity issues preference (preferred) shares that pay a fixed rate of dividend and that have a mandatory redemption feature at a future date, the substance is that they are a contractual obligation to deliver cash and, therefore, should be recognized as a liability. In contrast, preference shares that do not have a fixed maturity and where the issuer does not have a contractual obligation to make any payment are equity. In this example, even though both instruments are legally termed preference shares, they have different contractual terms and one is a financial liability, while the other one is equity.

A contractual right or obligation to receive or deliver a number of its own shares or other equity instruments that varies so that the fair value of the entity's own equity instruments to be received or delivered equals the fixed monetary amount of the contractual right or obligation is a financial liability.

When a derivative financial instrument gives one party a choice over how it is settled (for instance, the issuer or the holder can choose settlement net in cash or by exchanging shares for cash), it is a financial asset or a financial liability unless all of the settlement alternatives would result in it being an equity instrument. For rights issues offered for a fixed amount of foreign currency, current practice appears to require such issues to be accounted for as derivative liabilities. The amendment states that if such rights are issued pro rata to an entity's all existing shareholders in the same class for a fixed amount of currency, they should be classified as equity regardless of the currency in which the exercise price is denominated.

Some financial instruments—sometimes called compound instruments—have both a liability and an equity component from the issuer's perspective. In that case, ASBE No. 37 requires that the component parts be accounted for and presented separately according to their substance based on the definitions of liability and equity. The split is made at issuance and not revised for subsequent changes in market interest rates, share prices, or other event that changes the likelihood that the conversion option will be exercised.

To illustrate, a convertible bond contains two components. One is a financial liability, namely the issuer's contractual obligation to pay cash, and the other is an equity instrument, namely the holder's option to convert into common shares. Another example is debt issued with detachable share purchase warrants.

When the initial carrying amount of a compound financial instrument is required to be allocated to its equity and liability components, the equity component is assigned the residual amount after deducting from the fair value of the instrument as a whole the amount separately determined for the liability component.

Interest, dividends, gains, and losses relating to an instrument are classified as a liability that should be reported in profit or loss. This means that dividend payments on preferred shares classified as liabilities are treated as expenses. On the other hand, distributions (such as dividends) to holders of a financial instrument are classified as equity that should be charged directly against equity, not against earnings.

Transaction costs of an equity transaction are deducted from equity. Transaction costs related to an issue of a compound financial instrument are allocated to the liability and equity components in proportion to the allocation of proceeds.

The cost of an entity's own equity instruments that it has reacquired ("treasury shares") is deducted from equity. Gain or loss is not recognized on the purchase, sale, issue, or cancelation of treasury shares. Treasury shares may be acquired and held by the entity or by other members of the consolidated group. Consideration paid or received is recognized directly in equity. Costs of issuing or reacquiring equity instruments (other than in a business combination) are accounted for as a deduction from equity, net of any related income tax benefit.

Financial assets and financial liabilities shall be offset and presented on a net basis provided that certain criteria are met. Otherwise, they should be presented separately. Other introductions regard disclosure requirements.

41.11 Examples

On financial year N, Company X issues RMB 75,000,000, 5 % convertible bond for the same amount. The rate of conversion is set out to be RMB 1.00 of convertible bond for 1.00 of ordinary shares at any time starting from January 1st N + 1.

After the issuance in the primary market, the fair market interest rate is assessed to be 6.5 % per annum, and on the market, a straight bond with similar features (face value of RMB 75,000,000 and coupon rate 4 %) is sold at RMB 70,000,000. Company X classifies issued bonds as financial liabilities measured at their amortized cost.

In compliance with "split-accounting" provisions of ASBE No. 37, Company X has issues such as a debt security and a bond security at the same time. Therefore, the ASBE No. 37 requires in this case that the net proceeds of RMB 75,000,000 raised from the issuance of the convertible bond can be split in its liability and equity components.

In particular we have that:

Total cash proceeds of convertible bond issue: RMB 75,000,000
Liability component: RMB 70,000,000
Equity Component: RMB 5,000,000
Records in the journal entries should follow the distinction mentioned above.

Chapter 42
Accounting Standards for Business Enterprises No. 38—Initial Implementation of Accounting Standards for Enterprises

42.1 Chapter I: General Provisions

Article 1 According to the Accounting Standards for Enterprises—Basic Standards, these Standards is formulated in order to regulate the recognition and measurement of accounting elements, as well as the presentation of financial statements governed by the Initial Implementation of Accounting Standards for Enterprises, when the Accounting Standards for Enterprises is initially carried out.

Article 2 The phrase "initially implementing accounting standards for enterprises" means that the system of accounting standards for enterprises is first carried out, consisting of the basic standards, specific standards, and guidelines on the application of accounting standards.

Article 3 The Accounting Standards for Enterprises No. 28—Changes in Accounting Policies and Estimates and Corrections of Errors shall apply to the alteration of accounting policies occurring after initially carrying out accounting standards for enterprises.

42.2 Chapter II: Recognition and Measurement

Article 4 On the date of initial implementation, according to the Accounting Standards for Enterprises, an enterprise shall make classification, recognition, and measurement on all assets, liabilities, and the owner's equities again, and shall make a balance sheet for the initial period. As making a balance sheet for the initial period, the enterprise shall make no retroactive modulation to any item except for those to which retroactive modulations shall be made according to *Articles 5* through *19* of these Standards.

Article 5 A long-term equity investment on the date of initial implementation shall be respectively conducted according to the circumstances as follows:

L. Riccardi, *China Accounting Standards*,
DOI 10.1007/978-981-10-0006-5_42

1. In accordance with the Accounting Standards for Enterprises No. 20—Business Combination, if a long-term equity investment is generated from a business combination under common control, the unamortized equity investment difference shall be entirely sterilized, the retained earnings shall be modulated, and the book balance of the long-term equity investment after the sterilization of the equity investment difference shall be considered as the cost recognition on the date of initial implementation.
2. For any other long-term equity investment calculated by equity method except that mentioned in Item (1), in case there is any equity investment difference on the credit side, it shall sterilize the credit balance, the retained earnings shall be modulated, and the book balance of the long-term equity investment after the sterilization on the credit side shall be considered as the cost recognition on the date of initial implementation. In case there is any equity investment difference on the debit side, the book value of the long-term equity investment shall be considered as the cost recognition on the date of initial implementation.

Article 6 In case any conclusive evidence indicates that an investment real estate may be measured at fair value, it may be measured at fair value on the date of initial implementation and the retained earnings shall be modulated based on the difference between its book value and its fair value.

Article 7 On the date of initial implementation, for the discard expenses which meet the conditions for the recognition of expected liabilities but have not been charged to the asset costs prior to this date, the asset costs shall be increased and the related liabilities shall be recognized. Simultaneously, the retained earnings shall be modulated based on the depreciation (depletion) drawn complementarily.

Article 8 As to a plan on terminating the labor relationship with an employee which is already existing on the date of initial implementation, in case it meets the conditions described in the Accounting Standards for Enterprises No. 9—Wages and Salaries of Employees for the recognition of expected liabilities, the liability resulting from the compensation made for the cancelation of the labor relationship with the employee shall be recognized as well as the retained earnings shall be modulated.

Article 9 As to an investment formed in the operation of the enterprise annuity fund, it shall be measured at a fair value on the date of initial implementation and the retained earnings shall be modulated based on the difference between its book amount and the fair value.

Article 10 As to a share-based payment of which the vesting date is on or after the date of initial implementation, upon the provisions of the Accounting Standards for Enterprises No. 11—Share-based Payment, the retained earnings shall, in accordance with the fair value of the equity instrument, or service provided by any other party or liability assumed by any other party which is calculated and determined based on the equity instrument, be modulated at the amount of cost incurred during the vesting period before the date of initial implementation, and the owner's equities or liabilities shall be increased accordingly. Any retroactive modulation may not be made to any share-based payment made for any exercisable right before the date of initial implementation.

Article 11 On the date of initial implementation, according to the Accounting Standards for Enterprises No. 13—Contingencies, an enterprise shall recognize those restructuring obligations meeting the conditions for the recognition of expected liabilities as liabilities and shall modulate the retained earnings.

Article 12 On the date of initial implementation, in accordance with the provisions of the Accounting Standards for Enterprises No. 18—Income Tax, an enterprise shall make a retroactive modulation to the effect of the temporary difference between the carrying amount of an asset or liability and its tax based on income tax and shall modulate the retained earnings based on the affected amount.

Article 13 Other than the items as follows, any retroactive modulation may not be made to the business combinations occurring before the date of initial implementation:

1. As to a business combination under common control as prescribed in the Accounting Standards for Enterprises No. 20—Business Combination, the amortized value of the originally recognized business reputation shall be entirely sterilized and the retained earnings shall be modulated. As to a business combination not under common control as described in these Standards, the amortized value of the business reputation on the date of initial implementation shall be recognized as cost, and it shall not be amortized any more.
2. As to the business combination occurring before the date of initial implementation, in case it is stipulated in the combination contract or agreement that the combination cost should be modulated in accordance with the occurrence of future events, and the future events expected on the date of initial implementation are likely to occur and their effects on the combination cost can be measured reliably, the carrying amount of the already recognized business reputation shall be modulated based on the affected amount.
3. According to the Accounting Standards for Enterprises No. 8—Asset Impairment, an enterprise shall have an impairment test for the business reputation on the date of initial implementation, and if impaired, it shall be recognized with the amount after the impairment provision is made as well as the retained earnings shall be modulated.

Article 14 On the date of initial implementation, an enterprise shall divide the financial assets (excluding the investments under the Accounting Standards for Enterprises No. 2—Long-term Equity Investments) into financial assets, held-to-maturity investments, loans, receivables, and financial assets available for sale measured at their fair value and of which the alterations charged to the profits and losses in the current period.

1. As to those classified as financial assets measured at their fair value and of which the alterations charged to the profits and losses in the current period or available for sale, they shall be measured at their fair value on the initial date of

implementation, as well as the retained earnings shall be modulated based on the difference between the carrying amount and the fair value.

2. As to those classified as held-to-maturity investments, loans, and receivables, they shall, as of the date of initial implementation, be measured at their amortized cost in the subsequent accounting periods employing the actual interest rate method.

Article 15 As to a financial liability which on the date of first implementation is designated to be measured at its fair value and of which the alterations are charged to the profits and losses in the current period, it shall be measured at its fair value on the date of initial implementation as well as the retained earnings shall be modulated based on its carrying amount and fair value.

Article 16 As to a derivative financial instrument (excluding hedging instruments), which has not been recognized in the balance sheet, or which has been measured at its cost, it shall be measured at its fair value on the date of initial implementation and the retained earnings shall be modulated.

Article 17 As to an embedded financial instrument which shall be separated from the mixed instrument according to the Accounting Standards for Enterprises No. 22—Recognition and Measurement of Financial Instruments, on the date of initial implementation, it shall be separated from the mixed instrument and shall be conducted respectively, however, unless it is difficult to make a reasonable determination on the fair value of the embedded derivative financial instrument. As to a non-derivative financial instrument with liability and equity components which is issued by an enterprise, on the date of initial implementation, the liability component shall be separated from equity component according to the Accounting Standards for Enterprises No. 37—Presentation of Financial Instruments, unless it is difficult to make a reasonable determination on the fair value of the liability component.

Article 18 On the date of initial implementation, as to the hedges which do not meet the conditions for employing the hedge accounting methods described in the Accounting Standards for Enterprises No. 24—Hedging, the implementation of the original hedge accounting methods shall be brought to an end and shall be conducted according to the Accounting Standards for Enterprises No. 24—Hedging.

Article 19 On the date of initial implementation, a cession enterprise of reinsurance businesses shall recognize the related provisions which should be allocated back to the reinsurance acceptors as assets according to the Accounting Standards for Enterprises No. 26—Reinsurance Contracts as well as modulate the carrying amount of each provision.

42.3 Chapter III: Presentation

Article 20 During the period of preparation of the first annual financial statements after the date of initial implementation (referred to as the first annual financial statements hereinafter) according to the Accounting Standards for Enterprises, an enterprise shall make a balance sheet, profit statement, cash flow statement, statement on alternations of the owner's equities, and the notes in light of the Accounting Standards for Enterprises No. 30—Presentation of Financial Statements and the Accounting Standards for Enterprises No. 31—Cash Flow Statements. As to the enterprise which provides consolidated financial statements to outsiders, it shall be governed by the provisions in the Accounting Standards for Enterprises No. 33—Consolidated Financial Statements. As to the enterprise which provides interim financial reports during the period covered by the first annual financial statements, it shall be governed by the provisions in the Accounting Standards for Enterprises No. 32—Interim Financial Reports. An enterprise shall throw daylight on the alternations in the amount of the items of the financial statements upon initial implementation of Accounting Standards for Enterprises in its notes.

Article 21 The first annual financial statements shall at least consist of comparative information of the previous year presented according to the Accounting Standards for Enterprises. In case the presentation of the items of financial statements alters, the comparative figures of the previous year shall be modulated as required by the Accounting Standards for Enterprises concerning the presentation, unless it is impractical. As to a subsidiary company which was not included into the scope of consolidation, but should have been included into therein according to the Accounting Standards for Enterprises No. 33—Consolidated Financial Statements, the enterprise shall list it under the scope of consolidation for the comparative consolidated financial statements of the previous year. As to a subsidiary company which was included into the scope of consolidation, but should have not been included into therein according to these Standards, the enterprise shall not list the subsidiary company under the scope of consolidation for the comparative consolidated financial statements of the previous year. The minority shareholders' interests presented in the comparative financial statements of the previous year shall be listed under the category of the owner's equities according to these Standards. As to an enterprise that shall list the earnings per share, it shall calculate and list the earnings per share of the previous year in the comparative financial statements according to the Accounting Standards for Enterprises No. 34—Earnings Per Share. As to an enterprise that shall publish the segment information, it shall publish the segment information of the previous year in the comparative financial statements according to the Accounting Standards for Enterprises No. 35—Segment Reports.

42.4 Comments

ASBE No. 38 is applicable only to first-time adopters of the ASBEs issued in 2006. It describes the transactions and events that require adjustments when an enterprise adopts the ASBEs for the first time to prepare its financial statements (also called "the first annual financial statements"). The first annual financial statements shall include at least one year of comparative information prepared under the ASBEs. All items of income and expense recognized in a period must be included in profit or loss unless a Standard or an Interpretation requires otherwise. Some IFRSs require or permit some components to be excluded from profit or loss and instead to be included in other comprehensive income.

This standard applies to all general-purpose financial statements that are prepared and presented in accordance with International Financial Reporting Standards (IFRSs). For general-purposes financial statements are those intended to serve users who are not in a position to require financial reports tailored to their particular information needs.

The objective of ASBE No. 38 is to prescribe the basis for presentation of general-purpose financial statements, to ensure comparability both with the entity's financial statements of previous periods and with the financial statements of other entities. It sets out the overall requirements for the presentation of financial statements, guidelines for their structure, and minimum requirements for their content. Standards for recognizing, measuring, and disclosing specific transactions are addressed in other Standards and Interpretations.

Comparing ASBE No. 38 with the correspondent IFRS 1, the objective is the same. Similar to ASBE No. 38, IFRS 1 contains the transactions and events that require adjustments when an enterprise adopts IFRSs for the first time to prepare its financial statements.

42.5 Examples

Companies adopting ASBEs for the first time in 2006 should follow a reconciliatory statement for the differences occurred.

Item number	Name of item	Amount (RMB)
(a)	Owners' equity at December 31, 2006 (under previous accounting standards)	
1	Long-term equity investments' difference	
2	Investment properties measured under fair value model	
3	Prior-year depreciation provided, etc., on estimated costs of dismantling assets	
4	Termination compensation that meets the criteria of estimated liabilities	
5	Share-based payment	
6	Restructuring obligations that meet the criteria of estimated liabilities	
7	Business combinations	
8	Financial assets at fair value through profit or loss and available-for-sale financial assets	
9	Financial liabilities at fair value through profit or loss	
10	Increase in equity due to splitting of financial instruments	

(continued)

(continued)

Item number	Name of item	Amount (RMB)
11	Derivative financial instruments	
12	Income taxes	
13	Minority stakeholders' interest	
14	Special retrospective adjustment relating to listed companies on B shares, H shares, etc.	
15	Others	
(b)	Total of adjustments	
(c)	Increase in owners' equity	
(d)	Owners' equity at January 1, 2007 (new accounting standards)	

Chapter 43
Accounting Standards for Business Enterprises 2014

The Ministry of Finance—"MOF" issued in January 2014 three new Accounting Standards for Business Enterprises: Presentation of Financial Statements (ASBE 39), Employee Benefits (ASBE 40), and Fair Value Measurement (ASBE 41).

Moreover, in February and March 2014, the MOF revised Accounting Standards for Business Enterprises on long-term equity investments, consolidated financial statements, joint arrangements, and disclosure of interests in other entities.

43.1 Accounting Standards for Business Enterprises Reviewed in 2014

43.1.1 Accounting Standards for Business Enterprises No. 33—Consolidated Financial Statements

During the year 2014, the MOF edits the "Accounting Standers for Business Enterprises." The first ASBE they edited was the ASBE no. 33.

The main changes occurred in this principle are the following:

- In the ASBE 33, there is no mention to circumstances that allowed parent company not to prepare the consolidated financial statements. Under current PRC GAAPs, there are three types of enterprises that are required to prepare consolidated financial statements. Other enterprises may also choose to prepare consolidated financial statements voluntarily.
- Specifies the scope of consolidation shall be determined based on "control."
- All subsidiaries under the control of a parent shall be consolidated. The current ASBE introduces an exception: certain subsidiaries are exempted from consolidation, for example, where total assets, sales revenue, and profits of the subsidiary are less than 10 % of the corresponding amount of the group, subsidiaries declared bankrupt, subsidiaries engaged in specific industries, etc.
- A set of consolidated financial statements shall include a consolidated statement of changes in equity. However, the consolidated statement of profit appropriation is removed in the new ASBE 33.

L. Riccardi, *China Accounting Standards*,
DOI 10.1007/978-981-10-0006-5_43

- For a business combination not under common control, the identifiable net assets of the subsidiary shall be adjusted to their fair values at the date of acquisition when preparing consolidated financial statements.
- For a business combination involving enterprises under common control during the reporting period, the consolidated balance sheet includes the net assets of the combining entities using the book values; the consolidated income statements include the results of the combining entities for the full period (including the comparative periods).
- If the losses applicable to the minority shareholders in a subsidiary exceed the minority interest in that subsidiary's owners' equity at the beginning of the period, the excess is used to reduce minority interest in equity to the extent that the minority shareholder has a binding obligation and is able to make an additional investment to cover the losses. Otherwise, the excess is allocated against the owners' equity of the parent instead of being allocated to "unrecognized investment loss" (under current PRC GAAPs).
- In assessing an enterprise's ability to control another enterprise, the effect of "potential voting rights" shall be considered.
- The equity method instead of proportionate consolidation shall be used to account for equity interests in jointly controlled entities. The current ASBE 33 requires the use of proportionate consolidation methods.

43.1.2 Accounting Standards for Business Enterprises No. 35—Segment Reporting

The change occurred in ASBE 35 is related to the fact that the ASBE 35 requires one basis of segmentation to be primary and the other to be secondary, with considerably less information required to be disclosed for the secondary segment. It requires the same amount of information to be reported for both business segments and geographical segments.

43.1.3 Accounting Standards for Business Enterprises No. 37—Presentation of Financial Instruments

The main changes occurred in this principle are the following:

- ASBE 37 does not require anymore the issuer of a financial instrument to classify the instrument, or its component parts, on initial recognition as a financial liability or an equity instrument. If an instrument has both liability and equity components, the instrument needs to be split into two components and the components accounted for separately.

- Financial assets and financial liabilities shall be offset and presented on a net basis provided certain criteria are met. Otherwise, they shall be presented separately.
- Introduces significant disclosure requirements.

43.2 New Accounting Standards for Business Enterprises Added in 2014

43.2.1 Accounting Standards for Business Enterprises No. 39—Fair Value

43.2.1.1 Chapter I: General Provisions

Article 1 The first order of fair value measurement and disclosure norms, according to "Accounting Standards for Enterprises—Basic Standards," formulated guidelines.

Article 2 Fair values refer to the estimated value of all assets and liabilities of market participants at the date in which an orderly transaction occurs.

Article 3 This Article applies to other relevant accounting standards required to permit the measurement and disclosure of fair value.

Article 4 The following items apply to other measurement and disclosure of relevant accounting standards:

(A) If fair value measurement and disclosure are similar to other measurement attributes, such as standard net realizable value, apply "Accounting Standards for Enterprises No. 1—Inventories," standard present value of estimated future cash flow, apply "Enterprise Accounting Standards No. 10—Impairment of Assets," "Accounting Standards for Enterprises No. 1—Inventories," and "Accounting Standards for Enterprises No. 8—Impairment of Assets."
(B) Share-Based Payments and related measurement and disclosure of business apply "Enterprise Accounting Standards No. 11—Share-Based Payment."
(C) Leasing-related measurement and disclosure apply "Accounting Standards for Enterprises No. 21—Leases."

Article 5 The following is a disclosure of the application of other relevant accounting standards:

(A) For net fair value; it costs less to determine the recoverable amount of the asset disclosed, apply "Enterprise Accounting Standards No. 10—Impairment of Assets."
(B) The fair value of employees severance benefit plans to disclose assets apply "Enterprise Accounting Standards No. 10—Employee Benefits."
(C) To disclose the fair value of corporate pension fund investments apply "Enterprise Accounting Standards No. 10—The Enterprise Annuity Fund."

43.2.1.2 Chapter II: Covers the Underlying Asset or Liability

Article 6 Characteristics of business-related assets or liabilities should be considered before they are measured at fair value.

Characteristics of the underlying asset or liability refer to market participants at the measurement date pricing the asset or liability considered features, including the status and location of assets, restrictions on assets sold or used.

Article 7 Relevant assets or liabilities at fair value can be individual assets or liabilities (such as a financial instrument and a non-financial asset). They may also be the portfolio, or a combination of assets and liabilities (such as "Enterprise Accounting Standard No. 8—Impairment of Assets 'portfolio standard' and Accounting Standards for Enterprises No. 20—Business Combinations" standardized business). The related assets or liabilities of business both individual and joint are measured at fair value, depending on the measurement unit of the asset or liability.

Metering unit refers to the relevant assets, or liabilities counted alone or in combination. The minimum unit quantity when measuring unit-related assets or liabilities, other relevant accounting standards should be measured at fair value when required or permitted, except for the fair value of the guidelines outlining market risk or credit risk that can offset financial assets and financial liabilities.

43.2.1.3 Chapter III: Orderly Trading and Market

Article 8 Fair value of the underlying asset or liability shall be assumed by market participants when selling or transferring the assets and liabilities at the measurement date of the transaction.

This is an orderly transaction in the current market conditions.

An orderly transaction, in the measurement of time-related assets or liabilities have the usual market trading activities. Forced liquidation transactions are not orderly transactions.

Article 9 When an Enterprise is measuring related assets or liabilities at fair value, it should be assumed that the sale of assets or the transfer of liability will be an orderly transaction with major market-related asset or liability. In the absence of major markets, enterprises should assume that the transaction will include the most favorable market-related asset or liability.

The main market refers to the underlying assets or liabilities largest trading volume and the market with the highest level of trading activity.

Most advantageous market means after considering transaction costs and transport costs, the market that offers the maximum amount possible to sell the underlying asset or to transfer the minimum amount of market-related liabilities is the most advantageous.

Transaction costs means the costs directly attributable to the major markets of the underlying assets or liabilities (or most advantageous market), the incidence of the sale of the asset or liability transfer. Transaction costs are directly caused by the transaction. The exchange is necessary, but if assets or liabilities are not transferred, the fees will not occur.

Transportation costs refer to the major markets (or most advantageous market) costs incurred from the transportation of assets.

Article 10 When identifying a major market (or most advantageous market), an enterprise should consider all of the information that may be obtained reasonably, but there is no need to examine all markets.

Typically, the market that companies normally sell assets or liabilities can be considered as the main market (or most advantageous market).

Article 11 Business should be able to enter the primary market (or most advantageous market) at the measurement date, but this does not require companies to measure the actual date of the sale or transfer of assets and liabilities in the market.

Because different companies can enter different markets for different enterprises, identical assets or liabilities may have different major markets (or most advantageous market).

Article 12 An enterprise shall be measured by the prices of the major market-related assets or liabilities. If there is no major market, the fair value of the business should be measured at the most favorable market price of the underlying asset or liability.

Enterprises should not be adjusted in price due to asset costs. Transaction costs are not characteristics of the underlying assets or liabilities and are only related to the specific transaction.

Transaction costs do not include transportation costs.

Locations where the underlying asset is characteristic of the asset, where transport costs incurred enable the transfer of assets from the current position to the main market (or most advantageous market), enterprise transfer the assets according to the primary market from the current position (or most favorable markets). Transport costs should be adjusted to key market (or most advantageous market) prices.

Article 13 It does not exist when the measurement date can be offered for sale or transfer of assets and liabilities; when given relevant observable market price information, enterprises should view the market from the perspective of the participants who hold assets or liabilities, on the date occurred; the sale or transfer of assets and liabilities of the transaction should occur assuming the price of the transaction on the basis of measurement of the related assets or the fair value of the liability.

43.2.1.4 Chapter IV: Market Participants

Article 14 An enterprise using fair value of the underlying asset or liability should use the assumptions used by market participants when pricing the asset or liability to maximize the economic benefits for the realization of its use.

Market participants refer to the main market of the underlying asset or liability (or most advantageous market) and both of the following characteristics of the buyer and seller:

(A) Market participants should be independent of each other; there is no related party relationships described in "Enterprise Accounting Standards No. 36—Related Party Disclosures";
(B) Market participants should be familiar with the situation; according to information obtained by the relevant asset or liability, the transaction must have a reasonable perception;
(C) Market participants should be willing and able to trade the underlying asset or liability.

Article 15 Factors that should be considered in determining market participants are the measurement of the related assets or liabilities; the main market of the asset or liability (or most advantageous market) and the market corporate transactions and the other market participants identification of market participants in general.

43.2.1.5 Chapter V: Initially Measured at Fair Value

Article 16 An enterprise should be based on the nature and characteristics of the transaction related to the assets or liabilities, etc., to determine initially whether fair value recognized is equal to its trading price.

In an enterprise when concerning the assets or liabilities in the transaction; the transaction price is paid for by the acquired assets or liabilities at the received price (enter price). They can receive the required payment of fair value of the asset and liabilities sold or transferred (i.e., sell price). Fair value related to assets or liabilities, at the time of its initial recognition is normally equal to the transaction price, but in the following two cases, it may not be equal:

(A) Transactions between related parties where there is evidence that the companies' related party transactions are in the market except for some conditions.
(B) The transaction is forced.
(C) Metering unit represented by the transaction price and the measurement determined in accordance with *Article 7* of the guidelines of the different units.
(D) In the main markets, market is not related to assets or liabilities (or most advantageous market).

Article 17 Other relevant accounting standards require or allow companies to apply fair value. The underlying asset or liability and initially measured, and if the transaction price and fair value are not equal, the enterprise-related gains or losses are recognized in profit or loss, but other GAAPs are except as otherwise provided.

43.2.1.6 Chapter VI: Valuation Techniques

Article 18 Fair value of the underlying asset or liability should be used.

If it is applicable to the current situation and there is sufficient information available to support data and other valuation techniques.

Purpose of business use of valuation techniques is to estimate the measurement date under current market conditions, if market participant sells an asset or transfer a liability in an orderly price transactions.

When enterprise use fair value to measure assets or liabilities, the valuation techniques used include market approach, income approach, and cost approach. Enterprises should use measurement of one or more valuation technique, which are consistent with the fair value method. Select companies use a variety of techniques of measurement of fair value valuations. We should consider all valuation results as fair value.

Market approach is the use of the same or similar assets, liabilities or a combination of the price of assets and liabilities and other information including technology-related market transaction valuations.

Income approach is to convert future amounts to a single present value using valuation techniques.

Cost is a reflection of the current requirement to reset the required service capabilities and the amount of the underlying asset (often referred to current replacement cost) valuation techniques.

Article 19 When enterprises use the application of valuation techniques, they should use in preference to relevant observable inputs. You can use unobservable assets only if the relevant observable inputs cannot be obtained or are made impracticable under the circumstances.

Enter value refers to the assumption that market participants, when pricing the asset or liabilities related to the use, including observable inputs and unobservable inputs.

Observable inputs mean that the input value can be obtained from market data. The input value reflects the assumptions of market participants when pricing the related asset or liability to be used.

Unobservable inputs mean that the input value cannot be obtained from market data.

Enter value should be determined based on the best information available to market participants when pricing the asset or liability related to the use of assumptions.

The fair value of the transaction price should be used as the initial recognition of the enterprise and in the use of fair value in subsequent measurement involving unobservable inputs valuation techniques. Valuation techniques should be corrected in the valuation process, so the initial recognition of valuation techniques to determine the outcome of the transaction is equal to the price.

Article 20 Enterprises using valuation techniques are subsequently measured at fair value, particularly unobservable inputs shall ensure that the valuation technique reflects the measurement date of observable market data, such as prices for similar assets or liabilities and the like.

Article 21 With the exception of valuation techniques used in which fair value has been determined, it shall not be changed, but instead the valuation technique or its application that enables the measurement result in the present case shall be changed to be the same or more representative of fair value, including, but not limited to the following conditions:

(A) The emergence of new markets.
(B) New information cannot be obtained.
(C) It will no longer be able to obtain information before use.
(D) There are improved valuation techniques.
(E) The Market conditions change.

If Enterprise changes the valuation technique, its application shall be in accordance with "Accounting Standards for Enterprises No. 28—Accounting policies, changes in accounting estimates and correction of errors."

According to the disclosure requirements of the guidelines on the valuation of the technical change disclosed in its application, the provisions of the relevant change in accounting estimates will be disclosed in accordance with "Accounting Standards for Enterprises No. 28—Accounting policies, changes in accounting estimates and corrections of errors."

Article 22 When deciding fair value, using a valuation technique, select characteristics assets or liabilities should be used and market participants trading in the underlying asset or liability should consider consistent input values, including the liquidity premium or discount, control premium or discount, and other minority interests. This does not include metering and *Article 7* of this Code is inconsistent discount or premium unit.

Enterprises should consider the discount or premium on its large holdings of the underlying asset or liability that arises. If the discount or premium to reflect the market's normal daily trading volume is less than the number of companies in the current market-related asset or liability that sell or transfer its holdings, market participants adjust the asset or liability quotes.

Article 23 With underlying asset or liability at fair value, if bid and ask prices exist, companies should fair value be between the bid and ask prices of the most representative of the current fair values of the case to determine the fair value of the asset or liability. Businesses can use bid metering asset positions, or the use of asking metering liability positions.

This Standard does not restrict businesses using metering central parity pricing practices or other related assets or liabilities of market participants to use in practice between bid and asking price.

43.2.1.7 Noted in Chapter VII of the Fair Value Hierarchy

Article 24 Fair value of the input value used is divided into three levels, initially used is the first level input value, followed by a second level of the input value, and finally a third level of the input value. The first level of the input value is identical assets or liabilities at the measurement date and can be obtained in an unadjusted off of the active market. Active market refers to the underlying asset or liability trading volume and trading frequency sufficient to continue to provide market-pricing information.

The second level of the input value is the input value in addition to the first level of the input value of the underlying asset or liability, either directly or indirectly observable.

The third level of the input value is assets and liabilities related to unobservable inputs.

Level fair value measurement results belonging to the lowest level are determined by the input values and are important for the whole fair value belongings. Enterprises should be used to judge whether the input value is important in considering the relevant asset or liability on the basis of characteristics. Level fair value measurement results depend on the input value valuation techniques, rather than the valuation technique itself.

Article 25 The input value is the fair value hierarchy which provides the most reliable evidence. In all cases, when a company can get the same assets or liabilities quoted in an active market, the offer should be applied without adjustment of the fair value of the asset or liability, except in the following circumstances:

(A) Companies hold large amounts of similar but not identical assets or liabilities at fair value:
There is an active market price of these assets or liabilities, and it is difficult to obtain for each asset or liability at the date information pricing alone. In this case, companies can use other valuation models that do not rely solely on the offer.

(B) Fair value quoted in active markets that fails to be representative of the measurement date, as a result significant impact of events occurs that causes the failure to offer an active market on behalf of the fair value measurement date.

(C) The criteria of *Article 34* (B) of the situation.
Business due to the above circumstances for identical assets or liabilities quoted in an active market that adjust fair value measurement should be divided into the lower level.

Article 26 When using the second level of the input value, the underlying asset or liability is measured at fair value and should be based on the characteristics of the asset or liability, if the input value of the second level is to be adjusted. These features include asset condition or location, enter value associated with the degree of similar assets or liabilities (including the factor (ii) the provisions of *Article 34* of the Code), transaction input values that can be observed in the markets, and the level of activity and so on.

If the related assets or liabilities have specific term contract deadlines, the second level of the input value should be within almost the entire period that is observable.

The second level of the input values includes the following:

(A) The quoted active market for similar assets or liabilities;
(B) Non-active markets have the same or similar assets or liabilities quoted;
(C) Other observable inputs other than the quoted price, including interest rates and the yield curve during normal interval observable quotes, implied volatility and credit spreads;
(D) Markets verify input values and the like. Market-validated input value is obtained through correlation analysis or other means mainly from observable market data or observable market input values through data validation.

Companies use significant unobservable inputs on the second level of the input value adjustments, and the adjustments to the fair value measurement that are important for the overall fair value measurement results should be classified as the third level.

Article 27 The existence of market activity- or market activities-related assets or liabilities associated rarely leads to observable inputs that cannot be obtained or acquired practically without using a third-level input values, i.e., unobservable inputs value.

Unobservable inputs should reflect the market participants when pricing the asset or liability related to the use of assumptions, including assumptions about risk, such as the inherent risk and valuation techniques specific with input value valuation techniques.

Article 28 When determining unobservable inputs, the best information in the present case that can be reasonably obtained should be used, including all reasonable market participant assumptions that were made.

Businesses can use internal data as unobservable inputs, but if there is evidence that other market participants will use different internal data, or internal data that is business specific of these enterprises, or other market participants do not have business-related features, companies should make the appropriate adjustments to their internal data.

43.2.1.8 Chapter VIII: Fair Value of Non-financial Assets

Article 29 The enterprises are measured at fair value of non-financial assets. Market participants should consider the best use of the asset for the ability to produce economic benefits, or the sale of assets to other market participants that can use these assets to best use the ability to produce economic benefits.

The best use refers to market participants that realize the value of a portfolio of non-financial assets and liabilities or assets owned that maximize the use of non-financial assets.

Article 30 The enterprises that determine the best use of non-financial assets should consider whether the law permits the possibility of the physical as well as financial viability and other factors.

(A) Companies use to judge whether to allow non-financial assets in the law, these should be considered assets when the market participants consider the use of the asset for pricing restrictions in the law.
(B) If the business purpose of non-financial assets is determined on the kind of asset if possible, market participants should consider the physical characteristics of the asset when pricing the asset.
(C) Determining the use of non-financial assets of enterprises in the financial viability of the permit and the kind possible by law should be considered. If the use of the asset can generate enough income or cash flow, resulting in compensation for the asset after the cost of the use and that can still be able to meet the return on investment required by market participants.

Article 31 An enterprise shall determine the best use of non-financial assets from the perspective of the market participants.

Typically, companies use the existing non-financial assets that can be regarded as the best use unless market factors or other factors suggest that the market participants could use the asset in accordance with other uses to maximize value.

Article 32 If the enterprises are measured at fair value of non-financial assets, the following shall be determined based on the best use valuation premise:

(A) If market participants alone have a maximum value of non-financial assets, the fair value of the non-financial assets should be sold to the same market participants at the asset's current trading price.
(B) If market participants that have non-financial assets and other assets (or a combination of other assets or liabilities) in combination with the most value, the fair value of the non-financial assets should be used to sell them, to use the same combination of assets, market participants use the current trading price and the market participants can get a combination of other assets and liabilities. Among them, the liabilities include liabilities of companies to raise working capital, but do not include debt portfolio companies liabilities to raise funds arising from outside.

Best use purpose is assumed to be consistently applied in combination with the best use of all related assets.

It should be judged from the perspective of the enterprises market participant's best use of the assets that are used alone or in combination with other assets, or in combination with other assets and liabilities. But in the measurement of the fair value of financial assets, it should be assumed in accordance with these guidelines, determining the metering unit, to sell the assets.

43.2.1.9 Chapter IX: Liabilities Measured at Fair Value and Their Own Equity Instruments

Article 33 The enterprises that are measured at fair value of the liability should assume the liability at the measurement date that it is transferred to other market participants, and the debt continues to exist after the transfer by the transferee until the market participant fulfills the obligations.

If enterprises own equity instruments measured at fair value, it should be assumed at the measurement date that its own equity instruments are transferred to other market participants, also that its own equity instruments continue to exist after the transfer by the transferee as the market participants made the right tools related to assume corresponding obligations.

Article 34 Fair values of the liability or own equity instruments shall follow the following principles:

(A) The presence of the same or similar liabilities or equity instruments of their own observable market price of the offer should be determined on the basis of the fair value of their own debt or equity instruments.

(B) There are no identical or similar liabilities or equity instruments of their own observable market price, but the other side has a holding assets; companies should hold the asset at the measurement date to the asset that the fair value is determined based on the fair value of the liability or equity instrument itself in the perspective of the market participants.

While some features of the asset do not apply to the measure of their own liabilities or equity instruments, the firm should be adjusted according to the fair value of the asset to determine the fair value of the adjusted value of the liability or their own equity instrument. These features include the limited sale of assets and the measurement of assets and liabilities or equity instruments of their own similar but not identical, used to count and measure unit or business assets and liabilities of its own equity instruments and other units are that not identical.

(C) There are no identical or similar liabilities or equity instruments of their own observable market price, and the other party does not hold them as assets, enterprises should assume liabilities from the issuance of equity instruments or the market participants' point of view and the use of valuation techniques determining the fair value of their own debt or equity instruments.

Article 35 The enterprises that are measured at fair value of the liability should consider the risk of non-compliance and assume the risk of non-compliance before and after the transfer of liabilities remains unchanged.

Non-performance risk is the risk that companies does not fulfill their obligations, including but not limited to their own credit risk.

Article 36 In the fair value of the liability or own equity instruments and the liability or equity instrument itself, there are limited transfer factors. If the input fair value has been taken of this factor has been taken into account, companies should no longer be a separate provision of the relevant enter value, nor should it make relevant adjustment for other input values.

Article 37 In order to have a fair value of demand deposits and other features creditors may at any time request repayment of financial liabilities. The fair value of the financial liability should not be less than the amount payable when creditors demand repayment at any time, the creditor may request reimbursement from the discounted present value of the first day.

43.2.1.10 Chapter X: Market Risk or Credit Risk Can Be Offset by the Fair Value of Financial Assets and Financial Liabilities

Article 38 Enterprise net open market risk and credit risk-based management of financial assets and financial liabilities can orderly trade with market participants at the measurement date under current market conditions to sell a net long (i.e., assets) or transfer net short (i.e., liabilities) based on the price, the fair value of the portfolio of financial liabilities and financial assets.

Financial assets or financial liabilities and market risk or credit risk can be offset and "Enterprise Accounting Standards No. 22—Recognition and measurement of financial instruments" should be used to regulate financial assets and financial liabilities, including non-compliance with financial assets or financial liabilities, but according to the definition additional contract accounting treatment found in "Enterprise Accounting Standard No. 22—Financial Instruments Recognition and Measurement." Credit risk and market risk or to offset financial assets and financial liabilities related to presentation of financial statements should be applicable to other relevant accounting standards.

Article 39 In accordance with the provisions of *Article 38* of the present guidelines of fair value measurement of financial assets and financial liabilities combination, it shall meet the following conditions:

(A) Enterprises documented risk management or investment strategy has been enshrined, and net exposure to a particular market business risks or specific counter party credit risk is based on portfolio management of financial assets and financial liabilities;
(B) The net exposure to a particular market business risks or specific counterparty credit risk is based on a combination of financial reporting of financial assets and liabilities to corporate information and key management personnel;
(C) The enterprise at each balance sheet date provides fair value of the gold portfolio of financial assets and financial liabilities.

Article 40 If the enterprise and the fair value measurement of financial assets and liabilities of financial portfolio used in accordance with the provisions of *Article 38* of the present guidelines, the specific market risk and the duration of the financial assets and financial liabilities should be the same.

Enterprises, in accordance with the provisions of *Article 38* of this Code of fair value of financial assets and liabilities measured combination of financial, market participants considering all existing and assumed arrangements can reduce credit risk exposure, and companies should consider specifically net counterparty credit risk exposure or a specific impact on the opponent's net impact on the corporate credit exposure risk, and market participants expect the law to force the implementation of the possibility of such arrangements.

Article 41 The enterprises that adopt this Code, *Article 38* shall be in accordance with "Enterprise Accounting Standards No. 28 in accounting policies, changes in accounting estimates and correction of errors" to determine the relevant accounting policies, provisions, and these, once established, cannot be arbitrarily changed.

43.2.1.11 Chapter XI: Disclosure of the Fair Value

Article 42 An enterprise shall, according to the nature of the underlying asset or liability, characteristics, risk, and fair value hierarchy of the asset or liability, properly group and disclose fair value in accordance with group-related information.

To determine the categories of assets and liabilities, the enterprise should normally report (on the balance sheet) which items are due for further decomposition. An enterprise should disclose the information in each category and adjust statement presentation between projects.

Other relevant accounting standards specify the relevant asset or liability and its constituency grouping principles consistent with the provisions of this section. Companies can use this group to provide relevant information.

Article 43 An enterprise should distinguish between continuing and discontinued fair value measurement of fair value.

Continuing fair value refers to other relevant accounting standards requiring or allowing companies to continue measuring fair value at each balance sheet date.

Non-continuous fair value refers to other relevant accounting standards requiring or allowing measurement of corporate balance sheets in a particular case to the fair value.

Article 44 After the initial recognition of assets or liabilities related to each balance sheet date, the enterprise should continue to at least disclose the following information in each group of assets and liabilities at fair value in the notes:

(A) Other relevant accounting standards require or allow companies to continue to disclose fair value items and amounts on the balance sheet date.
(B) The fair value hierarchy.
(C) The amount and causes of the conversion between the various levels, as well as to determine the point of transition between the various levels of policy. Each level in the rollout should be separately disclosed.
(D) The fair value of the second level: Companies should disclose the valuation techniques and descriptive information used by the input value. When

changing the valuation of technology, and business, the change and reasons for change should be disclosed.

(E) For the third level of the fair value, the enterprise should disclose the valuation technique used, the input value and the valuation process of the descriptive information. When changing the valuation of technology to business, the reasons for the change should be disclosed. An enterprise should disclose important quantitative information and unobservable inputs which can be reasonably achieved in the use of fair value.

(F) For the third level of the fair value, the enterprise should disclose the opening balance and closing balance and adjust information between, including profit or loss, total realized gains or losses, unrealized gains or total loss, and confirm these gains and losses when they are unrealized gains or losses (such as the fair value of the underlying asset or liability changes and losses, etc.); also included is the current profits or losses in other comprehensive income totals, as well as disclosing relevant assets or liabilities purchase, sale, distribution, and settlement conditions.

(G) The fair value of the third level: when the amount of change of unobservable inputs may result in significant changes in fair value, the enterprise should disclose the sensitivity analysis of descriptive information.

The correlation between the input values and other unobservable inputs used in the enterprise should describe the relationship and its impact, in which unobservable inputs include at least a paragraph requiring the disclosure of unobservable inputs. For financial assets and financial liabilities, if it is to reflect a reasonably possible change in other assumptions and change one or more significant unobservable input leading to fair value, the enterprise should also disclose that fact, the impact of changes in the amount and the calculation method.

(H) When the best use of non-financial assets and their current use is not the same, the enterprise should disclose that fact and reason.

Article 45 After the initial recognition of assets or liabilities related to the balance sheet, companies should disclose at least the following information in each group, discontinued assets and liabilities measured at fair value in the notes:

(A) Other relevant accounting standards requiring or allowing companies to continue with the project and the amount non-measured at fair value, the amount measured at fair value and the reason in a particular case.

(B) The fair value hierarchy.

(C) For the second level of the fair value, the enterprise should disclose the valuation techniques and descriptive information used by the input value. When changing the valuation of technology, and business, the change and reason for change should be disclosed.

(D) For the third level of the fair value, the enterprise should disclose the valuation technique used, the input value, and the valuation process of descriptive information. When valuation techniques change, companies must change as well and disclose the reasons for the change. Important enterprise should disclose the fair value of the use of unobservable inputs quantitative information value.

(E) When the best use of non-financial assets and their current use is not at the same, the enterprise should disclose the fact and reason for this.

Article 46 Enterprise-level fair value adjustments related to the conversion point, accounting policy, should be consistent before and after each accounting period and should be disclosed in accordance with *Article 44* (C) of the provisions of the present guidelines. Enterprise-level fair value adjustments related to the conversion point accounting policy should be applied consistently, turn out the fair value hierarchy, and transfer to the fair value hierarchy.

Article 47 The enterprises to adopt the provisions of *Article 38* of this Code's accounting policies shall disclose that fact.

Article 48 For each group of assets and liabilities in the balance sheet at fair value but not disclosed as fair value, companies should follow this Code *Article 44*

Important (B), (D), (E), and (H) require the disclosure of information, but do not require disclosure of the third level of the valuation process measured at fair value and used in accordance with these guidelines *Article 44* (E) of unobservable inputs quantitative information value.

Article 49 For fair value at the time of issue with a third-party credit enhancement indivisible debt, the issuer shall disclose that fact, and whether the credit enhancement has been reflected in the fair value of the liability metering.

Article 50 An enterprise should disclose quantitative information required by these guidelines, in tabular form, unless the other form is more appropriate.

43.2.2 The Provisions of Chapter XII of Convergence

Article 51 Fair value prior to the date of this Standard is inconsistent with the requirements of this Code, and companies have not been restated.

Article 52 Of the guidelines, comparative financial statements disclosing information before the date of implementation of this Code are inconsistent requirements companies do not need to be adjusted in accordance with the provisions of the Code.

43.2.2.1 Chapter XIII: Supplementary

Article 53 The standard takes effect from July 1, 2014.

43.3 Summary

Article 39 covers the aspects of fair value in a joint venture enterprise. If assets are sold as a partnership; it is clear the capital must be distributed fairly among the parties.

Chapter I (General Provisions) covers the general accounting laws and refers to texts which lay a foundation for the script. Chapter II covers leases and the distribution of capital through this source of income, and it refers to assets which are measured in units (such as debt) and covers such liability and it covers the transportation costs which is essentially the markets in which the assets are in (if no market exists; the most advantageous market is used). Chapter III (orderly trading and market) advises of the attitude of the sale of the assets of a party; and the effects that this will have on the other parties. Specifically, a party should not trade if it significantly negatively affects other parties. These effects must be observable in the market and reasonable. The following chapter (Methodology for Determining Fair Value) concerns the proper measurement of fair value. Chapter V (Initial Fair Value Measurement) states that if information is available for better valuation techniques, this should be used. It also concerns the concept of "enter the value." Essentially, all relevant information should be used when valuing a company. Chapter VI (The Handling of Information for Trading) gives a disclosure of confidential information as this is tentative; moreover, it concerns the trading volume and frequency and its relation to the input values. Chapter VII (Movement of Assets Between Parties) gives the adjustment of the fair value (e.g., assets sold between parties).

Chapter VIII concerns how unobservable market fluctuations should be treated.

Chapter IX gives information on non-financial assets (e.g., laptops and computers) and how these are handled. Chapter X (gives introduction as to the purposes of a partnership) gives the guidelines for the purpose of the partnership. Chapter XI (The Distribution of Risks Throughout the Partnership) has information on how market and credit risks are distributed through the fair value concept. Chapter XI is similar to previous one but concerns financial assets (in a general sense). The last two chapters are the final disposals.

43.3.1 Accounting Standards for Business Enterprises No. 40—Joint Venture Arrangements

43.3.1.1 Chapter I: General Provisions

Article 1 This Article is for regulating the accounting treatment of joint venture in regard to identification, classification, and the equity of all participants.

Article 2 The arrangement of joint venture refers to an arrangement that is controlled by two or more parties.

Joint venture arrangements will have the following characteristics:

(A) All participants shall be restricted by the arrangement;
(B) Two or more of the participants exert common control.

No single participant will be able to control the arrangement individually; also any party with common control may stop other participants or combination of participants from exerting control alone.

Article 3 Joint venture does not require that all participants in the arrangements exert common control. The arrangement of joint venture does not only include participants who have common control, but also participants who do not have control.

Article 4 The disclosure of equity of the joint venture arrangement applies in *Article 41*.

43.3.1.2 Chapter II: The Identification and Classification of the Joint Venture Arrangements

Article 5 Common control refers to the common control associated with certain arrangements according to related commitments and relevant activities, which can only be decided when all participants sharing control approve.

Related activities mentioned in these guidelines refer to an activity that may have a huge impact.

An arrangement of related activities should be judged according to the specific circumstances.

This includes the sale and purchase of goods or services, financial management, asset purchase and GE, research and development activities, and financing activities.

Article 6 All participants or group of participants must agree before and arrangement of related activities may occur. In determining whether there is a common control, you should first determine all of the parties or collection of participants involved who have control of the arrangements and then determine the arrangement of related activities.

Article 7 If there are two or more parties combined to exert control, common control does not exist.

Article 8 Participants who only have protective rights do not share common control.

Article 9 Joint arrangement is divided into mutual management and joint venture.

Mutual Management refers to the participants who have the right to arrange relevant assets and liabilities.

The joint venture refers to a joint arrangement that only has rights in the business arrangements of net assets.

Article 10 Parties shall determine the classification of joint venture arrangements according to their rights and obligations in the joint venture agreements. The rights and obligations should be evaluated when considering the structure, legal form, and contractual terms of the arrangement and other factors.

Article 11 An arrangement that is not decided by single party should be classified as mutual operation.

Single entity refers to an entity which has separately identifiable financial structure including a separate legal entity which does not have legal recognition of the qualification subject.

Article 12 Joint venture arrangement should normally be divided for the joint venture. But Joint venture arrangements under the customs laws and regulations shall be divided into common business:

(A) The legal form of the joint arrangement suggests that joint venture arrangements, with respect to the phase of assets and liabilities, have rights and obligations.
(B) The contractual terms agreed upon for the joint venture arrangements suggest that joint venture arrangements, with respect to the phase of assets and liabilities, have rights and obligations.
(C) Other relevant facts and circumstances indicate that the arrangements in the joint venture enjoy rights and bear obligations related to assets and liabilities, respectively. Parties of the joint venture arrange virtually all outputs, and the arrangement of liability continuously relies upon the joint venture's support.

It is not solely dependent on a joint venture to provide debt guarantees to be considered as part of joint venture arrangements. Participants affording the payment of capital cannot be classified as affording relevant liabilities.

Article 13 Participants should reevaluate the classification of the joint arrangement if changes in facts and circumstances result in a change in the rights and obligations within the joint arrangement.

Article 14 For the completion of different activities for the establishment of a number of joint venture arrangements with an agreed upon framework, companies should determine the classification of each of the joint venture arrangements.

43.3.1.3 Chapter III: Accounting Treatment of Participants

Article 15 Joint venture parties should confirm and share common business interests in accordance with the following accounting standards.

(A) Confirm the assets held by the individual and confirm its share of common assets;
(B) Confirm the assumed liabilities of the individual, as well as their commitment to identify shared common liabilities;
(C) Confirm the revenue of its shares of joint operations;
(D) Share confirmation of the operating revenues generated by the sale of output;
(E) Recognize the costs incurred by the individual, as well as confirming their share of common costs.

Article 16 Before investing in or selling assets of the joint venture (except for the assets that constitute a business) to a third party, participants should confirm the profit and loss belonging to other participants involved in the common operation. The assets apply to the impairment in Article. The participants should confirm the whole amount.

Article 17 Profit and loss belonging to other participants, from purchasing assets (except for the assets constituting a business) for a common operation, must be confirmed before selling to a third party. The assets apply to the impairment in *Article 8*. The participants should confirm the whole amount.

Article 18 The participants that do not share common control, when sharing the rights and obligations on certain common operating assets should apply *Article 15* and *Article 17*. Otherwise, it should treat in accordance with relevant accounting standards.

43.3.1.4 Chapter IV: Accounting Entries for Joint Venture Participants

Article 19 The accounting treatment of joint venture should apply "Accounting Standards for Enterprise No. 2—long-term equity investment."

Article 20 Participants that do not share common control of the joint ventures should carry out their accounting according to its degree of impact on the joint venture:

(A) If it has a significant impact on the joint venture, it should be in accordance with the "Accounting Standard for Enterprise No. 2—Treatment for long-term equity investment."
(B) If it does not have a significant impact on the joint venture, it should be in accordance with "Accounting Standard for Enterprise No. 22—Recognition and measurement of financial instruments."

43.3.1.5 Chapter V: Cohesion Provisions

Article 21 Enterprises that apply this Article for the first time should be evaluated and confirmed according to the Article.

Article 22 Joint ventures that can be reclassified as a joint operation of the joint venture should terminate the long-term investments that apply equity method during the opening of the earliest period of comparable financial reports and other long-term equity that applies to joint venture. In the meantime, according to the related information that is given in the opening of the earliest period of comparable financial reports should be used to confirm the shares of assets (including goodwill) and liabilities. The difference between book value of confirmed assets and liabilities should apply the "Accounting Standard for Enterprise No. 18—Income tax." The difference that arises from the net amount of assets and liabilities and the book value of assets and liabilities should apply the following accounting standards:

(A) The former is larger that the latter—the difference should be deducted from the goodwill and then deducted from the retained earnings in the earliest comparable financial reports.
(B) The former is smaller than the latter—the difference should deducted from the retained earnings from the earliest comparable financial reports.

43.3.1.6 Chapter VI: Supplement

Article 23 This Article will be implemented from July 1, 2014.

43.4 Summary

The Article "Accounting Standard for Business Enterprises No. 40" is provided to supply information on joint venture arrangements. A joint venture arrangement refers to an arrangement that is controlled by two or more parties.

Chapter 1 of this Article provides information on the general provisions. This includes the basic characteristics of a joint venture arrangement and outlines, simply, the basis for control over a joint venture arrangement.

Following on from this, Chapter 2 outlines the process and regulations associated with the classification and identification of a joint venture agreement, including reference to common control, identification of when it exists and clarification of which parties share common control within the joint venture agreement.

Chapters 3 and 4 give an outline of the appropriate accounting treatments that participants within the joint venture agreement should apply, along with information on which of the accounting standards that participants should apply during the accounting treatment.

Finally, Chapter 5 gives an outline of the cohesion provisions belonging to this Article. This includes information about the reclassification of a joint venture arrangement the process that should be applied when reclassification occurs, as well as the accounting standards that should be followed.

43.4.1 Accounting Standard for Business Enterprises No. 41—Disclosure of Interest

43.4.1.1 Chapter I: General Provisions

Article 1 This Article is for regulating the disclosure of equity of other entities.

Article 2 The disclosed equity information of other entities should assist the users of financial reports to evaluate the nature and related risk of the equity of other entities. Also, the impact on the financial situation, result of operation, and cash flow can be evaluated by this disclosure.

Article 3 The equity of other entities mentioned in this Article refers to variable return equity earned by enterprises enabling them to join the related activities by other entities through contracts and other forms. The methods for participating in activities include holding the shares and debits of other entities or providing finance, current support, credit upgrading, and warranty for other entities.

Enterprises hold control, common control, or exert huge impact on other entities by these methods.

Other entities including subsidiaries, joint venture arrangement (including co-operation and joint venture), and associates and are not included in the consolidated financial reports of the structured body. Structured body refers to the body that does not have voting rights or similar rights as key elements when confirming the control party.

Article 4 This Article is applicable to equity disclosed for subsidiaries, joint venture arrangements (including joint operations and joint ventures), and associates that are excluded in the consolidated financial reports of the structured body. Enterprises provide both consolidated financial reports and financial reports of the individual parent company. Information required, according to this Article, should be disclosed in the notes of the consolidated financial reports. There is no need to disclose duplicate information in the single financial reports.

Article 5 The following disclosure applies to other related accounting standards:

(A) Welfare plans or other long-term welfare plans apply to "Accounting Standards for Enterprises No. 9—Employee Benefits."
(B) The equity in the joint venture arrangement applies to "Accounting Standards for Enterprises No. 37—Financial Instruments." Therefore, enterprises that have a huge impact on the joint venture arrangement or joint venture arrangement of the structural body apply these criteria.
(C) Enterprises that own the equity in other entities according to "Accounting Standards for Enterprises No. 22—Financial Instruments Recognition and Measurement," apply "Accounting Standards for Enterprises No. 37—Financial Instruments." Therefore, the equity is excluded from consolidated financial reports of the structured body, and the equity in joint ventures that is measured by fair value, applies these criteria.

43.4.1.2 Chapter II: The Disclosure of Important Judgment and Assumption

Article 6 Enterprises should disclose important judgments and assumptions on other entities with control, common control, or huge impact; also, the alteration of these judgments and assumptions should include but not be limited to the following:

(A) The assumption and judgment of enterprises holding 50 % or below of voting rights but which still have control over this entity, or enterprises holding 50 % or above of voting rights but which do not have control over this entity.
(B) The judgment and assumption of determining whether the joint venture arrangement is common operation or joint venture.
(C) The judgment and assumption of enterprises with 20 % or below of voting rights but holding huge influence, or enterprises with 20 % or above of voting rights but holding no huge influence.
(D) The judgment and assumptions on deciding whether enterprises are agent or client.

Article 7 Enterprises should disclose the important judgments and assumptions that are confirmed as investment subjects according to "Accounting Standards for enterprises No. 33—Consolidated Financial Statements." and reasons for enterprises defined as investment subjects, even if it does not fit with the nature of investment subject according to these criteria, enterprises (parent company) changing from non-investment subject to investment subject should disclose this change and the reasons for changing and should disclose the influence incurred by this change including fair value and disclosure items.

Enterprises (parent company) changing from investment subject to non-investment subject should disclose the alterations and reasons.

Article 8 Enterprises should disclose the constitution of disclosed corporation in the notes of the consolidated financial reports including the name of subsidiary, main operation area, the nature of business, and the percentage of shares.

The percentage of shares with minority shareholders of the subsidiary are important for the corporation and enterprises should disclose the following information in the notes of consolidated financial reports.

(A) The enterprises should disclose the percentage of voting rights when shares of minority shareholders in subsidiary are different from the holding voting rights.
(B) The equity and paid dividend that belong to the minority shareholder of the subsidiary in current the period.
(C) The accumulated amount for minority shareholders of the subsidiary in the current period.
(D) The main financial information of the subsidiary.

Article 9 There are major limitations on the asset usage and debt offsets. Enterprises should disclose the following information in the notes of their consolidated financial reports:

(A) The content of this limitation including limitations for cash and other assets transferring between the parent company and its subsidiaries and the limitations for dividends paid or profit distribution and debit withdrawals.
(B) The nature and extent of limitations when the minority shareholders own protective rights and these protective rights exert major limitations for asset usage or debt offsets.
(C) The amount of assets and debt in the consolidated financial reports related to the limitations.

Article 10 Enterprises' structural body that is included in the consolidated financial reports should disclose the following information in the notes of consolidated financial reports:

(A) The subsidiaries and certain companies that regulate by contract and provide financial support for the structural body should disclose the contract items including the issues that may cause loss.
(B) In the absence of the contract, enterprises or its subsidiaries that provide financial support or other supports for this structural body should disclose the type, amount, and reason for financial support including the situation for helping this structural body to gain financial support. Also the related elements for support should be disclosed when the financial support causes control over this structural body.
(C) Enterprises that have intention to provide financial support or other supports for this structural body should disclose this intention including the intention to help the structural body to gain financial support.

Article 11 If an enterprise changes the owners equity in its subsidiaries, and the change does not result in business loss of control of a subsidiary, the impact of the changes should be disclosed in the notes of the consolidated financial reports according to "Accounting Standards for enterprises No. 33—Consolidated Financial Statements":

(A) The profit and loss caused by losing control and some related, disclosed items.
(B) The profit and loss caused by recalculating the remaining shares with fair value at the time of losing control

Article 12 Enterprises that are subjects of investment and that include subsidiaries are excluded from consolidated financial reports and measured by fair value. This should be stated in the notes of financial reports. Meanwhile, the subsidiaries that are excluded from financial reports should disclose the following information:

(A) The name of subsidiary, main operation area and registration location.
(B) Enterprises should disclose the percentage of voting rights when the percentage of shares of the subsidiary is different from the percentage of voting rights. The subsidiaries that are subjects of investment and not included in the consolidated financial reports should disclose the related information according to the above requirements.

Article 13 Enterprises are subject to investment. The equity of subsidiaries that are not included in the financial reports should disclose related risk information:

(A) There are major limitations for subsidiaries that are excluded from consolidated financial reports, to pay cash dividend, to return loan, or to pay in advance. Enterprise should disclose the nature and extent of this limitation.
(B) When Enterprises have the intention to provide financial support for subsidiaries that are excluded from the consolidated financial reports, the promise and intention should be disclosed, including the promise and intention to help this subsidiary. Enterprises or subsidiaries that provide financial support or other support to subsidiaries that are excluded from the consolidated financial reports without contract regulation should disclose the nature, amount, and reason of this support.
(C) Subsidiaries that are excluded from the consolidated financial reports provide financial support for structural bodies controlled by enterprises. The enterprises should disclose the related contract items and the issues for loss that may be caused. In the absence of contract regulation, enterprises, and subsidiaries, that are excluded from the consolidated financial reports, and which provide financial support or other support for structural bodies that causes the enterprise to be the controller of the structural body, the enterprise should disclose the relative elements for support.

43.4.1.3 Chapter IV: The Disclosure of Equity in Common Operation Arrangement or Joint Venture

Article 14 The following information should be disclosed when important common operation arrangements and joint ventures exist:

(A) The name, main operation area, and registration location for common operation arrangements or joint venture.
(B) The nature of relationship between enterprises and joint ventures including common operation arrangements or joint venture nature and its beneficial strategy for enterprise activity.
(C) The enterprises should disclose the percentage of voting rights when the percentage of shares is different from the percentage of voting rights.

Article 15 For important common operation enterprises or joint ventures, enterprises should disclose the accounting treatment for common operation enterprises or joint venture investment, dividends received from common operation enterprises or joint ventures, and major financial information from common operation enterprises or joint ventures besides related information according with the Item 14. If enterprises apply equity method to common operation or joint ventures, the above major financial information should be the adjusted amount according to the equity method. Meanwhile, enterprises should disclose the adjustment procedure. The fair value should be disclosed if there is open market for this treatment.

Article 16 The equity of a single common operation company or joint venture is not important, and this information should be disclosed as common operation and joint venture:

(A) The total amount of book value of investment for common operations or joint ventures that is measured in equity method.
(B) Net profit for common operation enterprises or joint ventures, other comprehensive income, and comprehensive income for operation termination should be computed by the total amount of its shares.

Article 17 The enterprises should disclose the nature and extent of the limitation when there are limitations on common operation enterprises or joint ventures paying cash dividend, returning loans or paying in advance.

Article 18 Enterprises apply equity method to measure the investment of common operation enterprise or joint venture. If the investee has excess loss and the investor cannot afford the loss of shares, enterprises should disclose the loss of shares that are unconfirmed by common operation enterprises or joint ventures, including current shares and accumulated shares.

Article 19 Enterprises should disclose the unconfirmed commitment that is related to the investment to the common operation enterprises and the contingent liability that is related to the investment to the common operation enterprises or joint ventures.

Article 20 If the enterprises are subjects of investment, there is no need to disclose the related information in Item 15 and Item 16.

43.4.1.4 Chapter V: The Disclose of Equity in the Structural Subject that Excludes from Consolidated Financial Reports

Article 21 The following information should be disclosed for structural bodies that are excluded from consolidated financial reports:

(A) The nature, purpose, scale, activities, and financial way of the structural bodies that are excluded from the consolidated financial reports;
(B) The disclosure items and book value of assets and liabilities of structural bodies that are excluded from the consolidated financial reports;
(C) The maximum loss exposure and measurement of this loss exposure of structural bodies that are excluded from consolidated financial reports. If enterprises can measure this loss exposure, the facts and reason of this loss exposure should be disclosed;
(D) The comparison between the book value and the maximum loss exposure should be disclosed.

When enterprises that set up structural bodies but do not provide equity for this body in the financial reports to date, enterprises do not need to disclose information included in parts (B)–(D) from above, but should disclose the definition standards for the structural body, and disclose the profits, the type of profits, and the book value of assets transferred from this body.

Article 22 Enterprises should have intentions to provide financial support and other supports for structural bodies, including helping this body to get financial support. Enterprises should disclose the type, amount, and reason of this support while also helping this subject to get financial support.

Article 23 If enterprises are subjects of investment, the structural bodies that are controlled by enterprises but that are excluded from consolidated financial reports should disclose information according to Items 12 and 13. There is no need to apply this chapter.

43.4.1.5 Chapter VI: Connection Provision

Article 24 When disclosing the information in the comparable financial reports before the implemented date of this Article, it should be adjusted according to this Article and excluded from the consolidated financial reports of the structuring body.

43.4.1.6 Chapter VII: Supplement

Article 25 This Article was implemented from July 1, 2014.

43.5 Summary

The *Article* "Accounting Standard for Business Enterprises No. 41" provides information on the disclosure of interest.

Chapter 1 provides an outline of the general provisions surrounding the disclosure of interest. These general provisions provide information on the regulation of equity of other entities, as well as information to evaluate the nature and related risks of equity of other entities.

Also provided is a reference to equity for other entities and a brief description and examples of "other entities." These "other entities" include, for example, subsidiaries, joint venture arrangements, and associates.

Included next, in Chapter 2, is an outline on the disclosure of important judgments and assumptions surrounding the disclosure of interest and the processes involved. Along with this is a brief description of what is to be done, by companies, in a number of different situations and what should be disclosed when these situations occur.

Chapter 3 provides an outline of when enterprises should provide information in the notes of the consolidated financial reports, either due to an action taken by the enterprise or due to some occurrence within the business, and in each case what this information should be.

Following on from this, Chapter 4 provides information surrounding the disclosure of equity in common operation arrangement or joint venture. This includes what information should be disclosed when important common arrangement or joint venture exists.

The following chapter, Chapter 5, offers advice on the disclosure of equity in structural bodies that are excluded from the consolidated financial reports and what information should be excluded from these financial reports.

Finally, Chapter 6 provides information on connection provisions and advice on adjusting this information.

References

ACCA Global (2013) Does IFRS convergence affect financial reporting quality in China? Available at www.accaglobal.com/content/dam/acca/global/PDF-technical/financial-reporting/rr-131-002.pdf

Auditing Standards in China—a comparative analysis with relevant international standards and guidelines. Int J Acc 35(4) 2000

Bai Y (2011) The impact of mandatory adoption of IFRS on value relevance: the case of People's Republic of China. dare.uva.nl

Biondi Y, Zhang Q (2007) Accounting for the Chinese context: a comparative analysis of international and Chinese accounting standards focusing on business combination. Soc Econ Rev 5:695–724

Borker DR (2012) Accounting, culture, and emerging economies: IFRS in the BRIC countries. J Bus Econ Res (JBER). cluteinstitute.com

Cang Y, Chu Y, Lin TW (2014) An exploratory study of earnings management detectability, analyst coverage and the impact of IFRS adoption: evidence from China. J Acc Public Policy (Elsevier)

Chen Y, Jubb P, Tran A (1997) Problems of accounting reform in the People's Republic of China. Int J Acc 32(2):139–153

Chen CJP, Gul FA, Su XJ (1999) A comparison of reported earnings under Chinese GAAP vs IAS: evidence from the Shanghai stock exchange. Acc Horiz 13(2):91–111

China Briefing (2013) China GAAP vs. U.S. GAAP and IFRS. Available at http://www.china-briefing.com/news/2013/02/05/china-gaap-vs-u-s-gaap-and-ifrs.html

Chow LMY, Chau GKK, Gray SJ (1995) Accounting reform in China: cultural constraint on implementation and development. Acc Bus Res 26(1):29–49

Ding Y (2000) Harmonisation trends in Chinese accounting and remaining problems. Manag Financ 26(5):31–40

Ding Y, Su X (2008) Implementation of IFRS in a regulated market. J Acc Public Policy (Elsevier)

Eng LL, Sun L, Vichitsarawong T (2013) The valuation properties of earnings and book values reported under IAS, domestic GAAP and US GAAP: evidence from China, Hong Kong, Japan, Korea and Singapore. Adv Acc (Elsevier)

European Securities and Markets Authority (2011) Supplementary progress report on the equivalence of Chinese accounting standards with international financial reporting standards. Available at www.europarl.europa.eu/RegData/docs_autres_institutions/commission_europeenne/comitologie/info/2011/O018009-01/COM-AC_DI(2011)O018009-01(ANN2)_EN.pdf

He X, Wong TJ, Young D (2009) Challenges for implementation of fair value accounting in emerging markets: Evidence from IFRS adoption in China. tippie.uiowa.edu

Heng LCC, Noronha C (2011) Adv Acc 27:156–165 (incorporating Advances in International Accounting)

L. Riccardi, *China Accounting Standards*,
DOI 10.1007/978-981-10-0006-5

Heng LCC, Noronha C (2011) The impact of the new accounting standards for business enterprises (ASBE) on financial results of mainland Chinese listed companies. Adv Acc 27:156–165 (incorporating Advances in International Accounting)

Hou Q, Jin Q, Wang L (2014) Mandatory IFRS adoption and executive compensation: evidence from China. China J Acc Res (Elsevier)

InterChina Consulting (2009) Accounting in China. Available at www.casaasia.es/pdf/7209103358AM1246523638483.pdf

Ip CK, Noronha C (2007) The progress of accounting harmonization in China: a comparison of A-share and H-share financial results. Manag Auditing J 22(6):620–640

Ji XD (2001) Development of accounting and auditing systems in China. Ashgate, Aldershot

Lehman Brown (2014) Convergence of China GAAP to IAS. Available at www.lehmanbrown.com/peeling-the-onion/convergence-china-gaap-ias/

Moser R (2014) IFRS and convergence in China and the USA. J Technol Manage China. emeraldinsight.com

Nie P et al (2013) China's progress with IFRS convergence: interviews with Chinese professors. Issues Acc Edu 28(2)

Ng PPH, Lau C (2010) New PRC accounting standards—a milestone, part 1

Ng PPH, Lau C (2010) New PRC accounting standards—a milestone, part 2

Ng PPH, Lau C (2010) New PRC accounting standards—a milestone, part 3

Ng PPH, Ng EJ (2011) China master GAAP Guide, 8th edn. Wolters Kluwer, The Netherlands

Olesen K, Cheng F (2011) Convergence of accounting standards does not always lead to convergence of accounting practices: the case of China. Asian J Bus Acc 4(1):23–58

Peng SS, Bewley K (2009) Adaptability of fair value accounting in China: assessment of an emerging economy converging with IFRS. CAAA annual conference, 2009. papers.ssrn.com

Peng S, van der Laan Smith J (2010) Chinese GAAP and IFRS: an analysis of the convergence process. J Int Acc Auditing Tax (Elsevier)

Peng S, Tondkar RH, van der Laan Smith J, Harless DW (2008) Does convergence of accounting standards lead to the convergence of accounting practices?: A study from China. Int J Acc (Elsevier)

Qu X, Zhang G (2015) Value-relevance of earnings and book value over the institutional transition in China: the suitability of fair value accounting in this emerging market. Int J Acc (Elsevier)

Qu W, Fong M, Oliver J (2012) Does IFRS convergence improve quality of accounting information?—evidence from the Chinese stock market. Corp Ownersh Control

Ramanna K (2013) The international politics of IFRS harmonization. Acc, Econ Law. degruyter.com

Solas C, Ayhan S (2008) The historical evolution of accounting in China. Available at www.decomputis.org/dc/articulos_doctrinales/solas_ayhan8.pdf

Sito ufficiale IAS/IFRS: http://www.ifrs.org/Pages/default.aspx

Sito ufficiale MOF per gli ASBE: http://kjs.mof.gov.cn

Sun C (2011) The possible application of international accounting standards in China. Available at etheses.bham.ac.uk/4335/2/Sun13PhD.pdf

Tang Y (2000) Bumpy road toward leading to internationalization: a review of accounting development in China. Acc Horiz 14(1):93–102

Wang X, Wu M (2011) The quality of financial reporting in China: an examination from an accounting restatement perspective. China J Acc Res 4(4)

Wei F (2007) How is IFRS/IAS implemented in China. brage.bibsys.no

Wiley Insight (2011) Comparison of IFRS with China GAAP. Wiley international trends in financial reporting under IFRS: US GAAP, Chinese GAAP, and Indian GAAP. Available at ifrs.wiley.com/chapters/w9780470178447b05

Winkle GM, Huss HF, Chen XZ (1994) Accounting standards in the People's Republic of China: responding to economic reforms. Acc Horiz 8(3):48–57

World Bank (2009) Report on the observance of standards and codes (ROSC)—accounting and auditing. Available at www.worldbank.org/ifa/rosc_aa_chn.pdf

Wu S (2012) The impact of IFRS convergence on the effectiveness of accounting information for share valuation: evidence from the Mainland of China. Front Bus Res China

Yang Z (2012) The influence of the Chinese tax regime on IFRS convergence process in China: aligning the tax standards, CAS18 and IAS12. aut.researchgateway.ac.nz

Ying Z et al (2010) Fair value accounting in China: neoliberalisation and accounting change. Apira2010. econ.usyd.edu.au/conference_proceedings/APIRA-2010-201-Zhang-Fair-value-accounting-in-China.pdf

2015 International Financial Reporting Standards IFRS® Consolidated without early application. IFRS Foundation, London, UK

MIX
Papier aus verantwortungsvollen Quellen
Paper from responsible sources
FSC® C105338

If you have any concerns about our products,
you can contact us on
ProductSafety@springernature.com

In case Publisher is established outside the EU,
the EU authorized representative is:
Springer Nature Customer Service Center GmbH
Europaplatz 3, 69115 Heidelberg, Germany

Printed by Libri Plureos GmbH
in Hamburg, Germany